The Dred Scott Decision

LAW OR POLITICS?

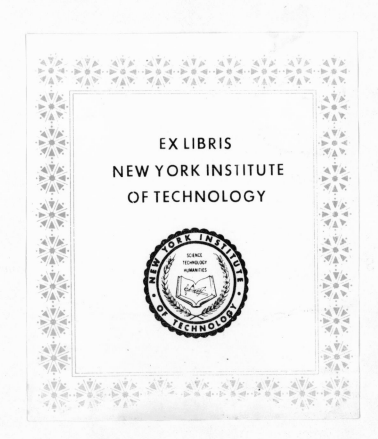

The Dred Scott Decision

Edited with an introduction by
STANLEY I. KUTLER, *University of Wisconsin*

★
★
★ # LAW OR POLITICS?
★
★

Houghton Mifflin Company · Boston

NEW YORK   ATLANTA   GENEVA, ILL.   DALLAS   PALO ALTO

COPYRIGHT © 1967 BY STANLEY I. KUTLER

A PREFATORY NOTE

With the following materials I have attempted to construct a multi-dimensional "biography" of a Supreme Court case — the Dred Scott decision. This case, perhaps more than any other in the history of the Court, constitutes a paradigm for portraying the rich and complex political, economic, social, and legal variables which contribute to American constitutional development. The origins and aftermath of the case no less than the decision itself help to illuminate the cataclysmic sectional struggle of the nineteenth century. Furthermore, Dred Scott as a legal precedent transcends its immediate historical context and serves as a timely illustration of the special role of the Supreme Court in the American constitutional and political system.

The main body of the volume consists of primary and contemporary sources. Generous abstracts from the three most important opinions of the justices should enable the reader to discern the clash of constitutional and legal issues within the Court. To complement the official utterances, I also have attempted to offer a broad survey of various lay responses to the decision, ranging from organs of public opinion, through politicians, and the legal community. Finally, I have included a number of interpretive historical essays selected and arranged so as to reflect the shifting views of historical interpretation. Indeed, the variety of interpretations the case has elicited comprise almost a separate study in themselves. For as if testifying to the perennial significance of this decision, the intervening years have produced historical reactions as diverse and heated as were the contemporary views of Dred Scott. It is always a pleasure to acknowledge the advice of colleagues and friends. I am indebted on this occasion especially to William Hanchett, Harold M. Hyman, Donald M. Roper, and Richard H. Sewell. I also wish to express my appreciation to Matthew Hodgson and Elizabeth Fox of Houghton Mifflin. Finally, I am grateful for the advice and encouragement of my wife, Sandra Sachs Kutler.

STANLEY I. KUTLER

Madison, Wisconsin
September 1966

v

CONTENTS

INTRODUCTION: THE
INCIDENCE OF DRED SCOTT

Senator William B. Allison of Iowa, in an 1887 commencement address, confronted the dilemma that still vexes any modern understanding of the coming of the Civil War. "When some future Tacitus shall record our annals," he said, "it will be difficult for him to explain to the student of our government how it was possible for . . . [slavery] to attain such proportions under a free constitution, and such mastery over a free people; and especially will he wonder by what process of alluring sophistry this [Supreme Court] . . . could have its eyes so dazed, and its intellect so blurred, as to seek to enthrone in the constitution the spirit of slavery, where the spirit of liberty had dwelt before."[1]

The Senator's perplexity three decades after the Dred Scott decision was to some extent valid. Indeed, considering that from its very birth, this nation boasted of being "conceived in liberty and dedicated to the proposition that all men are created equal," from the very moment of its formulation in 1857, the Court's ruling seemed grossly anachronistic. But the imperatives of politics govern American constitutional development quite as much as the niceties of law or the urgings of principle. Dred Scott's case illuminates the point. Decided in an hour of passionate division, it portrays vividly the eternal tension between principle and expediency, of which the often imperfect synthesis is constitutional law.

I

The case, like all others brought before the court, originated not on the plane of abstract principles, but in a concrete situation — here the status of one man. But tied as it was to the phenomenon of westward expansion, Dred Scott's personal history ultimately raised the question of the constitutional status of slavery in the territories. While Dred Scott waged a unique battle for freedom, his situation differed little from that of most other bondsmen. Born in Virginia around the turn of the century, Scott was owned for the first three decades of his life by the Peter Blow family.[2] In 1819, Blow, together with his family and slaves migrated to

---

[1] William B. Allison, *The Strength of our Government* . . . (Iowa City, 1887), 11.
[2] For a general study of the background of the case see Vincent C. Hopkins, *Dred Scott's Case* (New York, 1951), chs. 1–5.

more promising lands in Alabama. Eleven years later they moved again, this time to the thriving river city of St. Louis. When Blow died in 1832, the administrator of his estate sold Scott for five hundred dollars to an army surgeon, Dr. John Emerson of St. Louis. Accompanied by his new slave, Emerson served at posts in Missouri, Illinois, and in what is now the state of Minnesota. After the doctor's death in 1843, title to Dred Scott passed to Mrs. Emerson.

At that point Dred Scott attempted to purchase his freedom from his mistress. Unsuccessful, he thereupon brought suit for his freedom in the St. Louis circuit court in April 1846, alleging that under the provisions of the 1820 Missouri Compromise, his residence in Illinois and Minnesota had made him a free man. Although the jury decided for Mrs. Emerson, Scott's lawyers secured a retrial which began in January 1850. The plaintiff's counsel relied heavily on the Compromise of 1820, while Mrs. Emerson's attorney argued that Scott's "voluntary return" to Missouri, a slave-holding state, placed him under the local laws, with full rights reverting to the master. This time the jury found in favor of Scott. His freedom, however, proved temporary as on appeal, in 1852, the Missouri Supreme Court overturned the verdict. The state high court, reversing its previous practice by a two to one vote, refused to extend comity and honor the laws of other states.

Until 1852 no startling novelty had distinguished the Dred Scott case; similar pleas in behalf of slaves had been heard in the state courts throughout the century. In November 1853, however, Scott's lawyers maneuvered the controversy into the federal courts. After Mrs. Emerson remarried, her brother, John F. A. Sanford of New York, administered her affairs and property. Scott, claiming Missouri citizenship, charged that Sanford had assaulted him, and filed suit in federal court on grounds of diversity of citizenship. Sanford responded with a plea in abatement, a device to halt proceedings on the grounds that the court lacked jurisdiction.

This seemingly minor, yet vital, point soon matched in legal importance the substantive issue of Scott's freedom. Sanford's counsel contended that since Scott was a Negro of African descent, whose ancestors were brought and sold as slaves in this country, the court lacked jurisdiction. As a slave, no Negro could claim citizenship of the United States and therefore had no right to sue in a federal court. Federal Judge Robert Wells, however, denied the plea, held Scott to be a citizen, and advanced the somewhat novel and tenuous idea that residence and an ability to own property constituted citizenship. With the apparent disposal of the jurisdictional question, the trial proceeded on the substantive issue. Upon Judge Wells's instructions, the jury found Sanford not guilty, and Scott still to be the property of the defendant.

Scott's attorneys immediately moved for a writ of error to the United States Supreme Court. In addition, they girded themselves for the forthcoming battle by securing the services of the politically prominent Montgomery Blair. Among other factors, the Court's crowded docket prevented a hearing of *Scott v. Sandford* until February 1856, nearly two years after the lower court verdict.[3]

Given the Supreme Court's composition, only Scott's most naive supporters could have hoped for a favorable outcome. The venerable Chief Justice, Roger B. Taney, and four of his colleagues, James M. Wayne, John Catron, Peter Daniel, and John A. Campbell, were southerners, while two of the four northern justices, Samuel Nelson and Robert Grier, were conservative, states'-rights Democrats. Still another justice, Benjamin R. Curtis, a Whig and protegé of Daniel Webster, had earned a reputation in his native Massachusetts as a "slave-hounder" by his vigorous defense of the fugitive slave acts. Only John McLean of Ohio had any known sympathy for abolitionist or free soil advocates. An experienced group, with an average tenure of fifteen years, most of the justices had heard and participated in several other notable slavery cases.[4]

Montgomery Blair's presentation touched only briefly on Scott's citizenship status and his right to bring suit. Instead Blair stressed the importance of Scott's sojourn in Illinois and the Minnesota Territory, offering a vigorous defense of congressional power to regulate slavery in the territories. Senator Henry S. Geyer of Missouri, appearing for Sanford, shrewdly emphasized the citizenship question and Missouri's right to refuse comity to the laws of other states. Having heard three days' worth of arguments, the judges withdrew to confer together in privacy. Apparently an overwhelming majority of their number agreed to rule against Dred Scott's plea for freedom, but they could reach no common consensus as to the specific grounds for rejection. Four members — Taney, Curtis, Wayne, and Daniel — eagerly sought to discuss the lower court's disposal of the plea in abatement, and hence Scott's citizenship status. Justice Nelson tentatively supported the idea, but after a vote demonstrated the Court's close division, Nelson moved that new arguments be heard at the next term. Significantly, the delay foreclosed any possibility of a decision before the presidential election of 1856, thus dashing both Republican hopes for an issue and McLean's personal aspirations for the Republican nomination. The Ohioan from the outset had intended to dissent and to affirm the right of Congress to prohibit slavery in the territories.

One month after the Democratic triumph in November the Court prepared to hear new arguments. Both sides added distinguished constitutional authorities as associate counsel. Former Attorney General Reverdy Johnson, an intimate of Taney's, joined Geyer, while George T.

---

[3] The case is misspelled in the formal reports.
[4] See, for example, *Grove* v. *Slaughter*, 15 Peters 449 (1841); *Prigg* v. *Pennsylvania*, 16 Peters 539 (1842); *Jones* v. *Van Zandt*, 5 Howard 215 (1847); *Strader* v. *Graham*, 10 Howard 82 (1851).

Curtis, the Justice's brother, assisted Blair. The new attorneys hammered at the problem of congressional power and both proved able spokesmen for their respective viewpoints.

After the case went to a second conference, outside political pressures mounted on the justices. Newspapers filled columns with speculation and "inside" information as to what the Court would do, while political figures anxiously awaited results of what Alexander H. Stephens, with singular clairvoyance, called *the great case.*" By this time, only a fine line separated law from politics, and in a step of major importance, President-elect James Buchanan, anxious to offer the nation a definitive constitutional statement, erased it altogether by pointedly asking Justice Catron whether the Court would pronounce its opinion before the March 4 inauguration.[5] Catron replied that the matter was about to be decided in conference but warned Buchanan that the decision would "settle nothing" and be of little value to him and his administration. Indeed, events confirmed Catron's prediction, for the justices had decided to skirt the constitutional issues. Abandoning his earlier indecisiveness, Justice Nelson joined four other colleagues to hold that no plea in abatement lay before the Court. Moreover, a consensus now emerged which seemed disposed to ignore the question of congressional power in the territories. Assigned to write an opinion affirming the lower court decision, Nelson relied primarily upon the 1851 precedent of *Strader* v. *Graham* in which the Court decided to follow a state court's determination of a slave's status.

Justices McLean and Curtis immediately indicated their dissatisfaction and decided to discuss the substantive issues raised in the arguments. In turn, a few of the southern justices let it be known that while allowing Nelson's formula to serve as the opinion of the Court, they would respond to the dissents. Justice Wayne, however, according to a later statement by Justice Campbell, urged his colleagues to make the case a vehicle for resolving the constitutional issues, particularly the question of congressional power to regulate slavery in the territories. Wayne's suggestion carried, and Chief Justice Taney agreed to write an opinion. Significantly, Justice Nelson was absent.

Wayne's proposal must have passed only by a narrow majority, for on February 19, Catron wrote Buchanan suggesting that the President-elect contact Justice Grier and stress "how necessary it is — and how good the opportunity is, to settle the agitation by an affirmative decision of the Supreme Court. . . ." Not at all reticent about giving advice, Catron even prepared a draft statement for Buchanan's use in his inaugural address:

[5] John Bassett Moore, *Works of James Buchanan* (Philadelphia, 1912), X, 106–107; Philip Auchampaugh, "James Buchanan, the Court, and the Dred Scott Case," *Tennessee Historical Magazine*, IX (1926), 231–240; Philip S. Klein, *President James Buchanan: A Biography* (University Park, Pa., 1962).

That the question involving the constitutionality of the Missouri Compromise line is presented to the appropriate tribunal to decide; to wit, to the Supreme Court of the United States. It is due to its high and independent character to suppose that it will decide and settle a controversy which has so long and seriously agitated the country, and which *must* ultimately be decided by the Supreme Court. And until the case now before it, (on two arguments) presenting the direct question, is disposed of, I would deem it improper to express any opinion on the subject.

Buchanan immediately urged Grier, a fellow Pennsylvanian, to endorse the southern position. The pressure from Buchanan, the persuasive powers of Taney, and his own desire not to have "the line of latitude . . . mark the line of division" within the Court, contributed to Grier's conversion. The southerners now enjoyed outside support, and a more creditable margin.

Nevertheless, the attempt to settle definitively all questions with an "opinion of the Court" failed dismally; each of the nine justices presented separate and often contradictory statements, varying in length from expansive discussions by Taney and Curtis to brief concurring paragraphs by Grier and Wayne. Even Taney's effort, while reported as the "Opinion of the Court," did not win majority concurrence for all of its points. The Chief Justice contended that the Court could question the lower court's disposition of the plea in abatement. The circuit court, he said, had erred in its judgment, since the historical evidence demonstrated that no Negro — free or slave — could be a citizen within the meaning of the Constitution; hence no Negro could sue in the federal courts, and the lower court thus lacked jurisdiction. Despite this conclusion, Taney ventured into a lengthy analysis of the substantive questions relating to Dred Scott's personal status. Taney denied that Scott's residency in the Minnesota Territory and Illinois had made him a free man: first, the Act of 1820 deprived a slaveholder of the right to use his property and thus violated the due process clause of the Fifth Amendment of the Federal Constitution; second, the Illinois sojourn had no effect, for Scott automatically subjected himself to the laws of Missouri once he returned to that state. At the end Taney returned to his original point, reversing the judgment of the circuit court, and ordering the suit dismissed for want of jurisdiction.

Allying himself closely with the Taney opinion, Justice Wayne issued only a brief statement. Justice Daniel also agreed with the Chief Justice, but elaborated more fully the extreme southern "state sovereignty" thesis. Departing from the Taney thesis, Justices Campbell and Catron both treated the plea in abatement differently: Campbell refused to consider it, while Catron insisted that it was not properly a concern of the Court. Nevertheless, both accepted the Taney reasoning that proved the Missouri Compromise unconstitutional. Justice Grier, in a brief opinion, followed Taney on congressional power but dismissed the form of judgment as unimportant. Justice Nelson adhered to the opinion he wrote for the original majority.

The two other northern justices also differed somewhat between themselves. McLean held that the plea in abatement was not open, while Curtis consistently accepted Taney's position. Curtis, naturally, agreed with the lower court's disposition of the plea. McLean used both the Illinois and Minnesota residencies to find Scott a free man, while Curtis stressed the Minnesota sojourn and congressional power to prohibit slavery in a territory. With strict and unemotional adherence to constitutional intent and phraseology, as well as to the legislative record, he held the Missouri Compromise valid.

What did the Supreme Court "decide"? In one way or another, the justices ruled that Scott remained a slave. Beyond this, however, neither contemporaries of the event nor subsequent historians have ever concurred as to what a *majority* of the Court agreed upon. Was Taney's opinion on Negro citizenship and the unconstitutionality of the Missouri Compromise *obiter dicta?* Did at least five justices *properly* deny Scott's citizenship? Furthermore, was there a *proper* majority for ruling the Missouri Compromise unconstitutional? Could the Court so rule if a majority denied jurisdiction? Indeed, the jurisdictional knot — particularly whether the plea in abatement was before the Court — lies at the heart of these questions.[6]

Whatever genuine interest there may be in determining precisely what the Court decided, clearly most people in 1857, regardless of region or political affiliation, believed that the Court had sustained the constitutional position of the pro-slavery forces. Contemporary developments, however, soon made this question moot, for in 1862 Congress prohibited slavery in the territories — and this time without a judicial challenge. Therefore, a broader and more relevant inquiry might well center upon the political and institutional effects of the Court's action. Specifically, what role must be allotted the Dred Scott decision in an interpretation of the coming of the Civil War? And, with the war over and the slavery issue settled, what influence did the decision exercise on the development of constitutional law and the role of the Supreme Court in American government?

II

By 1857 the opposing positions on slavery in the territories clearly revolved around essentially abstract principles. As such, the Dred Scott

[6] A useful summary of the contemporary and historical literature on this problem is Frederick S. Allis, Jr., "The Dred Scott Labyrinth," in H. Stuart Hughes (ed.), *Teachers of History: Essays in Honor of Laurence Bradford Packard* (Ithaca, 1954) 341–368.

decision carried great symbolic import for both sides: it at once legitimatized the South's canons of slave expansion and afforded the Republican party the sinister glamour of a Cassandra. The Court's pronouncement, no matter how diffuse and ambiguous, offered a judicial imprimatur to Calhoun's state sovereignty doctrine rejecting congressional regulation of slavery in the territories. At the same time, Taney's opinion seemingly substantiated Republican charges that the South's boundless aggressive designs threatened to engulf the nation with slavery.

From the Compromise of 1820 until 1861, American constitutional and political history can be interpreted as a continuous dialogue centering on the territorial question, often bearing little or no relation to the reality of affairs. Beginning in the 1830's, the South, nettled by abolitionist attacks and bent on expansion, increasingly defended slavery as a "positive good." Indeed, following their most vigorous and promising spokesman, John C. Calhoun, the southerners buttressed their position with constitutional and legal sanction and elevated it into a social dogma.

Calhoun's constitutional exegesis reached maturity in his Senate speech of December 1837 on the "Importance of Domestic Slavery." Naturally, he relied on the notion of state sovereignty for the linchpin of his argument. The states, acting in their free, independent, and sovereign capacities, he contended, had acceded voluntarily to the Union to insure their security against domestic as well as foreign dangers. In creating a general government, however, the states reserved for themselves an exclusive power to regulate their own "domestic institutions." Any interference by other states, Calhoun maintained, would subvert the Union's intent, and therefore tend to weaken and destroy it. As the common agent of the states, the general government, moreover, had committed itself to protecting the domestic institutions of the several states. Therefore, any proposal to abolish slavery in either the District of Columbia or the territories "would be a direct and dangerous attack on the institutions of all the slaveholding States."

Initially, at least, the southern constitutional arguments aroused little national concern. Abolitionists were few in numbers and little heeded by the nation at large. When, however, the United States plunged into conflict with Mexico, the situation changed. Diverse opponents of the war soon found a useful rallying point in oppositon to an expansive, aggressive Slave Power. In August 1846, David Wilmot, an obscure Pennsylvania Democrat, offered a slogan and a symbol that buttressed northern opposition to the southern position. Borrowing directly from the Northwest Ordinance of 1787, Wilmot proposed that "neither slavery nor involuntary servitude shall ever exist" in any territory acquired from Mexico.

The Wilmot Proviso opened a new chapter of constitutional controversy. Few northerners disputed the right of states to maintain slavery free from outside interference. For the most part, they also conceded the South's constitutional right to recapture fugitive slaves, although many became increasingly concerned that its enforcement should not abridge the rights of free Negroes. But the extreme southern view of territorial nonintervention directly assaulted five decades of national political experience and practice. As Justice Curtis later explained in his Dred Scott dissent, from 1790 on, Congress regularly maintained a balance in its territorial legislation between prohibiting or permitting slavery.

Bearing in mind that there existed no widespread humanitarian opposition to slavery, the northern stance must also be understood beyond the realm of constitutional appeals. At bottom, the Wilmot ideology appealed to Northern self-interest. It "offered nothing to the slave," Professor Norman Graebner has written, but "to its potential adherents — the farmers, laborers, and capitalists of the North — it offered the opportunities of new lands free from the competition of slaveholders."[7] Here rested the fundamental tenet for the new free-soil appeal, a formulation which bridged the gap between the altruistic and materialistic antagonists of slavery, and created a united northern opposition. The Free-Soil party of 1848, like its later successor, the Republican party, symbolized the uneasy marriage of disparate motives.

Although southern power in the Senate precluded passage of the Wilmot Proviso, free-soilers, in strange alliance with Calhounites, prevented any extension of the Missouri Compromise theory. The dominant national Democratic party used the territorial settlements of the Compromise of 1850 to temporarily quash any direct confrontation. As the early 1850's wore on, moreover, compromise appeared even more difficult: a definitive political resolution of the constitutional conundrum began to look impracticable, if not impossible. But in the art of the impossible, the politic "solution" often is to do nothing, or to remove the problem to another arena. When, from a mixture of political and economic motives, Stephen A. Douglas, Democratic Senator from Illinois, formally initiated such a process in 1854, he sought to organize the Kansas-Nebraska territory on the basis of "popular sovereignty." His idea, which included specific repeal of the Missouri Compromise, flattered the South's nonintervention principle, yet politically, it backfired. For whatever Douglas's strategic considerations may have been, his proposal split the Democrats and stimulated the formulation of the Republican party. The free-soilers had a perfect appeal: Douglas's bill raised the spectre of a southern invasion of prized agrarian lands which had been guaranteed as free territory for over three decades. The mere opportunity for southern aggrandizement, whether attainable or not, proved a useful, indeed an invaluable, foil for anti-slavery politicians.

The new Republican party had its issue and exploited it in the presidential campaign of 1856. The Democrats, meanwhile, accepted the political solution of popular sovereignty for the sake of party unity. But

[7] Norman A. Graebner, "The Politicians and Slavery," in Graebner (ed.), *Politics and the Crisis of 1860* (Urbana, 1961), 13.

as political forces polarized on slavery questions, there was a growing demand to have the judiciary resolve the constitutional issues.[8]

The Supreme Court's "solution" in 1857 only hardened the diverse political positions. The most widely propagated aspects of the Dred Scott decision sustained southern constitutional theory; at the same time, the Republican party had to resist the decision or lose its very reason for existence. The response by Abraham Lincoln and others was determinable, necessary, and obvious. Paradoxically, the Court's action also exposed the tenuous character of the North-South alliance within the Democratic party and paved the path for its disruption.

The South rightfully regarded the decision as a great victory. From the southern viewpoint, Calhoun's logic had become the law of the land. But what southern Democrats regarded as a fundamental right proved either morally repugnant or politically suicidal for their northern and western colleagues. Stephen A. Douglas's relationship to his Illinois constituency offers a case in point. His notion of popular sovereignty rested essentially on the premise that territorial legislatures could determine the slavery question for themselves. Taney's opinion not only controverted this idea but also reinforced the southern position of nonintervention by either Congress *or* territorial legislature while the territorial status existed. Until the Supreme Court's pronouncement, the priority of party unity had submerged this significant difference. But after the decision, the rising Republican threat in Illinois prevented Douglas — whatever his actual beliefs — from ignoring or accepting the southern interpretation.

Douglas's opposition to the admission of Kansas in 1858 with the Lecompton constitution which permitted slavery presaged the imminent rupture of the Democratic party.[9] Allied with eastern Republicans, the Illinois senator successfully led the congressional battle to reject what he called the "Lecompton fraud." From that moment on, the leading candidate for the Democratic presidential nomination in 1860 was *persona non grata* with the South. Then, in October 1858, in his famous Freeport exchange with Abraham Lincoln, Douglas insisted that a territory could exclude slavery by failing to enact protective legislation. This so-called Freeport Doctrine sealed Douglas's fate, along with that of the Democratic party.

Abstractions revolved around a vicious political circle. In the Illinois senatorial contest of 1858, and elsewhere, the Dred Scott decision significantly strengthened the Republican party. Taney's remarks were interpreted in partisan fashion, and the Democratic schism shrewdly exploited. The Republican assault forced northern Democrats to circumvent or repudiate the extreme position of their southern political brethren, thus

[8] See Part I, *infra;* Wallace Mendelson, "Dred Scott's Case — Reconsidered," Part IV, *infra.*

[9] Don E. Fehrenbacher, *Prelude to Greatness: Lincoln in the 1850's* (Stanford, 1962), 128–142.

widening the growing party split. In turn, the defections by moderate Democrats added impetus to the South's drive for the substance — not the mere shadow — of what it claimed as its constitutional rights. Southern demands varied from a call for federal troops to protect slaveholders in the territories to the enactment of a uniform federal slave code for the territories. But all such attempts to convert constitutional abstractions into legislative facts proved to be politically impossible. The South's extremist interpretation and implementation of the Dred Scott decision only increased its isolation — an isolation which ultimately accelerated into separation.

In this sense, then, the Dred Scott decision bears directly upon the coming of the Civil War. The attempt to resolve the constitutional dilemma had solidified and strengthened the fledgling Republican party, which had in turn forced Democrats first to confront — and then to quarrel — over their own differences. The ensuing battle rent an already frail party fabric and insured the election of a Republican president in 1860. Lincoln's election, of course, made the southern constitutional position, along with Dred Scott, untenable and irrelevant.

III

Even after the Civil War had shorn the immediate questions of slavery and the nature of territorial government of meaning, the Dred Scott decision, with its myriad political, doctrinal, and institutional ramifications, remained much in evidence.

For one thing, the decision spurred demands for political reform of the federal judiciary, particularly the Supreme Court, branded by its southern majority. Malapportionment — in respect to population and geographic growth — was rife within the American governmental system, the Supreme Court not excepted. Until 1866, judicial tradition held it desirable that Supreme Court justices should be residents of the circuits in which they regularly heard cases. This tenet, together with the judiciary act of 1837, gave the South control of five of the nine judicial circuits — a number far out of proportion to its proper share. Furthermore, the existing nine circuits included none of the trans-Mississippi free states.

From 1855 on, in the face of determined and successful southern congressional opposition, the Republican party persistently agitated for reform of the circuit alignments. Once they achieved control of the legislative machinery, however, the Republicans redoubled their efforts. First in 1862, and then again in 1866, Congress reshaped the judicial circuits so as to leave only one composed exclusively of former slave states. The others were attached to northern or western states in order to reduce the chances of southern appointees. Various vacancies gave Lincoln five Supreme Court appointments, and naturally he took advantage of his new opportunities. All this served to make the judiciary safe for northern interests — and the Republican party.[10]

Political motivation notwithstanding, the reorganization of the Court speaks well of Republican moderation. Lingering bitterness from the Dred Scott decision prompted numerous extremist ideas, including abolition of the Court as then constituted. In general, however, political leaders made a careful distinction between the decision and the institution. Historical tradition and the recognized need for an impartial arbiter of the federal constitution proved decisive.

In the decades following the Dred Scott decision, the Supreme Court attained new heights of judicial power and, ironically enough, made liberal use of Taney's rationale of constitutional limitations. In his Dred Scott opinion, Taney held the Missouri Compromise unconstitutional on the grounds that it violated the Fifth Amendment and deprived persons of their property without due process of law. In this ruling he gave expression to the notion of a substantive limitation inherent in the due process idea which had been gathering momentum in state courts during the previous two decades; by applying it in Dred Scott, he sponsored its emergence into federal constitutional law.

Throughout the nineteenth and early twentieth centuries, the Supreme Court, drawing freely on the due process limitation, stood as a bulwark in defense of property interests. Citing the clauses in both the Fifth and the Fourteenth Amendments, the Court often invalidated or emasculated governmental attempts to regulate commerce and the economy. The particular property interest which Taney sought to secure may have become anachronistic, yet the principle he espoused in the Dred Scott case opened a whole new chapter in American constitutional law.

But more than the specific doctrine of due process, the Court in later years increasingly adhered to the conceptions of national power and of the judicial function underlying Dred Scott. The majority opinions in 1857 were marked by a negativist attitude toward the powers of what Taney called the "general government." Actually, the Dred Scott decision may be considered as the crowning touch to the Taney Court's modification of John Marshall's strongly nationalistic doctrines. And as a corollary, there was an awareness of the desirability for federal judicial authority to mediate and arbitrate differences between jealous and competing sovereignties. Justice Catron's messages to Buchanan reflected such an attitude. After the Civil War, this conception of the judicial function increasingly dominated the federal judiciary, and in part, accounted for the increased judicial activism.

The Dred Scott decision's more enduring relevance, however, lies in its negative symbolism. However real or exaggerated its contemporary

[10] Stanley I. Kutler, "Reconstruction and the Supreme Court: The Numbers Game Reconsidered," *The Journal of Southern History*, XXXII (1966), 56–58.

effects, it has stood as a monument of judicial indiscretion and as an instructive lesson in the virtues of judicial restraint. The late Justice Robert H. Jackson pungently observed of the case: "One such precedent is enough!" Criticism has dogged the history of the Supreme Court. From the late nineteenth century until 1937, an agrarian-labor-liberal coalition steadily assaulted the Court for its alleged pro-business inclinations and its preoccupation with property rights. Since the "constitutional revolution" of 1937, new cadres of critics have attacked the justices for their vigorous protection and advancement of civil rights and civil liberties. And through the years, the diverse criticism always has found common ground of expression within the real or imagined consequences of Dred Scott. Above all, then, Dred Scott's case persists as a constant reminder of the limits imposed on judicial power by political and social realities.

1

★ PROLOGUE

"Scarcely any question arises in the United States
that is not resolved, sooner or later, into a judicial
question."

ALEXIS DE TOCQUEVILLE, 1835

★ THE WAR WITH MEXICO and the subsequent acquisition of vast western lands intensified the long-smouldering sectional division over the question of slavery in the new territories. Beginning with the abortive Clayton Compromise of 1848, through the Compromise of 1850 and the Kansas-Nebraska Act of 1854, Congress wrestled with the problem but achieved only limited success. Traditional party alliances of Democrats and Whigs, rent by internal differences, experienced increasing strain and the legislative fruits they produced were, in consequence, vague, ambiguous, patchworks that offered little solution to the abiding basic problem. With existing legislation pleasing no one faction, political leaders in both sections increasingly spoke of the possibility of a judicial settlement — a possibility reflected in the legislation of the 1850's which facilitated jurisdictional avenues toward a decision by the Supreme Court. Whether Congress purposefully intended to turn the matter over to the Court is not entirely clear; the determination of legislative intent by historians being a treacherous thing at best. The abolitionists, naturally distrustful of many existing institutions and the men who guided them, represented a significant exception to the drive for a judicial solution. Nevertheless, the various statements in support of judicial participation certainly reflected the esteem and high regard in which the Court was held, and afforded a revealing contrast with the judicial image that prevailed after the Dred Scott decision.

1 *American Law Register*

(January 1856)

... [E]very disorganizing agency in the country appears to be at work. ... There are those ... who profess to deride systematically all warnings of danger to the Union. This is the security of ignorance. Those who stand ... upon the line which divides the sections now so unhappily at variance, and can survey without prejudice the movements on either side see and know too well the imminence of the peril. There is such exasperation on one side and determination on the other, as was never known before; and it will need the greatest caution and good sense, to prevent an explosion which would rend the Union into fragments. ... In such a crisis, it is the duty of all honest, thinking men to join in an endeavor to remove all those causes of controversy which are rankling and festering in the heart of the Nation, by submitting them to the peaceful arbitration of the Supreme Court. To leave them, in the present temper of local politics, in the hands of State Courts could only tend to organize passion by giving it the sanction of law, and to convert party quarrels into the conflicts of States. Admit that the Federal Judiciary may in its time have been guilty of errors, that it has occasionally sought to wield more power than was safe, that it is as fallible as every other human institution. Yet it has been and is a vast agency for good; it has averted many a storm which threatened our peace, and has lent its powerful aid in uniting us together in the bonds of law and justice. Its very existence has proved a beacon of safety. And now, when the black cloud is again on the horizon, when the trembling of the earth and the stillness of the air are prophetic to our fears, and we turn to it instinctively for protection, — let us ask ourselves, with all its imagined faults, what is there that can replace it? Strip it of its power, and what shall we get in exchange. Discord and confusion, statutes without obedience, Courts without authority, an anarchy of principles, and a chaos of decisions, till all law at last shall be extinguished by an appeal to arms. ...

---

1 "Appellate Jurisdiction of the Federal, over the State Courts." *American Law Register*, IV (January 1856), 150–152.

2 *Senator Stephen A. Douglas*

Democrat, Illinois (July 2, 1856)

My opinion in regard to the question . . . has been well known to the Senate for years. It has been repeated over and over again. . . . I [have said] it was a judicial question. . . . [I]f the Constitution carries slavery [into the territories] . . . let it go, and no power on earth can take it away; but, if the Constitution does not carry it there, no power but the people can carry it there. Whatever may be the true decision of that constitutional point, . . . I [have] stated I would not discuss this legal question, for by the [Kansas-Nebraska] bill we referred it to the courts. . . .

[I]ts [the Kansas-Nebraska bill's] opponents wish to know how I think the court will decide the constitutional question. I say I am willing to leave that to the Supreme Court of the United States, because the Constitution has intrusted it there.

3 *Senator Albert G. Brown*

Democrat, Mississippi (July 2, 1856)

My friend from Michigan [Senator Lewis Cass] and myself differ very widely as to what are the powers of a Territorial Legislature — he believing that they can exercise sovereign rights, and I believing no such thing; he contending that they have a right to exclude slavery, and I not admitting the proposition; but both of us concurring in the opinion that it is a question to be decided by the courts, and not by Congress.

2 *Congressional Globe,* 34th Congress, 1st Session, 797.
3 *Congressional Globe,* 34th Congress, 1st Session, Appendix, 801.

4

4 Abraham Lincoln

(July 23, 1856)

I grant you that an unconstitutional act is not a law; but I do not ask, and will not take your [Democrats'] construction of the Constitution. The Supreme Court of the United States is the tribunal to decide such questions, and we will submit to its decisions; and if you do also, there will be an end of the matter.

5 President James Buchanan

Inaugural Address (March 4, 1857)

A difference of opinion has arisen in regard to the point of time when the people of a Territory shall decide this question for themselves.

This is, happily, a matter of but little practical importance. Besides, it is a judicial question, which legitimately belongs to the Supreme Court of the United States, before whom it is now pending, and will, it is understood, be speedily and finally settled. To their decision, in common with all good citizens, I shall cheerfully submit. . . .

---

4 Roy P. Basler (ed.), *The Collected Works of Abraham Lincoln* (New Brunswick, Rutgers University Press, 1953), II, 355. In an autobiography written for the presidential campaign of 1860, Lincoln claimed to have no recollection of saying anything about a Supreme Court decision in 1856. *Ibid.*, IV, 67. The above report of his Galena, Illinois, speech of July 23, 1856, originally appeared in a local newspaper a week later.
5 *Inaugural Addresses of the Presidents of the United States*, House Document No. 540, 82nd Congress, 2nd Session (Washington, 1952), 104.

2

★ THE OPINIONS

★ AFTER A SECOND hearing of the Dred Scott case, the Supreme Court decided, in February 1857, to simply dispose of the matter without comment on Congress's power to prohibit slavery in the territories. Justice Samuel Nelson was selected to write a majority opinion which would follow the custom of adhering to a state court's interpretation of state laws. The majority thus concluded to give effect to the Missouri Supreme Court's ruling that Dred Scott was still a slave. Justices John McLean and Benjamin R. Curtis, however, announced their intention to dissent and discuss the merits of the case, including the problem of congressional power. The southern justices, with the backing of President-elect James Buchanan, believed that the case presented an opportunity for settling the constitutional issue and restoring sectional harmony. While Chief Justice Roger B. Taney ostensibly spoke for the majority, every member of the Court filed a separate opinion or comment. Three of these best represent the divergent viewpoints.. Taney's "opinion of the court" declared that Dred Scott remained a slave according to the laws of Missouri; that he was not a citizen; and that the Missouri Compromise was unconstitutional. Nelson presented his — and the Court's — original opinion deciding the case on the narrow issue. Curtis's dissent strongly affirmed congressional power to exclude slavery in the territories, and, in effect, refuted Taney's conclusions on that question and others.

1 Mr. Chief Justice Taney, the Opinion of the Court

. . . There are two leading questions presented by the record:

1. Had the Circuit Court of the United States jurisdiction to hear and determine the case between these parties? And

2. If it had jurisdiction, is the judgment it has given erroneous or not? . . .

[A]lthough [the government of the United States] . . . is sovereign and supreme in its appropriate sphere of action, yet it does not possess all the powers which usually belong to the sovereignty of a nation. Certain specified powers, enumerated in the Constitution, have been conferred upon it; and neither the legislative, executive, nor judicial departments of the Government can lawfully exercise any authority beyond the limits marked out by the Constitution. And in regulating the judicial department, the cases in which the courts of the United States shall have jurisdiction are particularly and specifically enumerated and defined; and they are not authorized to take cognizance of any case which does not come within the description therein specified. Hence, when a plaintiff sues in a court of the United States, it is necessary that he should show, in his pleading, that the suit he brings is within the jurisdiction of the court, and that he is entitled to sue there. And if he omits to do this, and should, by any oversight of the Circuit Court, obtain a judgment in his favor, the judgment would be reversed in the appellate court for want of jurisdiction in the court below. The jurisdiction would not be presumed, as in the case of a common-law English or State court, unless the contrary appeared. But the record, when it comes before the appellate court, must show, affirmatively, that the inferior court had authority under the Constitution, to hear and determine the case. And if the plaintiff claims a right to sue in a Circuit Court of the United States, under that provision of the Constitution which gives jurisdiction in controversies between citizens of different States, he must distinctly aver in his pleading that they are citizens of different States; and he cannot maintain his suit without showing that fact in the pleadings. . . .

If, however, the fact of citizenship is averred in the declaration, and the defendant does not deny it, and put it in issue by plea in abatement,

---

1 *Dred Scott* v. *John F. A. Sandford*, 19 Howard 393, 400–411, 426–432, 436–437, 446–452, 454.

he cannot offer evidence at the trial to disprove it, and consequently cannot avail himself of the objection in the appellate court, unless the defect should be apparent in some other part of the record. For if there is no plea in abatement, and the want of jurisdiction does not appear in any other part of the transcript brought up by the writ of error, the undisputed averment of citizenship in the declaration must be taken in this court to be true. In this case, the citizenship is averred, but it is denied by the defendant in the manner required by the rules of pleading, and the fact upon which the denial is based is admitted by the demurrer. And, if the plea and demurrer, and judgment of the court below upon it, are before us upon this record, the question to be decided is, whether the facts stated in the plea are sufficient to show that the plaintiff is not entitled to sue as a citizen in a court of the United States.

We think they are before us. The plea in abatement and the judgment of the court upon it, are a part of the judicial proceedings in the Circuit Court, and are there recorded as such; and a writ of error always brings up to the superior court the whole record of the proceedings in the court below. . . . And this being the case in the present instance, the plea in abatement is necessarily under consideration; and it becomes, therefore, our duty to decide whether the facts stated in the plea are or are not sufficient to show that the plaintiff is not entitled to sue as a citizen in a court of the United States.

This is certainly a very serious question, and one that now for the first time has been brought for decision before this court. But it is brought here by those who have a right to bring it, and it is our duty to meet it and decide it.

The question is simply this: Can a negro, whose ancestors were imported into this country, and sold as slaves, become a member of the political community formed and brought into existence by the Constitution of the United States, and as such become entitled to all the rights, and privileges, and immunities, guarantied by that instrument to the citizen? One of which rights is the privilege of suing in a court of the United States in the cases specified in the Constitution.

It will be observed, that the plea applies to that class of persons only whose ancestors were negroes of the African race, and imported into this country, and sold and held as slaves. The only matter in issue before the court, therefore, is, whether the descendants of such slaves, when they shall be emancipated, or who are born of parents who had become free before their birth, are citizens of a State, in the sense in which the word citizen is used in the Constitution of the United States. And this being the only matter in dispute on the pleadings, the court must be understood as speaking in this opinion of that class only, that is, of those persons who are the descendants of Africans who were imported into this country, and sold as slaves. . . .

We proceed to examine the case as presented by the pleadings.

The words "people of the United States" and "citizens" are synonymous terms, and mean the same thing. They both describe the political body who, according to our republican institutions, form the sovereignty, and who hold the power and conduct the Government through their representatives. They are what we familiarly call the "sovereign people," and every citizen is one of this people, and a constituent member of this sovereignty. The question before us is, whether the class of persons described in the plea in abatement compose a portion of this people, and are constituent members of this sovereignty? We think they are not, and that they are not included, and were not intended to be included, under the word "citizens" in the Constitution, and can therefore claim none of the rights and privileges which that instrument provides for and secures to citizens of the United States. On the contrary, they were at that time considered as a subordinate and inferior class of beings, who had been subjugated by the dominant race, and, whether emancipated or not, yet remained subject to their authority, and had no rights or privileges but such as those who held the power and the Government might choose to grant them.

It is not the province of the court to decide upon the justice or injustice, the policy or impolicy, of these laws. The decision of that question belonged to the political or law-making power; to those who formed the sovereignty and framed the Constitution. The duty of the court is, to interpret the instrument they have framed, with the best lights we can obtain on the subject, and to administer it as we find it, according to its true intent and meaning when it was adopted.

In discussing this question, we must not confound the rights of citizenship which a State may confer within its own limits, and the rights of citizenship as a member of the Union. It does not by any means follow, because he has all the rights and privileges of a citizen of a State, that he must be a citizen of the United States. He may have all of the rights and privileges of the citizen of a State, and yet not be entitled to the rights and privileges of a citizen in any other State. . . .

It is very clear, therefore, that no State can, by any act or law of its own, passed since the adoption of the Constitution, introduce a new member into the political community created by the Constitution of the United States. It cannot make him a member of this community by making him a member of its own. And for the same reason it cannot introduce any person, or description of persons, who were not intended to be embraced in this new political family, which the Constitution brought into existence, but were intended to be excluded from it.

The question then arises, whether the provisions of the Constitution, in relation to the personal rights and privileges to which the citizen of a State should be entitled, embraced the negro African race, at that time in this country, or who might afterwards be imported, who had then or should afterwards be made free in any State; and to put it in the power of a single State to make him a citizen of the United States, and endue him with the full rights of citizenship in every other State without their consent? Does the Constitution of the United States act upon him whenever he shall be made free under the laws of a State, and raised there to the rank of a citizen, and immediately clothe him with all the privileges of a citizen in every other State, and in its own courts?

The court think the affirmative of these propositions cannot be maintained. And if it cannot, the plaintiff in error could not be a citizen of the State of Missouri, within the meaning of the Constitution of the United States, and, consequently, was not entitled to sue in its courts.

It is true, every person, and every class and description of persons, who were at the time of the adoption of the Constitution recognised as citizens in the several States, became also citizens of this new political body; but none other; it was formed by them, and for them and their posterity, but for no one else. And the personal rights and privileges guarantied to citizens of this new sovereignty were intended to embrace those only who were then members of the several State communities, or who should afterwards by birthright or otherwise become members, according to the provisions of the Constitution and the principles on which it was founded. It was the union of those who were at that time members of distinct and separate political communities into one political family, whose power, for certain specified purposes, was to extend over the whole territory of the United States. And it gave to each citizen rights and privileges outside of his State which he did not before possess, and placed him in every other State upon a perfect equality with its own citizens as to rights of person and rights of property; it made him a citizen of the United States.

It becomes necessary, therefore, to determine who were citizens of the several States when the Constitution was adopted. And in order to do this, we must recur to the Governments and institutions of the thirteen colonies, when they separated from Great Britain and formed new sovereignties, and took their places in the family of independent nations. We must inquire who, at that time, were recognised as the people or citizens of a State, whose rights and liberties had been outraged by the English Government; and who declared their independence, and assumed the powers of Government to defend their rights by force of arms.

In the opinion of the court, the legislation and histories of the times, and the language used in the Declaration of Independence, show, that neither the class of persons who had been imported as slaves, nor their descendants, whether they had become free or not, were then acknowledged as a part of the people, nor intended to be included in the general words used in that memorable instrument.

It is difficult at this day to realize the state of public opinion in relation to that unfortunate race, which prevailed in the civilized and enlightened portions of the world at the time of the Declaration of Independence, and when the Constitution of the United States was framed and adopted. But the public history of every European nation displays it in a manner too plain to be mistaken.

They had for more than a century before been regarded as beings of an inferior order, and altogether unfit to associate with the white race, either in social or political relations; and so far inferior, that they had no rights which the white man was bound to respect; and that the negro might justly and lawfully be reduced to slavery for his benefit. He was bought and sold, and treated as an ordinary article of merchandise and traffic, whenever a profit could be made by it. This opinion was at that time fixed and universal in the civilized portion of the white race. It was regarded as an axiom in morals as well as in politics, which no one thought of disputing, or supposed to be open to dispute; and men in every grade and position in society daily and habitually acted upon it in their private pursuits, as well as in matters of public concern, without doubting for a moment the correctness of this opinion.

And in no nation was this opinion more firmly fixed or more uniformly acted upon than by the English Government and English people. They not only seized them on the coast of Africa, and sold them or held them in slavery for their own use; but they took them as ordinary articles of merchandise to every country where they could make a profit on them, and were far more extensively engaged in this commerce than any other nation in the world.

The opinion thus entertained and acted upon in England was naturally impressed upon the colonies they founded on this side of the Atlantic. And, accordingly, a negro of the African race was regarded by them as an article of property, and held, and bought and sold as such, in every one of the thirteen colonies which united in the Declaration of Independence, and afterwards formed the Constitution of the United States. The slaves were more or less numerous in the different colonies, as slave labor was found more or less profitable. But no one seems to have doubted the correctness of the prevailing opinion of the time.

The legislation of the different colonies furnishes positive and indisputable proof of this fact. . . .

The language of the Declaration of Independence is equally conclusive:

It begins by declaring that, "when in the course of human events it becomes necessary for one people to dissolve the political bands which have connected them with another, and to assume among the powers of the earth the separate and equal station to which the laws of nature and nature's God entitle them, a decent respect for the opinions of mankind requires that they should declare the causes which impel them to the separation."

It then proceeds to say: "We hold these truths to be self-evident: that all men are created equal; that they are endowed by their Creator with certain unalienable rights; that among them is life, liberty, and the pursuit of happiness; that to secure these rights, Governments are instituted, deriving their just powers from the consent of the governed."

The general words above quoted would seem to embrace the whole human family, and if they were used in a similar instrument at this day would be so understood. But it is too clear for dispute, that the enslaved African race were not intended to be included, and formed no part of the people who framed and adopted this declaration; for if the language, as understood in that day, would embrace them, the conduct of the distinguished men who framed the Declaration of Independence would have been utterly and flagrantly inconsistent with the principles they asserted; and instead of the sympathy of mankind, to which they so confidently appealed, they would have deserved and received universal rebuke and reprobation.

Yet the men who framed this declaration were great men — high in literary acquirements — high in their sense of honor, and incapable of asserting principles inconsistent with those on which they were acting. They perfectly understood the meaning of the language they used, and how it would be understood by others; and they knew that it would not in any part of the civilized world be supposed to embrace the negro race, which, by common consent, had been excluded from civilized Governments and the family of nations, and doomed to slavery. They spoke and acted according to the then established doctrines and principles, and in the ordinary language of the day, and no one misunderstood them. The unhappy black race were separated from the white by indelible marks, and laws long before established, and were never thought of or spoken of except as property, and when the claims of the owner or the profit of the trader were supposed to need protection.

This state of public opinion had undergone no change when the Constitution was adopted, as is equally evident from its provisions and language.

The brief preamble sets forth by whom it was formed, for what purposes, and for whose benefit and protection. It declares that it is formed by the *people* of the United States; that is to say, by those who were members of the different political communities in the several States; and its great object is declared to be to secure the blessings of liberty to themselves and their posterity. It speaks in general terms of the *people* of the United States, and of *citizens* of the several States, when it is providing for the exercise of the powers granted or the privileges secured to the citizen. It does not define what description of persons are intended to be included under these terms, or who shall be regarded as a citizen and one of the people. It uses them as terms so well understood, that no further description or definition was necessary.

But there are two clauses in the Constitution which point directly and specifically to the negro race as a separate class of persons, and show clearly that they were not regarded as a portion of the people or citizens of the Government then formed.

One of these clauses reserves to each of the thirteen States the right to import slaves until the year 1808, if it thinks proper. And the importation which it thus sanctions was unquestionably of persons of the race of which we are speaking, as the traffic in slaves in the United States had always been confined to them. And by the other provision the States pledge themselves to each other to maintain the right of property of the master, by delivering up to him any slave who may have escaped from his service, and be found within their respective territories. . . .

No one, we presume, supposes that any change in public opinion or feeling, in relation to this unfortunate race, in the civilized nations of Europe or in this country, should induce the court to give to the words of the Constitution a more liberal construction in their favor than they were intended to bear when the instrument was framed and adopted. Such an argument would be altogether inadmissible in any tribunal called on to interpret it. If any of its provisions are deemed unjust, there is a mode described in the instrument itself by which it may be amended; but while it remains unaltered, it must be construed now as it was understood at the time of its adoption. It is not only the same in words, but the same in meaning, and delegates the same powers to the Government, and reserves and secures the same rights and privileges to the citizen; and as long as it continues to exist in its present form, it speaks not only in the same words, but with the same meaning and intent with which it spoke when it came from the hands of its framers, and was voted on and adopted by the people of the United States. Any other rule of construction would abrogate the judicial character of this court, and make it the mere reflex of the popular opinion or passion of the day. This court was not created by the Constitution for such purposes. Higher and graver trusts have been confided to it, and it must not falter in the path of duty.

What the construction was at that time, we think can hardly admit of doubt. We have the language of the Declaration of Independence and of the Articles of Confederation, in addition to the plain words of the Constitution itself; we have the legislation of the different States, before, about the time, and since, the Constitution was adopted; we have the legislation of Congress, from the time of its adoption to a recent period; and we have the constant and uniform action of the Executive Department, all concurring together, and leading to the same result. And if anything in relation to the construction of the Constitution can be regarded as settled, it is that which we now give to the word "citizen" and the word "people."

And upon a full and careful consideration of the subject, the court is of opinion, that, upon the facts stated in the plea in abatement, Dred Scott was not a citizen of Missouri within the meaning of the Constitution of the United States, and not entitled as such to sue in its courts; and, consequently, that the Circuit Court had no jurisdiction of the case, and that the judgment on the plea in abatement is erroneous.

We are aware that doubts are entertained by some of the members of the court, whether the plea in abatement is legally before the court upon this writ of error; but if that plea is regarded as waived, or out of the case upon any other ground, yet the question as to the jurisdiction of the Circuit Court is presented on the face of the bill of exception itself, taken by the plaintiff at the trial; for he admits that he and his wife were born slaves, but endeavors to make out his title to freedom and citizenship by showing that they were taken by their owner to certain places, hereinafter mentioned, where slavery could not by law exist, and that they thereby became free and upon their return to Missouri became citizens of that State.

Now, if the removal of which he speaks did not give them their freedom, then by his own admission he is still a slave; and whatever opinions may be entertained in favor of the citizenship of a free person of the African race, no one supposes that a slave is a citizen of the State or of the United States. If, therefore, the acts done by his owner did not make them free persons, he is still a slave, and certainly incapable of suing in the character of a citizen.

The principle of law is too well settled to be disputed, that a court can give no judgment for either party, where it has no jurisdiction; and if, upon the showing of Scott himself, it appeared that he was still a slave, the case ought to have been dismissed, and the judgment against him and in favor of the defendant for costs, is, like that on the plea in abatement, erroneous, and the suit ought to have been dismissed by the Circuit Court for want of jurisdiction in that court.

But, before we proceed to examine this part of the case, it may be proper to notice an objection taken to the judicial authority of this court to decide it; and it has been said, that as this court has decided against the jurisdiction of the Circuit Court on the plea in abatement, it has no right to examine any question presented by the exception; and that anything it may say upon that part of the case will be extra-judicial, and mere obiter dicta.

This is a manifest mistake; there can be no doubt as to the jurisdiction of this court to revise the judgment of a Circuit Court, and to reverse it for any error apparent on the record, whether it be the error of giving judgment in a case over which it had no jurisdiction, or any other material error; and this, too, whether there is a plea in abatement or not. . . .

It is the duty of the appellate tribunal to correct this error; but that could not be done by dismissing the case for want of jurisdiction here — for that would leave the erroneous judgment in full force, and the injured party without remedy. And the appellate court therefore exercises the power for which alone appellate courts are constituted, by reversing the judgment of the court below for this error. It exercises its proper and appropriate jurisdiction over the judgment and proceedings of the Circuit Court, as they appear upon the record brought up by the writ of error.

The correction of one error in the court below does not deprive the appellate court of the power of examining further into the record, and correcting any other material errors which may have been committed by the inferior court. There is certainly no rule of law — nor any practice — nor any decision of a court — which even questions this power in the appellate tribunal. On the contrary, it is the daily practice of this court, and of all appellate courts where they reverse the judgment of an inferior court for error, to correct by its opinions whatever errors may appear on the record material to the case; and they have always held it to be their duty to do so where the silence of the court might lead to misconstruction or future controversy, and the point has been relied on by either side, and argued before the court.

In the case before us, we have already decided that the Circuit Court erred in deciding that it had jurisdiction upon the facts admitted by the pleadings. And it appears that, in the further progress of the case, it acted upon the erroneous principle it had decided on the pleadings, and gave judgment for the defendant, where, upon the facts admitted in the exception, it had no jurisdiction.

We are at a loss to understand upon what principle of law, applicable to appellate jurisdiction, it can be supposed that this court has not judicial authority to correct the last-mentioned error, because they had before corrected the former; or by what process of reasoning it can be made out, that the error of an inferior court in actually pronouncing judgment for one of the parties, in a case in which it had no jurisdiction, cannot be looked into or corrected by this court, because we have decided a similar question presented in the pleadings. The last point is distinctly presented by the facts contained in the plaintiff's own bill of exceptions, which he himself brings here by this writ of error. It was the point which chiefly occupied the attention of the counsel on both sides in the argument — and the judgment which this court must render upon both errors is precisely the same. It must, in each of them, exercise jurisdiction over the judgment, and reverse it for the errors committed by the court below; and issue a mandate to the Circuit Court to conform its judgment to the opinion pronounced by this court, by dismissing the case for want of jurisdiction in the Circuit Court. This is the constant and invariable practice of this court, where it reverses a judgment for want of jurisdiction in the Circuit Court.

It can scarcely be necessary to pursue such a question further. The want of jurisdiction in the court below may appear on the record without any plea in abatement. This is familiarly the case where a court of chancery has exercised jurisdiction in a case where the plaintiff had a plain and adequate remedy at law, and it so appears by the transcript when brought here by appeal. So also where it appears that a court of admiralty has exercised jurisdiction in a case belonging exclusively to a court of common law. In these cases there is no plea in abatement. And for the same reason, and upon the same principles, where the defect of jurisdiction is patent on the record, this court is bound to reverse the judgment, although the defendant has not pleaded in abatement to the jurisdiction of the inferior court. . . .

We proceed, therefore, to inquire whether the facts relied on by the plaintiff entitled him to his freedom. . . .

In considering this part of the controversy, two questions arise: 1. Was he, together with his family, free in Missouri by reason of the stay in the territory of the United States hereinbefore mentioned? And 2. If they were not, is Scott himself free by reason of his removal to Rock Island, in the State of Illinois, as stated in the above admissions?

We proceed to examine the first question.

The act of Congress, upon which the plaintiff relies, declares that slavery and involuntary servitude, except as a punishment for crime, shall be forever prohibited in all that part of the territory ceded by France, under the name of Louisiana, which lies north of thirty-six degrees thirty minutes north latitude, and not included within the limits of Missouri. And the difficulty which meets us at the threshold of this part of the inquiry is, whether Congress was authorized to pass this law under any of the powers granted to it by the Constitution; for if the authority is not given by that instrument, it is the duty of this court to declare it void and inoperative, and incapable of conferring freedom upon any one who is held as a slave under the laws of any one of the States.

The counsel for the plaintiff has laid much stress upon that article in the Constitution which confers on Congress the power "to dispose of and make all needful rules and regulations respecting the territory or other property belonging to the United States;" but, in the judgment of the court, that provision has no bearing on the present controversy, and the power there given, whatever it may be, is confined, and was intended to be confined, to the territory which at that time belonged to, or was claimed by, the United States, and was within their boundaries as set-tled by the treaty with Great Britain, and can have no influence upon a territory afterwards acquired from a foreign Government. It was a special provision for a known and particular territory, and to meet a present emergency, and nothing more.

A brief summary of the history of the times, as well as the careful and measured terms in which the article is framed, will show the correctness of this proposition. . . .

[T]he clause was . . . intended for a specific purpose. . . . It was to transfer to the new Government the property then held in common by the States, and to give to that Government power to apply it to the objects for which it had been destined by mutual agreement among the States before their league was dissolved. It applied only to the property which the States held in common at that time, and has no reference whatever to any territory or other property which the new sovereignty might afterwards itself acquire.

The language used in the clause, the arrangement and combination of the powers, and the somewhat unusual phraseology it uses, when it speaks of the political power to be exercised in the government of the territory, all indicate the design and meaning of the clause to be such as we have mentioned. It does not speak of *any* territory, nor of *Territories*, but uses language which, according to its legitimate meaning, points to a particular thing. The power is given in relation only to *the* territory of the United States — that is, to a territory then in existence, and then known or claimed as the territory of the United States. It begins its enumeration of powers by that of disposing, in other words, making sale of the lands, or raising money from them, which, as we have already said, was the main object of the cession, and which is accordingly the first thing provided for in the article. It then gives the power which was necessarily associated with the disposition and sale of the lands — that is, the power of making needful rules and regulations respecting the territory. And whatever construction may now be given to these words, every one, we think, must admit that they are not the words usually employed by statesmen in giving supreme power of legislation. They are certainly very unlike the words used in the power granted to legislate over territory which the new Government might afterwards itself obtain by cession from a State, either for its seat of Government, or for forts, magazines, arsenals, dock yards, and other needful buildings.

And the same power of making needful rules respecting the territory is, in precisely the same language, applied to the *other* property belonging to the United States — associating the power over the territory in this respect with the power over movable or personal property — that is, the ships, arms, and munitions of war, which then belonged in common to the State sovereignties. And it will hardly be said, that this power, in relation to the last-mentioned objects, was deemed necessary to be thus specially given to the new Government, in order to authorize it to make needful rules and regulations respecting the ships it might itself build, or arms and munitions of war it might itself manufacture or provide for the public service.

No one, it is believed, would think a moment of deriving the power of Congress to make needful rules and regulations in relation to property of this kind from this clause of the Constitution. Nor can it, upon any fair construction, be applied to any property but that which the new Government was about to receive from the confederated States. And if this be true as to this property, it must be equally true and limited as to the territory, which is so carefully and precisely coupled with it — and like it referred to as property in the power granted. The concluding words of the clause appear to render this construction irresistible; for, after the provisions we have mentioned, it proceeds to say, "that nothing in the Constitution shall be so construed as to prejudice any claims of the United States, or of any particular State. . . ."

This brings us to examine by what provision of the Constitution the present Federal Government, under its delegated and restricted powers, is authorized to acquire territory outside of the original limits of the United States, and what powers it may exercise therein over the person or property of a citizen of the United States, while it remains a Territory, and until it shall be admitted as one of the States of the Union.

There is certainly no power given by the Constitution to the Federal Government to establish or maintain colonies bordering on the United States or at a distance, to be ruled and governed at its own pleasure; nor to enlarge its territorial limits in any way, except by the admission of new States. That power is plainly given; and if a new State is admitted, it needs no further legislation by Congress, because the Constitution itself defines the relative rights and powers, and duties of the State, and the citizens of the State, and the Federal Government. But no power is given to acquire a Territory to be held and governed permanently in that character.

And indeed the power exercised by Congress to acquire territory and establish a Government there, according to its own unlimited discretion, was viewed with great jealousy by the leading statesmen of the day. And in the Federalist, (No. 38,) written by Mr. Madison, he speaks of the acquisition of the Northwestern Territory by the confederated States, by the cession from Virginia, and the establishment of a Government there, as an exercise of power not warranted by the Articles of Confederation, and dangerous to the liberties of the people. And he urges the adoption of the Constitution as a security and safeguard against such an exercise of power.

We do not mean, however, to question the power of Congress in this respect. The power to expand the territory of the United States by the admission of new States is plainly given; and in the construction of this power by all the departments of the Government, it has been held to authorize the acquisition of territory, not fit for admission at the time, but to be admitted as soon as its population and situation would entitle it to admission. It is acquired to become a State, and not to be held as a colony and governed by Congress with absolute authority; and as the propriety of admitting a new State is committed to the sound discretion of Congress, the power to acquire territory for that purpose, to be held by the United States until it is in a suitable condition to become a State upon an equal footing with the other States, must rest upon the same discretion. It is a question for the political department of the Government, and not the judicial; and whatever the political department of the

Government shall recognise as within the limits of the United States, the judicial department is also bound to recognise, and to administer in it the laws of the United States, so far as they apply, and to maintain in the Territory the authority and rights of the Government, and also the personal rights and rights of property of individual citizens, as secured by the Constitution. All we mean to say on this point is, that, as there is no express regulation in the Constitution defining the power which the General Government may exercise over the person or property of a citizen in a Territory thus acquired, the court must necessarily look to the provisions and principles of the Constitution, and its distribution of powers, for the rules and principles by which its decision must be governed.

Taking this rule to guide us, it may be safely assumed that citizens of the United States who migrate to a Territory belonging to the people of the United States, cannot be ruled as mere colonists, dependent upon the will of the General Government, and to be governed by any laws it may think proper to impose. The principle upon which our Governments rest, and upon which alone they continue to exist, is the union of States, sovereign and independent within their own limits in their internal and domestic concerns, and bound together as one people by a General Government, possessing certain enumerated and restricted powers, delegated to it by the people of the several States, and exercising supreme authority within the scope of the powers granted to it, throughout the dominion of the United States. A power, therefore, in the General Government to obtain and hold colonies and dependent territories, over which they might legislate without restriction, would be inconsistent with its own existence in its present form. Whatever it acquires, it acquires for the benefit of the people of the several States who created it. It is their trustee acting for them, and charged with the duty of promoting the interests of the whole people of the Union in the exercise of the powers specifically granted. . . .

[I]t is undoubtedly necessary that some Government should be established, in order to organize society, and to protect the inhabitants in their persons and property; and as the people of the United States could act in this matter only through the Government which represented them, and through which they spoke and acted when the Territory was obtained, it was not only within the scope of its powers, but it was its duty to pass such laws and establish such a Government as would enable those by whose authority they acted to reap the advantages anticipated from its acquisition, and to gather there a population which would enable it to assume the position to which it was destined among the States of the Union. The power to acquire necessarily carries with it the power to preserve and apply to the purposes for which it was acquired. The form of government to be established necessarily rested in the discretion of Congress. It was their duty to establish the one that would be best suited for the protection and security of the citizens of the United States, and other inhabitants who might be authorized to take up their abode there, and that must always depend upon the existing condition of the Territory, as to the number and character of its inhabitants, and their situation in the Territory. . . .

But the power of Congress over the person or property of a citizen can never be a mere discretionary power under our Constitution and form of Government. The powers of the Government and the rights and privileges of the citizen are regulated and plainly defined by the Constitution itself. And when the Territory becomes a part of the United States, the Federal Government enters into possession in the character impressed upon it by those who created it. It enters upon it with its powers over the citizen strictly defined, and limited by the Constitution, from which it derives its own existence, and by virtue of which alone it continues to exist and act as a Government and sovereignty. It has no power of any kind beyond it; and it cannot, when it enters a Territory of the United States, put off its character, and assume discretionary or despotic powers which the Constitution has denied to it. It cannot create for itself a new character separated from the citizens of the United States, and the duties it owes them under the provisions of the Constitution. The Territory being a part of the United States, the Government and the citizen both enter it under the authority of the Constitution, with their respective right defined and marked out; and the Federal Government can exercise no power over his person or property, beyond what that instrument confers, nor lawfully deny any right which it has reserved.

A reference to a few of the provisions of the Constitution will illustrate this proposition.

For example, no one, we presume, will contend that Congress can make any law in a Territory respecting the establishment of religion, or the free exercise thereof, or abridging the freedom of speech or of the press, or the right of the people of the Territory peaceably to assemble, and to petition the Government for the redress of grievances.

Nor can Congress deny to the people the right to keep and bear arms, nor the right to trial by jury, nor compel any one to be a witness against himself in a criminal proceeding.

These powers, and others, in relation to rights of person, which it is not necessary here to enumerate, are, in express and positive terms, denied to the General Government; and the rights of private property have been guarded with equal care. Thus the rights of property are united with the rights of person, and placed on the same ground by the fifth amendment to the Constitution, which provides that no person shall be deprived of life, liberty, and property, without due process of law. And an act of Congress which deprives a citizen of the United States of his liberty or property, merely because he came himself or brought his property into a particular Territory of the United States, and who had committed no offence against the laws, could hardly be dignified with the name of due process of law.

So, too, it will hardly be contended that Congress could by law quarter a soldier in a house in a Territory without the consent of the owner, in time of peace; nor in time of war, but in a manner prescribed by law. Nor could they by law forfeit the property of a citizen in a Territory who was convicted of treason, for a longer period than the life of the person convicted; nor take private property for public use without just compensation.

The powers over person and property of which we speak are not only not granted to Congress, but are in express terms denied, and they are forbidden to exercise them. And this prohibition is not confined to the States, but the words are general, and extend to the whole territory over which the Constitution gives it power to legislate, including those portions of it remaining under Territorial Government, as well as that covered by States. It is a total absence of power everywhere within the dominion of the United States, and places the citizens of a Territory, so far as these rights are concerned, on the same footing with citizens of the States, and guards them as firmly and plainly against any inroads which the General Government might attempt, under the plea of implied or incidental powers. And if Congress itself cannot do this — if it is beyond the powers conferred on the Federal Government — it will be admitted, we presume, that it could not authorize a Territorial Government to exercise them. It could confer no power on any local Government, established by its authority, to violate the provisions of the Constitution.

It seems, however, to be supposed, that there is a difference between property in a slave and other property, and that different rules may be applied to it in expounding the Constitution of the United States. And the laws and usages of nations, and the writings of eminent jurists upon the relation of master and slave and their mutual rights and duties, and the powers which Governments may exercise over it, have been dwelt upon in the argument.

But in considering the question before us, it must be borne in mind that there is no law of nations standing between the people of the United States and their Government, and interfering with their relation to each other. The powers of the Government, and the rights of the citizen under it, are positive and practical regulations plainly written down. The people of the United States have delegated to it certain enumerated powers, and forbidden it to exercise others. It has no power over the person or property of a citizen but what the citizens of the United States have granted. And no laws or usages of other nations, or reasoning of statesmen or jurists upon the relations of master and slave, can enlarge the powers of the Government, or take from the citizens the rights they have reserved. And if the Constitution recognises the right of property of the master in a slave, and makes no distinction between that description of property and other property owned by a citizen, no tribunal, acting under the authority of the United States, whether it be legislative, executive, or judicial, has a right to draw such a distinction, or deny to it the benefit of the provisions and guarantees which have been provided for the protection of private property against the encroachments of the Government.

Now, as we have already said in an earlier part of this opinion, upon a different point, the right of property in a slave is distinctly and expressly affirmed in the Constitution. The right to traffic in it, like an ordinary article of merchandise and property, was guarantied to the citizens of the United States, in every State that might desire it, for twenty years. And the Government in express terms is pledged to protect it in all future time, if the slave escapes from his owner. This is done in plain words — too plain to be misunderstood. And no word can be found in the Constitution which gives Congress a greater power over slave property, or which entitles property of that kind to less protection than property of any other description. The only power conferred is the power coupled with the duty of guarding and protecting the owner in his rights.

Upon these considerations, it is the opinion of the court that the act of Congress which prohibited a citizen from holding and owning property of this kind in the territory of the United States north of the line therein mentioned, is not warranted by the Constitution, and is therefore void; and that neither Dred Scott himself, nor any of his family, were made free by being carried into this territory; even if they had been carried there by the owner, with the intention of becoming a permanent resident.

We have so far examined the case, as it stands under the Constitution of the United States, and the powers thereby delegated to the Federal Government.

But there is another point in the case which depends on State power and State law. And it is contended, on the part of the plaintiff, that he is made free by being taken to Rock Island, in the State of Illinois, independently of his residence in the territory of the United States; and being so made free, he was not again reduced to a state of slavery by being brought back to Missouri.

Our notice of this part of the case will be very brief; for the principle on which it depends was decided in this court, upon much consideration, in the case of Strader et al. *v.* Graham, reported in 10th Howard, 82. In that case, the slaves had been taken from Kentucky to Ohio, with the consent of the owner, and afterwards brought back to Kentucky. And this court held that their *status* or condition, as free or slave, depended upon the laws of Kentucky, when they were brought back into that State, and not of Ohio; and that this court had no jurisdiction to revise the judgment of a State court upon its own laws. This was the point directly before the court, and the decision that this court had not jurisdiction turned upon it, as will be seen by the report of the case.

So in this case. As Scott was a slave when taken into the State of Illinois by his owner, and was there held as such, and brought back in that character, his *status*, as free or slave, depended on the laws of Missouri, and not of Illinois. . . .

Upon the whole, therefore, it is the judgment of this court, that it appears by the record before us that the plaintiff in error is not a citizen of Missouri, in the sense in which that word is used in the Constitution; and that the Circuit Court of the United States, for that reason, had no jurisdiction in the case, and could give no judgment in it. Its judgment for the defendant must, consequently, be reversed, and a mandate issued, directing the suit to be dismissed for want of jurisdiction.

2 *Mr. Justice Nelson*

With respect to the plea in abatement, which went to the citizenship of the plaintiff, and his competency to bring a suit in the Federal courts, the common-law rule of pleading is, that upon a judgment against the plea on demurrer, and that the defendant answer over, and the defendant submits to the judgment, and pleads over to the merits, the plea in abatement is deemed to be waived, and is not afterwards to be regarded as a part of the record in deciding upon the rights of the parties. There is some question, however, whether this rule of pleading applies to the peculiar system and jurisdiction of the Federal courts. As, in these courts, if the facts appearing on the record show that the Circuit Court had no jurisdiction, its judgment will be reversed in the appellate court for that cause, and the case remanded with directions to be dismissed.

In the view we have taken of the case, it will not be necessary to pass upon this question, and we shall therefore proceed at once to an examination of the case upon its merits. The question upon the merits, in general terms, is, whether or not the removal of the plaintiff, who was a slave, with his master, from the State of Missouri to the State of Illinois, with a view to a temporary residence, and after such residence and return to the slave State, such residence in the free State works an emancipation. . . .

Our opinion is, that the question is one which belongs to each State to

---

2 *Dred Scott* v. *John F. A. Sandford*, 19 Howard 393, 458–466, 468–469

decide for itself, either by its Legislature or courts of justice; and hence, in respect to the case before us, to the State of Missouri — a question exclusively of Missouri law, and which, when determined by that State, it is the duty of the Federal courts to follow it. In other words, except in cases where the power is restrained by the Constitution of the United States, the law of the State is supreme over the subject of slavery within its jurisdiction.

As a practical illustration of the principle, we may refer to the legislation of the free States in abolishing slavery, and prohibiting its introduction into their territories. Confessedly, except as restrained by the Federal Constitution, they exercised, and rightfully, complete and absolute power over the subject. Upon what principle, then, can it be denied to the State of Missouri? The power flows from the sovereign character of the States of this Union; sovereign, not merely as respects the Federal Government — except as they have consented to its limitation — but sovereign as respects each other. Whether, therefore, the State of Missouri will recognise or give effect to the laws of Illinois within her territories on the subject of slavery, is a question for her to determine. Nor is there any constitutional power in this Government that can rightfully control her.

Every State or nation possesses an exclusive sovereignty and jurisdiction within her own territory; and, her laws affect and bind all property and persons residing within it. It may regulate the manner and circumstances under which property is held, and the condition, capacity, and state, of all persons therein; and, also, the remedy and modes of administering justice. And it is equally true, that no State or nation can affect or bind property out of its territory, or persons not residing within it. No State, therefore, can enact laws to operate beyond its own dominions, and, if it attempts to do so, it may be lawfully refused obedience. Such laws can have no inherent authority extra-territorially. This is the necessary result of the independence of distinct and separate sovereignties.

Now, it follows from these principles, that whatever force or effect the laws of one State or nation may have in the territories of another, must depend solely upon the laws and municipal regulations of the latter, upon its own jurisprudence and polity, and upon its own express or tacit consent. . . .

Nations, from convenience and comity, and from mutual interest, and a sort of moral necessity to do justice, recognise and administer the laws of other countries. But, of the nature, extent, and utility, of them, respecting property, or the state and condition of persons within her territories, each nation judges for itself; and is never bound, even upon the ground of comity, to recognise them, if prejudicial to her own interests. The recognition is purely from comity, and not from any absolute or paramount obligation. . . .

These principles fully establish, that it belongs to the sovereign State of Missouri to determine by her laws the question of slavery within her jurisdiction, subject only to such limitations as may be found in the Federal Constitution; and, further, that the laws of other States of the Confederacy, whether enacted by their Legislatures or expounded by their courts, can have no operation within her territory, or affect rights growing out of her own laws on the subject. This is the necessary result of the independent and sovereign character of the State. The principle is not peculiar to the State of Missouri, but is equally applicable to each State belonging to the Confederacy. The laws of each have no extra-territorial operation within the jurisdiction of another, except such as may be voluntarily conceded by her laws or courts of justice. To the extent of such concession upon the rule of comity of nations, the foreign law may operate, as it then becomes a part of the municipal law of the State. When determined that the foreign law shall have effect, the municipal law of the State retires, and gives place to the foreign law.

In view of these principles, let us examine a little more closely the doctrine of those who maintain that the law of Missouri is not to govern the status and condition of the plaintiff. They insist that the removal and temporary residence with his master in Illinois, where slavery is inhibited, had the effect to set him free, and that the same effect is to be given to the law of Illinois, within the State of Missouri, after his return. Why was he set free in Illinois? Because the law of Missouri, under which he was held as a slave, had no operation by its own force extra-territorially; and the State of Illinois refused to recognise its effect within her limits, upon principles of comity, as a state of slavery was inconsistent with her laws, and contrary to her policy. But, how is the case different on the return of the plaintiff to the State of Missouri? Is she bound to recognise and enforce the law of Illinois? For, unless she is, the status and condition of the slave upon his return remains the same as originally existed. Has the law of Illinois any greater force within the jurisdiction of Missouri, than the laws of the latter within that of the former? Certainly not. They stand upon an equal footing. Neither has any force extra-territorially, except what may be voluntarily conceded to them. . . .

We come now to the decision of this court in the case of Strader et al. *v.* Graham, (10 How., p. 2.) The case came up from the Court of Appeals, in the State of Kentucky. The question in the case was, whether certain slaves of Graham, a resident of Kentucky, who had been employed temporarily at several places in the State of Ohio, with their master's consent, and had returned to Kentucky into his service, had thereby become entitled to their freedom. The Court of Appeals held that they had not. The case was brought to this court under the twenty-fifth section of the judiciary act. This court held that it had no jurisdiction, for the reason, the question was one that belonged exclusively to the State of Kentucky. The Chief Justice, in delivering the opinion of the court observed that "every State has an undoubted right to determine the status or domestic and social condition of the persons domiciled within its territory, except in so far as the powers of the States in this respect are restrained, or duties and obligations imposed upon them, by the Constitution of the United States. There is nothing in the Constitution of the United States, he observes, that can in any degree control the law of Kentucky upon this subject. And the condition of the negroes, therefore, as to freedom or slavery, after their return, depended altogether upon the laws of that State, and could not be influenced by the laws of Ohio. It was exclusively in the power of Kentucky to determine, for herself, whether their employment in another State should or should not make them free on their return."

It has been supposed, in the argument on the part of the plaintiff, that the eighth section of the act of Congress passed March 6, 1820, (3 St. at Large, p. 544,) which prohibited slavery north of thirty-six degrees thirty minutes, within which the plaintiff and his wife temporarily resided at Fort Snelling, possessed some superior virtue and effect, extra-territorially, and within the State of Missouri, beyond that of the laws of Illinois, or those of Ohio in the case of Strader et al *v.* Graham. A similar ground was taken and urged upon the court in the case just mentioned, under the ordinance of 1787, which was enacted during the time of the Confederation, and re-enacted by Congress, after the adoption of the Constitution, with some amendments adapting it to the new Government. (1 St. at Large, p. 50.)

In answer to this ground, the Chief Justice, in delivering the opinion of the court, observed: "The argument assumes that the six articles which that ordinance declares to be perpetual, are still in force in the States since formed within the territory, and admitted into the Union. If this proposition could be maintained, it would not alter the question; for the regulations of Congress, under the old Confederation or the present Constitution, for the government of a particular Territory, could have no force beyond its limits. It certainly could not restrict the power of the States, within their respective territories, nor in any manner interfere with their laws and institutions, nor give this court control over them.

"The ordinance in question, he observes, if still in force, could have no more operation than the laws of Ohio in the State of Kentucky, and could not influence the decision upon the rights of the master or the slaves in the State."

This view, thus authoritatively declared, furnishes a conclusive answer to the distinction attempted to be set up between the extra-territorial effect of a State law and the act of Congress in question.

It must be admitted that Congress possesses no power to regulate or abolish slavery within the States; and that, if this act had attempted any such legislation, it would have been a nullity. And yet the argument here, if there be any force in it, leads to the result, that effect may be given to such legislation; for it is only by giving the act of Congress operation within the State of Missouri, that it can have any effect upon the question between the parties. Having no such effect directly, it will be difficult to maintain, upon any consistent reasoning, that it can be made to operate indirectly upon the subject.

The argument, we think, in any aspect in which it may be viewed, is utterly destitute of support upon any principles of constitutional law, as, according to that, Congress has no power whatever over the subject of slavery within the State; and is also subversive of the established doctrine of international jurisprudence, as, according to that, it is an axiom that the laws of one Government have no force within the limits of another, or extra-territorially, except from the consent of the latter. . . .

Our conclusion, therefore, is, upon this branch of the case, that the question involved is one depending solely upon the law of Missouri, and that the Federal court sitting in the State, and trying the case before us, was bound to follow it.

The remaining question for consideration is, What is the law of the State of Missouri on this subject? And it would be a sufficient answer to refer to the judgment of the highest court of the State. . . . The [state] court placed the decision upon the temporary residence of the master with the slaves in the State and Territory to which they removed, and their return to the slave State; and upon the principles of international law, that foreign laws have no extra-territorial force, except such as the State within which they are sought to be enforced may see fit to extend to them, upon the doctrine of comity of nations.

This is the substance of the grounds of the decision.

The same question has been twice before that court since, and the same judgment given, (15 Misso. R., 595; 17 Ib., 434.) It must be admitted, therefore, as the settled law of the State, and, according to the decision in the case of Strader et al. *v.* Graham; is conclusive of the case in this court. . . .

Upon the whole, it must be admitted that the current of authority, both in England and in this country, is in accordance with the law as declared by the courts of Missouri in the case before us, and we think the court below was not only right, but bound to follow it. . . .

A question has been alluded to, on the argument, namely: the right of the master with his slave of transit into or through a free State, on business or commercial pursuits, or in the exercise of a Federal right, or the discharge of a Federal duty, being a citizen of the United States, which is not before us. This question depends upon different considerations and principles from the one in hand, and turns upon the rights and privileges secured to a common citizen of the republic under the Constitution of the United States. When that question arises, we shall be prepared to decide it.

Our conclusion is, that the judgment of the court below should be affirmed.

3 *Mr. Justice Curtis, Dissenting*

. . . Now, the plea to the jurisdiction in this case does not controvert the fact that the plaintiff resided in Missouri at the date of the writ. If he did then reside there, and was also a citizen of the United States, no provisions contained in the Constitution or laws of Missouri can deprive the plaintiff of his right to sue citizens of States other than Missouri, in the courts of the United States.

So that, under the allegations contained in this plea, and admitted by the demurrer, the question is, whether any person of African descent, whose ancestors were sold as slaves in the United States, can be a citizen of the United States. If any such person can be a citizen, this plaintiff has the right to the judgment of the court that he is so; for no cause is shown by the plea why he is not so, except his descent and the slavery of his ancestors.

The first section of the second article of the Constitution uses the language, "a citizen of the United States at the time of the adoption of the Constitution." One mode of approaching this question is, to inquire who were citizens of the United States at the time of the adoption of the Constitution.

Citizens of the United States at the time of the adoption of the Constitution can have been no other than citizens of the United States under the Confederation. By the Articles of Confederation, a Government was organized, the style whereof was, "The United States of America." This Government was in existence when the Constitution was framed and proposed for adoption, and was to be superseded by the new Government of the United States of America, organized under the Constitution. When, therefore, the Constitution speaks of citizenship of the United States, existing at the time of the adoption of the Constitution, it must necessarily refer to citizenship under the Government which existed prior to and at the time of such adoption. . . .

To determine whether any free persons, descended from Africans held in slavery, were citizens of the United States under the Confederation, and consequently at the time of the adoption of the Constitution of the United States, it is only necessary to know whether any such persons were citizens of either of the States under the Confederation, at the time of the adoption of the Constitution.

---

3 *Dred Scott* v. *John F. A. Sandford,* 19 Howard 393, 571–76, 582–84, 588–94, 604–06, 608–10, 613, 615–19, 624–27, 633.

Of this there can be no doubt. At the time of the ratification of the Articles of Confederation, all free native-born inhabitants of the States of New Hampshire, Massachusetts, New York, New Jersey, and North Carolina, though descended from African slaves, were not only citizens of those States, but such of them as had the other necessary qualifications possessed the franchise of electors, on equal terms with other citizens. . . .

New York, by its Constitution of 1820, required colored persons to have some qualifications as prerequisites for voting, which white persons need not possess. And New Jersey, by its present Constitution, restricts the right to vote to white male citizens. But these changes can have no other effect upon the present inquiry, except to show, that before they were made, no such restrictions existed; and colored in common with white persons, were not only citizens of those States, but entitled to the elective franchise on the same qualifications as white persons, as they now are in New Hampshire and Massachusetts. I shall not enter into an examination of the existing opinions of that period respecting the African race, nor into any discussion concerning the meaning of those who asserted, in the Declaration of Independence, that all men are created equal; that they are endowed by their Creator with certain inalienable rights; that among these are life, liberty, and the pursuit of happiness. My own opinion is, that a calm comparison of these assertions of universal abstract truths, and of their own individual opinions and acts, would not leave these men under any reproach of inconsistency; that the great truths they asserted on that solemn occasion, they were ready and anxious to make effectual, wherever a necessary regard to circumstances, which no statesman can disregard without producing more evil than good, would allow; and that it would not be just to them, nor true in itself, to allege that they intended to say that the Creator of all men had endowed the white race, exclusively, with the great natural rights which the Declaration of Independence asserts. But this is not the place to vindicate their memory. As I conceive, we should deal here, not with such disputes, if there can be a dispute concerning this subject, but with those substantial facts evinced by the written Constitutions of States, and by the notorious practice under them. And they show, in a manner which no argument can obscure, that in some of the original thirteen States, free colored persons, before and at the time of the formation of the Constitution, were citizens of those States.

The fourth of the fundamental articles of the Confederation was as follows: "The free inhabitants of each of these States, paupers, vagabonds, and fugitives from justice, excepted, shall be entitled to all the privileges and immunities of free citizens in the several States."

The fact that free persons of color were citizens of some of the several States, and the consequence, that this fourth article of the Confederation would have the effect to confer on such persons the privileges and immunities of general citizenship, were not only known to those who framed and adopted those articles, but the evidence is decisive, that the fourth article was intended to have that effect, and that more restricted language, which would have excluded such persons, was deliberately and purposely rejected. . . .

Did the Constitution of the United States deprive them or their descendants of citizenship?

That Constitution was ordained and established by the people of the United States, through the action, in each State, of those persons who were qualified by its laws to act thereon, in behalf of themselves and all other citizens of that State. In some of the States, as we have seen, colored persons were among those qualified by law to act on this subject. These colored persons were not only included in the body of "the people of the United States," by whom the Constitution was ordained and established, but in at least five of the States they had the power to act, and doubtless did act, by their suffrages, upon the question of its adoption. It would be strange, if we were to find in that instrument anything which deprived of their citizenship any part of the people of the United States who were among those by whom it was established.

I can find nothing in the Constitution which, *proprio vigore*, deprives of their citizenship any class of persons who were citizens of the United States at the time of its adoption, or who should be native-born citizens of any State after its adoption; nor any power enabling Congress to disfranchise persons born on the soil of any State, and entitled to citizenship of such State by its Constitution and laws. And my opinion is, that, under the Constitution of the United States, every free person born on the soil of a State, who is a citizen of that State by force of its Constitution or laws, is also a citizen of the United States. . . .

It has been often asserted that the Constitution was made exclusively by and for the white race. It has already been shown that in five of the thirteen original States, colored persons then possessed the elective franchise, and were among those by whom the Constitution was ordained and established. If so, it is not true, in point of fact, that the Constitution was made exclusively by the white race. And that it was made exclusively for the white race is, in my opinion, not only an assumption not warranted by anything in the Constitution, but contradicted by its opening declaration, that it was ordained and established by the people of the United States, for themselves and their posterity. And as free colored persons were then citizens of at least five States, and so in every sense part of the people of the United States, they were among those for whom and whose posterity the Constitution was ordained and established. . . .

One [State] may confine the right of suffrage to white male citizens; another may extend it to colored persons and females; one may allow all persons above a prescribed age to convey property and transact business; another may exclude married women. But whether native-born women, or persons under age, or under guardianship because insane or spend-thrifts, be excluded from voting or holding office, or allowed to do so, I apprehend no one will deny that they are citizens of the United States. Besides, this clause of the Constitution does not confer on the citizens of one State, in all other States, specific and enumerated privileges and immunities. They are entitled to such as belong to citizenship, but not to such as belong to particular citizens attended by other qualifications. Privileges and immunities which belong to certain citizens of a State, by reason of the operation of causes other than mere citizenship, are not conferred. Thus, if the laws of a State require, in addition to citizenship of the State, some qualification for office, or the exercise of the elective franchise, citizens of all other States, coming thither to reside, and not possessing those qualifications, cannot enjoy those privileges, not because they are not to be deemed entitled to the privileges of citizens of the State in which they reside, but because they, in common with the native-born citizens of that State, must have the qualifications prescribed by law for the enjoyment of such privileges, under its Constitution and laws. It rests with the States themselves so to frame their Constitutions and laws as not to attach a particular privilege or immunity to mere naked citizenship. If one of the States will not deny to any of its own citizens a particular privilege or immunity, if it confer it on all of them by reason of mere naked citizenship, then it may be claimed by every citizen of each State by force of the Constitution; and it must be borne in mind, that the difficulties which attend the allowance of the claims of colored persons to be citizens of the United States are not avoided by saying that, though each State may make them its citizens, they are not thereby made citizens of the United States, because the privileges of general citizenship are secured to the citizens of each State. The language of the Constitution is, "The citizens of each State shall be entitled to all privileges and immunities of citizens in the several States." If each State may make such persons its citizens, they become, as such, entitled to the benefits of this article, if there be a native-born citizenship of the United States distinct from a native-born citizenship of the several States. . . .

The conclusions at which I have arrived on this part of the case are:

First. That the free native-born citizens of each State are citizens of the United States.

Second. That as free colored persons born within some of the States are citizens of those States, such persons are also citizens of the United States.

Third. That every such citizen, residing in any State, has the right to sue and is liable to be sued in the Federal courts, as a citizen of that State in which he resides.

Fourth. That as the plea to the jurisdiction in this case shows no facts, except that the plaintiff was of African descent, and his ancestors were sold as slaves, and as these facts are not inconsistent with his citizenship of the United States, and his residence in the State of Missouri, the plea to the jurisdiction was bad, and the judgment of the Circuit Court over-ruling it was correct.

I dissent, therefore, from that part of the opinion of the majority of the court, in which it is held that a person of African descent cannot be a citizen of the United States; and I regret I must go further, and dissent both from what I deem their assumption of authority to examine the constitutionality of the act of Congress commonly called the Missouri compromise act, and the grounds and conclusions announced in their opinion.

Having first decided that they were bound to consider the sufficiency of the plea to the jurisdiction of the Circuit Court, and having decided that this plea showed that the Circuit Court had not jurisdiction, and consequently that this is a case to which the judicial power of the United States does not extend, they have gone on to examine the merits of the case as they appeared on the trial before the court and jury, on the issues joined on the pleas in bar, and so have reached the question of the power of Congress to pass the act of 1820. On so grave a subject as this, I feel obliged to say that, in my opinion, such an exertion of judicial power transcends the limits of the authority of the court, as described by its repeated decisions, and, as I understand, acknowledged in this opinion of the majority of the court. . . .

I do not consider it to be within the scope of the judicial power of the majority of the court to pass upon any question respecting the plaintiff's citizenship in Missouri, save that raised by the plea to the jurisdiction; and I do not hold any opinion of this court, or any court, binding, when expressed on a question not legitimately before it. (Carroll v. Carroll, 16 How., 275.) The judgment of this court is, that the case is to be dismissed for want of jurisdiction, because the plaintiff was not a citizen of Missouri, as he alleged in his declaration. Into that judgment, according to the settled course of this court, nothing appearing after a plea to the merits can enter. A great question of constitutional law, deeply affecting the peace and welfare of the country, is not, in my opinion, a fit subject to be thus reached.

But as, in my opinion, the Circuit Court had jurisdiction, I am obliged to consider the question whether its judgment on the merits of the case should stand or be reversed.

The residence of the plaintiff in the State of Illinois, and the residence of himself and his wife in the territory acquired from France lying north of latitude thirty-six degrees thirty minutes, and north of the State of Missouri, are each relied on by the plaintiff in error. As the residence in the territory affects the plaintiff's wife and children as well as himself, I must inquire what was its effect.

The general question may be stated to be, whether the plaintiff's *status,* as a slave, was so changed by his residence within that territory, that he was not a slave in the State of Missouri, at the time this action was brought.

In such cases, two inquiries arise, which may be confounded, but should be kept distinct.

The first is, what was the law of the Territory into which the master and slave went, respecting the relation between them?

The second is, whether the State of Missouri recognises and allows the effect of that law of the Territory on the *status* of the slave, on his return within its jurisdiction.

As to the first of the questions, the will of States and nations, by whose municipal laws slavery is not recognised, has been manifested in three different ways.

One is, absolutely to dissolve the relation, and terminate the rights of the master existing under the law of the country whence the parties came. . . .

The second is, where the municipal law of a country not recognising slavery, it is the will of the State to refuse the master all aid to exercise any control over his slave; and if he attempt to do so, in a manner justifiable only by that relation, to prevent the exercise of that control. But no law exists, designed to operate directly on the relation of master and slave, and put an end to that relation. . . .

The third is, to make a distinction between the case of a master and his slave only temporarily in the country, *animo non manendi,* and those who are there to reside for permanent or indefinite purposes. . . . It is necessary in this case to keep in view this distinction between those countries whose laws are designed to act directly on the *status* of a slave, and make him a freeman, and those where his master can obtain no aid from the laws to enforce his rights.

It is to the last case only that the authorities, out of Missouri, relied on by defendant, apply, when the residence in the nonslaveholding Territory was permanent. . . .

But if the acts of Congress on this subject are valid, the law of the Territory of Wisconsin, within whose limits the residence of the plaintiff and his wife, and their marriage and the birth of one or both of their children, took place, falls under the first category, and is a law operating directly on the *status* of the slave. By the eighth section of the act of March 6, 1820, (3 Stat. at Large, 548,) it was enacted that, within this Territory, "slavery and involuntary servitude, otherwise than in the punishment of crimes, whereof the parties shall have been duly convicted, shall be, and is hereby, forever prohibited: *Provided, always,* that any person escaping into the same, from whom labor or service is lawfully claimed in any State or Territory of the United States, such fugitive may be lawfully reclaimed, and conveyed to the person claiming his or her labor or service, as aforesaid."

By the act of April 20, 1836, (4 Stat. at Large, 10,) passed in the same month and year of the removal of the plaintiff to Fort Snelling, this part of the territory ceded by France, where Fort Snelling is, together with so much of the territory of the United States east of the Mississippi as now constitutes the State of Wisconsin, was brought under a Territorial Government, under the name of the Territory of Wisconsin. By the eighteenth section of this act, it was enacted, "That the inhabitants of this Territory shall be entitled to and enjoy all and singular the rights, privileges, and advantages, granted and secured to the people of the Territory of the United States northwest of the river Ohio, by the articles of compact contained in the ordinance for the government of said Territory, passed on the 13th day of July, 1787; and shall be subject to all the restrictions and prohibitions in said articles of compact imposed upon the people of the said Territory." The sixth article of that compact is, "there shall be neither slavery nor involuntary servitude in the said Territory, otherwise than in the punishment of crimes, whereof the party shall have been duly convicted. *Provided, always,* that any person escaping into the same, from whom labor or service is lawfully claimed in any one of the original States, such fugitive may be lawfully reclaimed, and conveyed to the person claiming his or her labor or service, as aforesaid." By other provisions of this act establishing the Territory of Wisconsin, the laws of the United States, and the then existing laws of the State of Michigan, are extended over the Territory; the latter being subject to alteration and repeal by the legislative power of the Territory created by the act.

Fort Snelling was within the Territory of Wisconsin, and these laws were extended over it. . . .

It would not be easy for the Legislature to employ more explicit language to signify its will that the *status* of slavery should not exist within the Territory, than the words found in the act of 1820, and in the ordinance of 1787; and if any doubt could exist concerning their application to cases of masters coming into the Territory with their slaves to reside, that doubt must yield to the inference required by the words of exception. That exception is, of cases of fugitive slaves. An exception from a prohibition marks the extent of the prohibition; for it would be absurd, as well as useless, to except from a prohibition a case not contained within it. . . . I must conclude, therefore, that it was the will of Congress that the state of involuntary servitude of a slave, coming into the Territory with his master, should cease to exist. . . .

I have thus far assumed, merely for the purpose of the argument, that the laws of the United States, respecting slavery in this Territory, were constitutionally enacted by Congress. It remains to inquire whether they are constitutional and binding laws.

In the argument of this part of the case at bar, it was justly considered by all the counsel to be necessary to ascertain the source of the power of Congress over the territory belonging to the United States. Until this is ascertained, it is not possible to determine the extent of that power. On the one side it was maintained that the Constitution contains no express grant of power to organize and govern what is now known to the laws of the United States as a Territory. That whatever power of this kind exists, is derived by implication from the capacity of the United States to hold and acquire territory out of the limits of any State, and the necessity for its having some government.

On the other side, it was insisted that the Constitution has not failed to make an express provision for this end, and that it is found in the third section of the fourth article of the Constitution.

To determine which of these is the correct view, it is needful to advert to some facts respecting this subject, which existed when the Constitution was framed and adopted. It will be found that these facts not only shed much light on the question, whether the framers of the Constitution omitted to make a provision concerning the power of Congress to organize and govern Territories, but they will also aid in the construction of any provision which may have been made respecting this subject. . . .

It appears . . . that when the Federal Constitution was framed, and presented to the people of the several States for their consideration, the unsettled territory was viewed as justly applicable to the common benefit, so far as it then had or might attain thereafter a pecuniary value; and so far as it might become the seat of new States, to be admitted into the Union upon an equal footing with the original States. And also that the relations of the United States to that unsettled territory were of different kinds. The titles of the States of New York, Virginia, Massachusetts, Connecticut, and South Carolina, as well of soil as of jurisdiction, had been transferred to the United States. North Carolina and Georgia had not actually made transfers, but a confident expectation, founded on their appreciation of the justice of the general claim, and fully justified by the results, was entertained, that these cessions would be made. The ordinance of 1787 had made provision for the temporary government of so much of the territory actually ceded as lay northwest of the river Ohio.

But it must have been apparent, both to the framers of the Constitution and the people of the several States who were to act upon it, that the Government thus provided for could not continue, unless the Constitution should confer on the United States the necessary powers to continue it. . . .

The Congress of the Confederation had assumed the power not only to dispose of the lands ceded, but to institute Governments and make laws for their inhabitants. In other words, they had proceeded to act under the cession, which, as we have seen, was as well of the jurisdiction as of the soil. This ordinance was passed on the 13th of July, 1787. The Convention for framing the Constitution was then in session at Philadelphia. The proof is direct and decisive, that it was known to the Convention. . . .

The importance of conferring on the new Government regular powers commensurate with the objects to be attained, and thus avoiding the alternative of a failure to execute the trust assumed by the acceptance of the cessions made and expected, or its execution by usurpation, could scarcely fail to be perceived. That it was in fact perceived, is clearly shown by the Federalist, (No. 38,) where this very argument is made use of in commendation of the Constitution.

Keeping these facts in view, it may confidently be asserted that there is very strong reason to believe, before we examine the Constitution itself, that the necessity for a competent grant of power to hold, dispose of, and govern territory, ceded and expected to be ceded, could not have escaped the attention of those who framed or adopted the Constitution; and that if it did not escape their attention, it could not fail to be adequately provided for.

Any other conclusion would involve the assumption that a subject of the gravest national concern, respecting which the small States felt so much jealousy that it had been almost an insurmountable obstacle to the formation of the Confederation, and as to which all the States had deep pecuniary and political interests, and which had been so recently and constantly agitated, was nevertheless overlooked; or that such a subject was not overlooked, but designedly left unprovided for, though it was manifestly a subject of common concern, which belonged to the care of the General Government, and adequate provision for which could not fail to be deemed necessary and proper. . . .

That Congress has some power to institute temporary Governments over the territory, I believe all agree; and, if it be admitted that the necessity of some power to govern the territory of the United States could not and did not escape the attention of the Convention and the people, and that the necessity is so great, that, in the absence of any express grant, it is strong enough to raise an implication of the existence of that power, it would seem to follow that it is also strong enough to afford material aid in construing an express grant of power respecting that territory; and that they who maintain the existence of the power, without finding any words at all in which it is conveyed, should be willing to receive a reasonable interpretation of language of the Constitution, manifestly intended to relate to the territory, and to convey to Congress some authority concerning it.

It would seem, also, that when we find the subject-matter of the growth and formation and admission of new States, and the disposal of the territory for these ends, were under consideration, and that some provision therefor was expressly made, it is improbable that it would be, in its terms, a grossly inadequate provision; and that an indispensably necessary power to institute temporary Governments, and to legislate for the inhabitants of the territory, was passed silently by, and left to be deduced from the necessity of the case. . . .

There was to be established by the Constitution a frame of government, under which the people of the United States and their posterity were to continue indefinitely. To take one of its provisions, the language of which is broad enough to extend throughout the existence of the Government, and embrace all territory belonging to the United States throughout all time, and the purposes and objects of which apply to all territory of the United States, and narrow it down to territory belonging to the United States when the Constitution was framed, while at the same time it is admitted that the Constitution contemplated and authorized the acquisition, from time to time, of other and foreign territory, seems to me to be an interpretation as inconsistent with the nature and purposes of the instrument, as it is with its language, and I can have no hesitation in rejecting it. . . .

But it is insisted, that whatever other powers Congress may have respecting the territory of the United States, the subject of negro slavery forms an exception.

The Constitution declares that Congress shall have power to make *"all needful rules and regulations"* respecting the territory belonging to the United States.

The assertion is, though the Constitution says all, it does not mean all — though it says all, withont [*sic*] qualification, it means all except such as allow or prohibit slavery. It cannot be doubted that it is incumbent on those who would thus introduce an exception not found in the language of the instrument, to exhibit some solid and satisfactory reason, drawn from the subject-matter or the purposes and objects of the clause, the context, or from other provisions of the Constitution, showing that the words employed in this clause are not to be understood according to their clear, plain, and natural signification. . . .

It has already been stated, that after the Government of the United States was organized under the Constitution, the temporary Government of the Territory northwest of the river Ohio could no longer exist, save under the powers conferred on Congress by the Constitution. Whatever legislative, judicial, or executive authority should be exercised therein could be derived only from the people of the United States under the Constitution. And, accordingly, an act was passed on the 7th day of August, 1789, (1 Stat. at Large, 50,) which recites: "Whereas, in order that the ordinance of the United States in Congress assembled, for the government of the territory northwest of the river Ohio, *may continue to have full effect*, it is required that certain provisions should be made, so as to adapt the same to the present Constitution of the United States. . . ."

I consider the passage of this law to have been an assertion by the first Congress of the power of the United States to prohibit slavery within this part of the territory of the United States; for it clearly shows that slavery was thereafter to be prohibited there, and it could be prohibited only by an exertion of the power of the United States, under the Constitution; no other power being capable of operating within that territory after the Constitution took effect.

On the 2d of April, 1790, (1 Stat. at Large, 106,) the first Congress passed an act accepting a deed of cession by North Carolina of that territory afterwards erected into the State of Tennessee. The fourth express condition contained in this deed of cession, after providing that the inhabitants of the Territory shall be temporarily governed in the same manner as those beyond the Ohio, is followed by these words: *"Provided, always,* that no regulations made or to be made by Congress shall tend to emancipate slaves."* . . .

Without going minutely into the details of each case, I will now give reference to two classes of acts, in one of which Congress has extended the ordinance of 1787, including the article prohibiting slavery, over different Territories, and thus exerted its power to prohibit it; in the other, Congress has erected Governments over Territories acquired from France and Spain, in which slavery already existed, but refused to apply to them that part of the Government under the ordinance which excluded slavery. . . .

[There] . . . are eight distinct instances, beginning with the first Congress, and coming down to the year 1848, in which Congress has excluded slavery from the territory of the United States; and six distinct instances in which Congress organized Governments of Territories by which slavery was recognised and continued, beginning also with the first Congress, and coming down to the year 1822. These acts were severally signed by seven Presidents of the United States, beginning with General Washington, and coming regularly down as far as Mr. John Quincy Adams, thus including all who were in public life when the Constitution was adopted.

If the practical construction of the Constitution contemporaneously with its going into effect, by men intimately acquainted with its history from their personal participation in framing and adopting it, and continued by them through a long series of acts of the gravest importance, be entitled to weight in the judicial mind on a question of construction, it would seem to be difficult to resist the force of the acts above adverted to. . . .

Looking at the power of Congress over the Territories as of the extent just described, what positive prohibition exists in the Constitution, which restrained Congress from enacting a law in 1820 to prohibit slavery north of thirty-six degrees thirty minutes north latitude?

The only one suggested is that clause in the fifth article of the amendments of the Constitution which declares that no person shall be deprived of his life, liberty, or property, without due process of law. I will now proceed to examine the question, whether this clause is entitled to the effect thus attributed to it. It is necessary, first, to have a clear view of the nature and incidents of that particular species of property which is now in question.

Slavery, being contrary to natural right, is created only by municipal law. This is not only plain in itself, and agreed by all writers on the subject, but is inferable from the Constitution, and has been explicitly declared by this court. The Constitution refers to slaves as "persons held to service in one State, under the laws thereof." Nothing can more clearly describe a *status* created by municipal law. In Prigg *v.* Pennsylvania, (10 Pet., 611,) this court said: "The state of slavery is deemed to be a mere municipal regulation, founded on and limited to the range of territorial laws." In Rankin *v.* Lydia, (2 Marsh., 12, 470,) the Supreme Court of Appeals of Kentucky said: "Slavery is sanctioned by the laws of this State, and the right to hold them under our municipal regulations is unquestionable. But we view this as a right existing by positive law of a municipal character, without foundation in the law of nature or the unwritten common law." I am not acquainted with any case or writer questioning the correctness of this doctrine. . . .

Is it conceivable that the Constitution has conferred the right on every citizen to become a resident on the territory of the United States with his slaves, and there to hold them as such, but has neither made nor provided for any municipal regulations which are essential to the existence of slavery?

Is it not more rational to conclude that they who framed and adopted the Constitution were aware that persons held to service under the laws of a State are property only to the extent and under the conditions fixed by those laws; that they must cease to be available as property, when their owners voluntarily place them permanently within another jurisdiction, where no municipal laws on the subject of slavery exist; and that, being aware of these principles, and having said nothing to interfere with or displace them, or to compel Congress to legislate in any particular manner on the subject, and having empowered Congress to make all needful rules and regulations respecting the territory of the United States, it was their intention to leave to the discretion of Congress what regulations, if any, should be made concerning slavery therein? Moreover, if the right exists, what are its limits, and what are its conditions? If citizens of the United States have the right to take their slaves to a Territory, and hold them there as slaves, without regard to the laws of the Territory, I suppose this right is not to be restricted to the citizens of slaveholding States. A citizen of a State which does not tolerate slavery can hardly be denied the power of doing the same thing. And what law of slavery does either take with him to the Territory? If it be said to be those laws respecting slavery which existed in the particular State from which each slave last came, what an anomaly is this? Where else can we find, under the law of any civilized country, the power to introduce and permanently continue diverse systems of foreign municipal law, for holding persons in slavery? I say, not merely to introduce, but permanently to continue, these anomalies. For the offspring of the female must be governed by the foreign municipal laws to which the mother was subject; and when any slave is sold or passes by succession on the death of the owner, there must pass with him, by a species of subrogation, and as a kind of unknown *jus in re*, the foreign municipal laws which constituted, regulated, and preserved, the *status* of the slave before his exportation. Whatever theoretical importance may be now supposed to belong to the maintenance of such a right, I feel a perfect conviction that it would, if ever tried, prove to be as impracticable in fact, as it is, in my judgment, monstrous in theory. . . .

Nor, in my judgment, will the position, that a prohibition to bring slaves into a Territory deprives any one of his property without due process of law, bear examination.

It must be remembered that this restriction on the legislative power is not peculiar to the Constitution of the United States; it was borrowed from *Magna Charta;* was brought to America by our ancestors, as part of their inherited liberties, and has existed in all the States, usually in the very words of the great charter. It existed in every political community in America in 1787, when the ordinance prohibiting slavery north and west of the Ohio was passed.

And if a prohibition of slavery in a Territory in 1820 violated this principle of *Magna Charta,* the ordinance of 1787 also violated it; and what power had, I do not say the Congress of the Confederation alone, but the Legislature of Virginia, or the Legislature of any or all the States of the Confederacy, to consent to such a violation? The people of the States had conferred no such power. I think I may at least say, if the Congress did then violate *Magna Charta* by the ordinance, no one discovered that violation. Besides, if the prohibition upon all persons, citizens as well as others, to bring slaves into a Territory, and a declaration that if brought they shall be free, deprives citizens of their property without due process of law, what shall we say of the legislation of many of the slaveholding States which have enacted the same prohibition? . . . I am not aware that such laws, though they exist in many States, were ever supposed to be in conflict with the principle of *Magna Charta* incorporated into the State Constitutions. It was certainly understood by the Convention which framed the Constitution, and has been so understood ever since, that, under the power to regulate commerce, Congress could prohibit the importation of slaves; and the exercise of the power was restrained till 1808. A citizen of the United States owns slaves in Cuba, and brings them to the United States, where they are set free by the legislation of Congress. Does this legislation deprive him of his property without due process of law? If so, what becomes of the laws prohibiting the slave trade? If not, how can a similar regulation respecting a Territory violate the fifth amendment of the Constitution? . . .

. . . I am of opinion that so much of the several acts of Congress as prohibited slavery and involuntary servitude within that part of the Territory of Wisconsin lying north of thirty-six degrees thirty minutes north latitude, and west of the river Mississippi, were constitutional and valid laws.

I have expressed my opinion, and the reasons therefor, at far greater length than I could have wished, upon the different questions on which I have found it necessary to pass, to arrive at a judgment on the case at bar. These questions are numerous, and the grave importance of some of them required me to exhibit fully the grounds of my opinion. I have touched no question which, in the view I have taken, it was not absolutely necessary for me to pass upon, to ascertain whether the judgment of the Circuit Court should stand or be reversed. I have avoided no question on which the validity of that judgment depends. To have done either more or less, would have been inconsistent with my views of my duty.

In my opinion, the judgment of the Circuit Court should be reversed, and the cause remanded for a new trial.

3

★ DRED SCOTT AND
THE NATION

1857–1865

A

Editorial Comment:
The Republican Assault

Most Republican newspapers expressed outrage at the Dred Scott decision; some advocated outright defiance of the Court's ruling. A few moderate Republican voices argued that despite the decision, "natural" laws of labor and production would limit slavery's expansion.

1 *New York Tribune*

March 7, 1857

The long trumpeted decision of the Supreme Court in the Dred Scott case was pronounced by Judge Taney yesterday, having been held over from last year in order not too flagrantly to alarm and exasperate the Free States on the eve of an important Presidential election. Its cardinal points are reported as follows:

1. A negro, because of his color, is denied the rights of a citizen of the United States — even the right to sue in our Courts for the redress of the most flagrant wrongs.

2. A slave, being taken by his master into a Free State and thence returning under his master's sway, is not therefore entitled to his freedom.

3. *Congress has no rightful power to prohibit Slavery in the Territories:* hence the Missouri Restriction was unconstitutional.

Justice Nelson, we are happy to say, does not fully concur in this abominable judgment. Justice McLean of course dissents *in toto;* so, we presume, does Justice Curtis in the main, despite his eminence in Union saving. Justice Grier, we presume, went all lengths with the five slaveholders who compose a majority of the Court, leaving but four-ninths to the immense preponderance of population in the Free States.

The decision, we need hardly say, is entitled to just as much moral weight as would be the judgment of a majority of those congregated in any Washington bar-room. It is a *dictum* prescribed by the stump to the bench — the Bowie-knife sticking in the stump ready for instant use if needed. It is of a piece with the votes . . . for the Annexation of Texas with the boundary of the Rio Grande.

This judgment annihilates all Compromises and brings us face to face with the great issue in the right shape. Slavery implies slave laws — that is laws sustaining and enforcing the claim of one man to own and sell another. In the absence of such laws, Slavery cannot exist; and a Republican ascendancy in the nation, insuring Republican rule over the Territories, will prove a shield against the enactment of any such laws. Under any other rule, all our Territories are henceforth Slave Territories on the way to be ripened into Slave States. . . .

Let not Slavery exult over this as a second and separate triumph from the inauguration and inaugural of Buchanan. They are parts of one whole, and as such will be regarded and met in the spirit of Freemen.

2 *Chicago Tribune*

March 12, 1857

[O]ur highest Judicial officers . . . have . . . set their flinty faces against the policy of *our* part, whether that policy rested upon the goodly doctrine of the common law, or the noble sentiments of the Declaration of Independence.

We must confess we are shocked at the violence and servility of the Judicial Revolution caused by the decision of the Supreme Court of the United States. We scarcely know how to express our detestation of its inhuman dicta, or to fathom the wicked consequences which may flow from it. The blood of the early day — of the times that tried mens ['] souls — was all healthful and strong, and lived, or was shed, for Liberty as freely as water. That is now changed *legally*. This decision has sapped the constitution of its glorious and distinctive features, and seeks to pervert it into a barbarous and unchristian channel.

Jefferson feared this Supreme Court, and foretold its usurpation of the legislative power of the Federal Government. His prophecy is now reality. The terrible evil he dreaded is upon us.

To say or suppose, that a Free People can respect or will obey a decision so fraught with disastrous consequences to the People and their Liberties, is to dream of impossibilities. No power can take away their rights. They will permit no power to abridge them. No servility of Judges or of Presidents, no servility of Congresses can taint their spirit or subdue it. The contest has come, and in that contest, the Supreme Court, we are sorry to say, will be shorn of its moral power — will lose that prestige, that authority, which instinctively insures respect and commands obedience. By its own bad act it has impaired its organization. Fortunate will it be, if that act does not destroy its utility. . . .

That there has been for long years a conspiracy against Freedom in this Republic, and that certain members of the Supreme Court were engaged in it, we do not doubt. How this has happened, or why, it is needless to discuss now. It is enough to know, that a continued residence at Washington — the breathing in of its central and polluted atmosphere makes, or tends to make, those in authority, at once obedient and servile to the ruling dynasty, and callous to the purer and higher instincts and principles of the people. The Judiciary has proved no exception. We would, therefore, apply the remedy which JEFFERSON urged, and JACKSON recommended — *decentralization*. Strip the President of every power which the people can exercise. Let every office which *they* are able to fill, be filled by them. Confide into their hands the election of the Judges of the United States, and thus infuse into these Judges a knowledge of their interests, a spirit and a purpose kindred with theirs, an independence of the Executive worthy of them.

3 *Harper's Weekly*

March 28, 1857

The opinions of the Court in this case are not yet before the public. One or two of the dissenting opinions have leaked out somewhat irregularly, but we have as yet no authentic mode of knowing precisely what the Court, as such, has decided. It is therefore premature, and somewhat unsafe, to attempt to criticise a judgment the reasons of which are not before us; but as it is generally understood that we have the *points* which have been ruled, it may not be amiss to consider what is likely to be the practical effect of the decision which is, in certain quarters, producing such a fervid heat.

It is understood, then, that the Court has decided that free negroes are not citizens of the United States. This is a point that has been so held heretofore by the State Courts of Connecticut, which has been disposed of administratively in the same way by the Department of State in refusing passports to free Africans, and which our commentator, Kent, states as a point of nicety and difficulty. Nor does it appear that the question of the citizenship of our free black population is a question likely to take any practical shape capable of profoundly agitating the public mind. We are indeed a consistent and reasonable people! We have among us a small representation of a tropical race of human beings, marked off from us by the unmistakable line of color, if by nothing else, and over whom we daily arrogate to ourselves of the Caucasian stock a complete and absolute superiority. We will not marry with them, we will not eat with them, as a general rule we do not let them vote, we will let them hold no office. We do not allow them to kneel beside us to worship the Great Father of all; not even when we approach the end of our weary journey will we allow our miserable dust to repose side by side with theirs in the common receptacle of humanity. And yet, when half a dozen old lawyers at Washington, after racking their heads for two years over a question that has bothered the Robe for half a century, announce as their decision that *free blacks are not citizens of the United States,* and as such not permitted to sue in certain courts of limited and special jurisdiction, we fume, and fret, and bubble, and squeak, as if some dreadful injustice and oppression were committed. It really does not seem to us that this part of the Dred Scott decision is likely to produce any very serious practical results.

In the second place, the Supreme Court have decided that the Missouri Compromise was unconstitutional, and that Congress has no power to prohibit slavery in the Territories. If this question had been so decided three years ago, it might have been considered formidable, but of what practical effect is it now? The party in power — certain to be in power in two branches of the Government at least for the next four years — have announced it as their fixed and unalterable determination to leave the question of slavery to the Territories themselves. When then, or how is the case to arise, which shall give to this branch of the decision any practical force?

In the third place, the Supreme Court have decided, that if a black, who is a slave in a slave State, is taken into a State by the laws of which he becomes free, and subsequently returns into the State whence he came, he reverts to his original condition of slavery. It is constantly stated that the Supreme Court has decided the right of transit, as it is called; that is to say, that slave-owners have a right to come into or pass through the free States with their slaves, and that as long as they do not fix their residence in a free State, their right of property will be held sacred. It is very obvious that nothing of the kind has been decided in the Dred Scott case. Whatever may be the inclination of the Supreme Court on this point, they have as yet not touched it.

But suppose they had — suppose they do — what will be the practical effect of the decision? . . . Suppose in the Lemon case (all these slave cases are sour enough) they do decide this very question? As an abstract or theoretical question, it is one of the most delicate that could be started; for if our Southern brethren are to come on to Saratoga or to Newport for the season, with their sable dependents, and if during their sojourn the domestic institution is to be hedged round and protected with all the majesty of the law, it is plain that the occasions of contest, collision, difficulty, and turmoil would be endless.

Practically, however, the question is probably not so serious. It is idle — unfortunately, perhaps, but very certainly — it is idle to attempt to enforce any laws in this country against a general public opinion. There is not a State, nor a county in a State where it can be done; and simply because the Government has no force to compel obedience to its mandates. We have seen it in multitudinous cases. The Anti-Rent difficulty — the Native American disputes in Philadelphia, Cincinnati, and Louisville — the fate of the gamblers at Vicksburg — the destruction of the convent at Boston — everywhere it is the same thing. We have seen it, and are seeing it every day, in regard to this very subject of slavery. A Fugitive Slave law was passed six years ago, giving the master stringent provisions to recover his property, and the assistance of the whole Federal authority to reclaim him. What has been the result? One poor devil of a fugitive was returned — it cost $100,000, more or less; and since then, in the Eastern States, and New York at all events, the law has practically been a dead letter, and the slaves are making their way northward all the while. The idea that any decision of the Supreme Court can reestablish slavery in the Free States is a bugbear — an absurdity.

The only result, therefore, that we can arrive at is, that however repugnant the Dred Scott decision may be to the feelings of a portion of the Northern States, it can have no practical effects injurious to our tranquility, or to our institutions. The subject of slavery will be left to be decided, as it ultimately must be, by the laws which govern labor and production.

It is, indeed, most devoutly to be desired that this great question could be left to be determined exclusively by those laws, free from the interference of the hot-heads of the press and of the pulpit. If we would but permit Nature to have her own way for only a few short years. . . .

B

Editorial Comment:
The Democratic Defense

Nearly all southern and Democratic spokesmen regarded the Supreme Court's action with great satisfaction. Their long-held views had been vindicated, and they urged the nation to unite and accept the judicial solution.

1 *The [Washington D.C.] Daily Union*

March 12, 1857

On the 6th instant the Chief Justice of the United States delivered an elaborate opinion of the Supreme Court declaring the Missouri Compromise unconstitutional. We have not yet had the satisfaction of perusing a full and authenticated report of that opinion, and therefore can only refer to it in general terms. That it will constitute a prominent era in our judicial history all will admit. It will receive universal attention in the country, from the fact that almost every reading man, to whatever party he may belong, has read the discussion of the history and validity of the Missouri Compromise, and is qualified to understand the reasoning of the court.

We cherish a most ardent and confident expectation that this decision will meet a proper reception from the great mass of our intelligent countrymen; that it will be regarded with soberness and not with passion; and that it will thereby exert a mighty influence in diffusing sound opinions and restoring harmony and fraternal concord throughout the country. It comes at an auspicious period. Had it been pronounced — which could hardly have been possible — during the excitement of a presiden-

51

tial canvass, its useful effect, for the present at least, would have been lost. Though no less just and constitutional than it is, it would have been temporarily overwhelmed in the surges of party clamor. Now, however, the excitement and strife of the late canvass are happily abated. The sober second thought has returned to the people; and they are well prepared to receive the judgment of the highest tribunal in the land, even if it, in many instances, differs from their own favorite political opinions.

The court which has settled the vexed constitutional question as to the power of Congress over Territories is entirely independent of the legislative branch of the government. It is elevated above the schemes of party politics, and shielded alike from the effects of sudden passion and of popular prejudice. Little motive, therefore, can the venerable jurists who compose that tribunal have for a deviation from the true principles of law.

It would be fortunate, indeed, if the opinion of that court on this important subject could receive the candid and respectful acquiescence which it merits. Such an exhibition of the moral conservatism of the people would well correspond with that sublime example of the fitness of the people for self-government lately witnessed in the laying down and taking up of high executive trusts in the midst of orderly enthusiasm. But we expect this decision will for a while be questioned, and even ridiculed by the anti-slavery press. The judges who concurred in it will be abused. "We have a race of agitators all over the country," said Daniel Webster in his speech at Buffalo in 1851; "their livelihood consists in agitating; their freehold, their copyhold, their capital, their all in all, depend on the excitement of the public mind." To this class, which still exists, this decision will be a fresh topic of sectional agitation.

In 1842 the Supreme Court decided, in the case of Prigg vs. Pennsylvania, that Congress had the constitutional power to legislate for the return of fugitive slaves. The opinion of the court was on that occasion delivered by Mr. Justice Story, one of the ablest jurists of the country. Learned tribunals in various States have concurred in that decision. The unimpassioned judgment of the people approves of it. Nevertheless, when local prejudices were to be inflamed, or party purposes were to be served, that decision has been attacked by the press and by itinerant lecturers as if it was nothing more than the harangue of a stump orator. From similar sources we may apprehend that this decision will meet with similar treatment.

We refer to the judgment of the court in this case in no spirit of triumph. We would not subject it to the mere uses of party. Many men supported the Nebraska-Kansas act who believed Congress had the right to exclude slavery from the Territories, but who deemed it inexpedient to have the right exercised. They wished to keep the subject out of Congress. They thought as Mr. Webster did when he favored the organization of New Mexico without the application of the Wilmot proviso.

These men may be unprepared for this decision. We know that in the non-slave-holding states there are many who sincerely deprecated the repeal of the Missouri Compromise. There are many who have been brought up in the faith of the Wilmot proviso. They, perhaps, have not examined both sides of the question, and will feel a regret at this decision as deep as the pleasure of our southern friend is ardent. We would appeal to such men in a spirit of candor and patriotism; and, without censuring them for sentiments which they have long honestly cherished, only invite them to review their opinions, and to conform their action to the adjudication of the highest judicial tribunal in the land.

Never perhaps, in the history of the country, has there existed so much bitterness between the North and the South as within the past year. And it is remarkable that this bitterness has resulted not from measures so much as from transient excesses. The troubles in Kansas and some other accidental acts contributed to this state of things. But the chief cause of alienation was the unbridled license of a portion of the press and the intemperate language employed by many of our public speakers. It has been common for some of the ablest journals of the North to misrepresent and vilify the institutions and the people of the South. And these attacks have been reciprocated by some of the radical papers of the South. Orators have resorted to the same practice. Under such circumstances, what else but bitterness and alienation could follow? What else but distrust be excited? No state or community is perfect. The North and the South have different institutions. Each State is alone responsible for its institutions, and it is morally and constitutionally wrong for the people of one State to assail the institutions of another State. Nor is it at all remarkable to expect that people who have been differently educated by social habits, by tradition, by paternal precept, will think entirely alike. There must be toleration, and there must be forbearance.

It is gratifying to see that a better feeling is beginning to exist between both sections of the country; and we invoke the temperate and intelligent public opinion of the country, so potent for wise purposes, to withhold every vestige of support from that class whose livelihood is to create sectional animosity. In this way their shafts will fall impotent in the dust, and the wounds they have before made will become healed.

2 Charleston [South Carolina]
Daily Courier, March 9, 1857

... [T]he decision of the Supreme Court, just pronounced, in the Dred Scott case, that the Missouri Compromise is unconstitutional (an opinion we have always entertained and maintained,) and that free negroes have no rights as citizens, under the Constitution of the United States, that is, are unknown as such to the federal compact, (whatever may be their anomalous condition in their respective States,) will, we confidently believe, settle these vexed questions forever, quiet the country, and relieve it of abolition agitation, and tend greatly to perpetuate our Union — our Constitutional Union — the greatest political boon ever vouchsafed by God to man. The ordinance of 1787 was the first great error, and the Missouri Compromise line, the second great error, of the Southern States, suicidally striking at their own constitutional equality with their confederate sisters — God be praised, they are now both adjudged to be unconstitutional, and are obliterated forever. Let the South never again compromise her equality, but maintain it, as she would her life-blood.

3 Cincinnati Daily Enquirer
March 8, 1857

The decision of the United States Supreme Court in the famous "Dred Scott" case . . . is an event of great political importance. The court of last resort, which has jurisdiction over questions appertaining to the powers of the Federal Government, decided that Congress has no power under the Constitution to legislate upon slavery in the Territories, and that all such legislation as the so-called Missouri Compromise, which undertook to do so, is null and void. This is a complete vindication of the doctrine of the Nebraska Bill, which, now, it is judicially determined only swept an illegal and unconstitutional measure from the statute-book. To the friends of the "Wilmot Proviso" and the Abolition legislation for the Territories this decision of the Supreme Court will be most crushing and annihilating. Hereafter they will have no pretense whatever for keeping Congress and the country in a turmoil on that subject, as it would be no use for Congress to pass laws on a subject which the Supreme Court would immediately annul, in accordance with this decision. The whole question of slavery, in its judicial aspects, has been argued by the best lawyers before the Court which, after mature and long deliberation, have come to the conclusion announced above. The influence of their action upon the country must necessarily be immense. The whole people, without distinction of party, have confidence in that august tribunal, the Supreme Court of the United States, which by virtue of the age, eminent legal attainments of its members, their life tenure, which places them beyond the influence of party feeling, have no motive whatever in the world to bias and corrupt their decision.

Additional force will be given it when it is known that the bench, composed of Northern and Southern members, was nearly unanimous on the main point, there being but two dissenters out of the nine Justices who compose the Court. One of them, Judge McLean, of this city, had previously volunteered an opinion on the subject years ago, before it was argued or came before him judicially; and, sustaining this unfortunate position, his dissent was naturally anticipated. It is to be regretted that he should thus have unnecessarily committed himself on a point that he was liable to be called upon to determine as a Judge.

While thus anticipating a general acquiescence in the decision of the Supreme Court, it would be too much to expect that it will escape attack and censure from disappointed and embittered partisans, whose political capital and hope of office will wither before it. They will doubtless blackguard and assail the Court; but it will still further weaken their cause among sober and intelligent men, who will never countenance their foray upon an honest and intelligent Judiciary. The men who aided in the passage of the Nebraska Bill of 1854, and sustained it against an unrestraining and infatuated opposition, will, by this decision, be placed in an enviable attitude before the country, and will have a good position assigned them in history. Coming after the result of the late election and the new President's inaugural, it is the last of a series of triumphs, political and judicial, to which hereafter they will refer with pleasure and pride.

C

The Political Arena

In the aftermath of the decision, northern Republicans attacked the Supreme Court in confident expectation of a rich political harvest. Interpreting the decision as clear evidence of the Slave Power's aggressive and sinister ambitions, prominent spokesmen such as William H. Seward hinted darkly that a web of conspiracy prevailed in the highest councils of the national government, while William P. Fessenden insisted that the Republican party had no intention of adhering to any such mistaken "decision" of the Court. In the political arena, Abraham Lincoln effectively capitalized on both these tacks to bolster his cause in the famous Illinois senatorial campaign of 1858. Furthermore, within the Democratic party the Dred Scott case advanced a long-developing split down the road to outright schism. Stephen A. Douglas, driven to a choice between his cherished notion of "popular sovereignty" and Taney's opinion with all its implications, adopted a position guaranteed to incur him hostility in the South. For their part, southern Democrats increasingly demanded laws from Congress implementing the judicial decree that slavery was entitled to federal protection in the territories. The vehemence of the southern demands alienated many erstwhile northern sympathizers, as evidenced by Ohio Senator George E. Pugh's response.

1 *Senator William Pitt Fessenden*

(Republican-Maine)

I desire . . . to advert to one other position which . . . has been alluded to again to-day — that this matter has been settled by the judicial forum. It is said that it has been carried to the Supreme Court of the United

1 *Congressional Globe*, 35th Congress, 1st Session, 616–17, 620 (February 8, 1858).

States, and settled there. Does the honorable Senator from Louisiana [Judah P. Benjamin], as a lawyer, undertake to tell me that the question has been settled by a judicial decision in that court? Did that question ever arise and present itself to the mind of the court with reference to any necessity of the case? To what extent does the honorable Senator, or anybody else who is a lawyer, undertake to say that the decision of the court is binding? It is binding so far, and so far alone, as it can issue its mandate. Its opinion is of force only upon the question which settles the cause. Am I bound to follow out a set of opinions that may be advanced by any set of judges in any court simply because, after they have decided a cause, they undertake to give their opinions? They may be bad men, they may be weak men, but their mandate in the case before them must be obeyed; and I will go as far and as readily as any man to obey the mandate of any court to which I am bound to render obedience; and I am bound to render obedience to the Supreme Court of the United States; but when they undertake to settle questions not before them, I tell them those questions are for me as well as for them. When they undertake to give opinions on collateral matters which are not involved in their decision, and they are not called upon to decide them, I tell them they are men like myself and others, and their opinions are of no value, except so far as they enforce them by sufficient and substantial reasons; and if they give bad reasons or bad logic, I would treat them as I should anybody else who would try to convince my judgment in such a way. . . .

If these are mere party decisions, let us understand it. It seems that when the decisions are one way by the Supreme Court of the United States, gentlemen of the South say "the judges are partisan judges; they cannot settle constitutional questions for us; those are political matters." When, however, they undertake extra-judicially to give opinions not called for by the point before them; to lay down doctrines at variance with the whole history and precedents of the country from its very foundation, to overturn the decisions of their own predecessors, greater men than ever they can hope to be, and to reverse all the decisions of the legislative department of the Government, on questions of a political character and description, on their own mere say-so, we are told all this is law.

Sir, I was perfectly aware, from the course of proceeding, what this decision would be. When I saw the dictum, or the dogma, if you please to call it so, laid down in the Cincinnati platform, that there was no power in the people of a Territory to exclude slavery, and when I saw that that question had been brought to the Supreme Court of the United States, and that the Supreme Court, after hearing the argument, had adjourned from one day before the election of President over to another day after the election of President, I knew what the strength of the slavery party was; I felt what the decision was to be; and I felt as well, and I do not hesitate to say it here, that had the result of that election been otherwise, and had not the party triumphed on the dogma which they had thus introduced, we should never have heard of a doctrine so utterly at variance with all truth; so utterly destitute of all legal logic; so founded on error, and unsupported by anything like argument, as is the opinion of the Supreme Court.

I should like, if I had time, to attempt to demonstrate the fallacy of that opinion. I have examined the view of the Supreme Court of the United States on the question of the power of the Constitution to carry slavery into free territory belonging to the United States, and I tell you that I believe any fairly respectable lawyer in the United States can show, beyond all question, to any fair and unprejudiced mind, that the decision has nothing to stand upon except assumption, and bad logic from the assumptions made. The main proposition on which that decision is founded; the corner-stone of it, without which it is nothing; without which it fails entirely to satisfy the mind of any man, is this: that the Constitution of the United States recognizes slavery as property, and protects it as such. I deny it. It neither recognizes slavery as property, nor does it protect slavery as property.

Fortunately for my assertion, the Supreme Court, in making that the very corner-stone of their decision, without which the whole fails, state the clauses on which they ground these assertions. On what do they found the assertion that the Constitution protects slavery as property? On the provision of the Constitution by which Congress is prohibited from passing a law to prevent the African slave trade for twenty years; and therefore they say the Constitution recognizes it as property. Will not anybody see that this constitutional provision, if it works one way, must work the other? If, by protecting the slave trade for twenty years, we recognize it as property, when we say that at the end of the twenty years we will cease to protect it, or may cease to do so, is not that denying that it is property after that period elapses? Suppose I yield to the court all the force they demand, and admit that here is a distinct recognition that this is property, because we recognize that the African slave trade may exist for twenty years; yet, when we say that after that period has elapsed that protection shall no longer exist, do we not say that after that period of time it no longer is property, and ceases to be at the expiration of twenty years? Certainly if the argument will work the one way, it must work the other. If you derive the power under the Constitution, because for twenty years it is property, you lose it when the twenty years elapse, by the same method of argument. . . .

That is my argument, and it is my answer to the assumption of the Supreme Court of the United States. If it is an assumption on my part, it is certainly an assumption on theirs. But I leave it to every fair man, on every principle of logic. It depends on that, does it? That died twenty years after the Constitution went into operation. Did not the recognition die with it? Does the Constitution recognize it after the twenty years have elapsed? The power is gone. So far as you draw any recognition from that clause, it ceased with the expiration of the period.

Again, the court say it is recognized as property by the provisions that persons held to service escaping from one State into another shall be delivered up. Are they not spoken of as "persons?" Are they spoken of as property? Is there anything said about their being property? Does not that provision of the Constitution apply just as well to white apprentices, held under the laws of the different States for a term of years, as it does to slaves? Will you pretend that by the Constitution of the United States, white persons, held as apprentices for a term of years, are property? Certainly no such position can exist. Your argument, if it works at all, must go the whole length, and you must find that the word "person" means property, and may be regularly and legally construed as property. I have not time now to pursue this topic.

Then, sir, to sum up the substance of my argument, I wish to say again that what I consider this original scheme to have been, was to assert popular sovereignty in the first place with a view of rendering the repeal of the Missouri compromise in some way palatable; then to deny it and avow the establishment of slavery; then to legalize this by a decision of the Supreme Court of the United States, and claim that it had become established. I sincerely believe that decision of the Supreme Court of the United States was a part of the programme. It was to be had, if having it would avail; but if not, it would never have been had. . . .

[It is charged] that I am undermining the institutions of the country by attacking the Supreme Court of the United States! I attack not their decision, for they have made none; it is their opinion. My belief is, my position is, that that very opinion, if carried into practice, undermines the institutions of this country. Sir, the institutions of this country stood firm; they stood upon the doctrines of freedom, not of slavery. When the Supreme Court of the United States lay down the doctrine that the Constitution of the United States recognizes slavery, I do not deny it. The position I assumed was, that the Constitution of the United States does not recognize slaves as property; does not protect them as property. It recognizes slavery as an institution existing in the States; it provides for certain contingencies; those contingencies I neither repudiate nor deny, nor attempt to cavil at; but I do deny the position which is assumed by the Supreme Court of the United States, applied to property as recognized by the Constitution beyond the limits of those States.

I assume, as I have always assumed, that in the Territories no State has any right. There is no such thing as the right of States in a Territory. The rights, if they exist, are the rights of the people of the States — personal rights; and when an individual, a citizen of a State, leaves that State with a design to go to another, and passes beyond its limits, he loses every right which he had as a citizen of that State, for he ceases to be its citizen. It being a personal right, if you wish to put it on that ground, and wish to divide this Territory according to the interest the people have in it, in proportion to numbers, how much, I ask, would the slaveholders of the Union be entitled to? How much would the half a million of slaveholders, with their wives and children, be entitled to out of the Territories of the United States when put against the more than twenty millions of free people, who have the same rights with themselves? And yet the doctrine is taught here that because in some of the States of the Union slavery exists, therefore we are to take the number of States, and on the ground of State rights claim that the territory is to be equally divided, with equal privileges.

Sir, it is a personal privilege. So far as you may be a slaveholder, and desire to go to the territories, you have all the privilege which belongs to you as an individual. If the Constitution enables and authorizes you to carry slaves there, take them there and try it. I deny the fact. It never was so held until very recently, when individuals of the Supreme Court gave that opinion. When Mr. Calhoun broached the doctrine in the Senate of the United States, it was received with derision, and it died. It hardly had an existence long enough to have it said that it lived; and when Mr. Calhoun, at a later day, said, as he did say, that if the Supreme Court should decide that the doctrine was not a true one, that decision would be entitled to no respect, to no observance, pray, was not he uttering sentiments undermining the Constitution of the United States and our institutions? He said then, in a supposed case, what I say now. He said that if the Supreme Court established the doctrine that the Constitution did not carry slavery into the Territories, that opinion of theirs would be entitled to no respect. I say they have decided according to his wish, and that decision is entitled to no respect, for it is opposed to all the precedents of this Government, and opposed to all the doctrines which lie at the foundation of our institutions, and opposed to the previous decisions of that court. . . .

2 Senator William H. Seward

(Republican-New York)

The new President [Buchanan] . . . before coming into office . . . approached or was approached by the Supreme Court of the United States. On their docket was, through some chance or design, an action which an

---

2 Congressional Globe, 35th Congress, 1st Session, 941, 943 (March 3, 1858).

obscure negro man in Missouri had brought for his freedom against his reputed master. The court had arrived at the conclusion, on solemn argument, that insomuch as this unfortunate negro had, through some ignorance or chicane in special pleading, admitted what could not have been proved, that he had descended from some African who had once been held in bondage, that therefore he was not, in view of the Constitution, a citizen of the United States and therefore could not implead the reputed master in the Federal courts; and on this ground the Supreme Court were prepared to dismiss the action, for want of jurisdiction over the suitor's person. This decision, certainly as repugnant to the Declaration of Independence and to the spirit of the Constitution, as to the instincts of humanity, nevertheless would be one which would exhaust all the power of the tribunal, and exclude consideration of all other questions that had been raised upon the record. The counsel who had appeared for the negro had volunteered from motives of charity, and, ignorant of course of the disposition which was to be made of the cause, had argued that his client had been freed from slavery by operation of the Missouri prohibition of 1820. The opposing counsel, paid by the defending slaveholder, had insisted, in reply, that that famous statute was unconstitutional. The mock debate had been heard in the chamber of the court in the basement of the Capitol, in the presence of the curious visitors at the seat of Government, whom the dullness of a judicial investigation could not disgust. The court did not hesitate to please the incoming President, by seizing this extraneous and idle forensic discussion, and converting it into an occasion for pronouncing an opinion that the Missouri prohibition was void; and that, by force of the Constitution, slavery existed, with all the elements of property in man over man, in all the Territories of the United States, paramount to any popular sovereignty within the Territories, and even to the authority of Congress itself.

In this ill-omened act, the Supreme Court forgot its own dignity, which had always been maintained with just judicial jealousy. They forgot that the province of a court is simply *"jus dicere,"* and not at all *"jus dare."* They forgot, also, that one "foul sentence does more harm than many foul examples; for the last do but corrupt the stream, while the former corrupteth the fountain." And they and the President alike forgot that judicial usurpation is more odious and intolerable than any other among the manifold practices of tyranny.

The day of inauguration came — the first one among all the celebrations of that great national pageant that was to be desecrated by a coalition between the executive and judicial departments, to undermine the National Legislature and the liberties of the people. The President, attended by the usual lengthened procession, arrived and took his seat on the portico. The Supreme Court attended him there, in robes which yet exacted public reverence. The people, unaware of the import of the whisperings carried on between the President and the Chief Justice, and imbued with veneration for both, filled the avenues and gardens far away as the eye could reach. The President addressed them in words as bland as those which the worst of all the Roman Emperors pronounced when he assumed the purple. He announced (vaguely, indeed, but with self-satisfaction) the forthcoming extra-judicial exposition of the Constitution, and pledged his submission to it as authoritative and final. The Chief Justice and his associates remained silent. The Senate, too, were there — constitutional witnesses of the transfer of administration. They, too, were silent, although the promised usurpation was to subvert the authority over more than half of the empire which Congress had assumed contemporaneously with the birth of the nation, and had exercised without interruption for near seventy years. It cost the President, under the circumstances, little exercise of magnanimity now to promise to the people of Kansas, on whose neck he had, with the aid of the Supreme Court, hung the millstone of slavery, a fair trial in their attempt to cast it off, and hurl it to the earth, when they should come to organize a state government. Alas! that even this cheap promise, uttered under such great solemnities, was only made to be broken!

The pageant ended. On the 5th of March, the judges, without even exchanging their silken robes for courtiers' gowns, paid their salutations to the President, in the Executive palace. Doubtlessly the President received them as graciously as Charles I did the judges who had, at his instance subverted the statutes of English liberty. On the 6th of March, the Supreme Court dismissed the negro suitor, Dred Scott, to return to his bondage; and having thus disposed of that private action for an alleged private wrong, on the ground of want of jurisdiction in the case, they proceeded, with amusing solemnity, to pronounce the opinion that if they had had such jurisdiction, still the unfortunate negro would have had to remain in bondage, unrelieved, because the Missouri prohibition violates rights of general property involved in slavery, paramount to the authority of Congress. A few days later copies of this opinion were multiplied by the Senate's press, and scattered in the name of the Senate broadcast over the land, and their publication has not yet been disowned by the Senate. Simultaneously, Dred Scott, who had played the hand of *dummy* in this interesting political game, unwittingly, yet to the complete satisfaction of his adversary, was voluntarily emancipated; and thus received from his master, as a reward, the freedom which the Court had denied him as a right. . . .

The Supreme Court . . . can reverse its spurious judgment more easily than we could reconcile the people to its usurpation. Sir, the Supreme Court of the United States attempts to command the people of the United States to accept the principles that one man can own other men; and that they must guaranty the inviolability of that false and pernicious property. The people of the United States never can, and they never will, accept principles so unconstitutional and so abhorrent. Never, never. Let the court recede. Whether it recedes or not, we shall reorganize the court, and thus reform its political sentiments and practices, and bring them into harmony with the Constitution and with the laws of nature. In doing so, we shall not only reassume our own just authority, but we shall restore that high tribunal itself to the position it ought to maintain, since so many invaluable rights of citizens, and even of States themselves, depend upon impartiality and its wisdom. . . .

3 Senator Judah P. Benjamin

(Democrat-Louisiana)

As a member of that committee which is charged in the Senate with the examination of all subjects touching the judiciary of the country, it is my duty to make answer to those charges which are brought against the highest judges of the land with a violence, a recklessness, and, I regret to be compelled to add, with a disregard of truth and decency which will yet bring down upon their authors the indignant condemnation of their outraged countrymen.

Mr. President, the whole subject of slavery, so far as it is involved in the issue now before the country, is narrowed down at last to a controversy on the solitary point, whether it be competent for the Congress of the United States, directly or indirectly, to exclude slavery from the Territories of the Union. The Supreme Court of the United States have given a negative answer to this proposition, and it shall be my first effort to support that negation by argument, independently of the authority of the decision.

It seems to me that the radical, fundamental error which underlies the argument in affirmation of this power, is the assumption that slavery is the creature of the statute law of the several States where it is established; that it has no existence outside of the limits of those States; that slaves are not property beyond those limits; and that property in slaves is neither recognized nor protected by the Constitution of the United States, nor by international law. I controvert all these propositions. . . .

Now, sir, because the Supreme Court of the United States says — what is patent to every man who reads the Constitution of the United States — that it does guaranty property in slaves, it has been attacked with vituperation here, on this floor, by Senators on all sides. Some have ab-

---

stained from any indecent, insulting remarks in relation to the court. Some have confined themselves to calm and legitimate argument. To them I am about to reply. To the others, I shall have something to say a little later. What says the Senator from Maine, [Mr. FESSENDEN?]. . . .

The Senator . . . says that the Constitution does not recognize slaves as property, nor protect them as property, and his reasoning, a little further on, is somewhat curious. He says:

> "On what do they found the assertion that the Constitution recognizes slavery as property? On the provision of the Constitution by which Congress is prohibited from passing a law to prevent the African slave trade for twenty years; and therefore they say the Constitution recognizes slaves as property."

I should think that was a pretty fair recognition of it. On this point the gentleman declares:

> "Will not anybody see that this constitutional provision, if it works one way, must work the other? If, by allowing the slave trade for twenty years, we recognize slaves as property, when we say that at the end of twenty years we will cease to allow it, or may cease to do so, is not that denying them to be property after that period elapses?"

That is the argument. Nothing but my respect for the logical intellect of the Senator from Maine could make me treat this argument as serious, and nothing but having heard it myself would make me believe that he ever uttered it. What, sir! The Constitution of our country says to the South, "you shall count as the basis of your representation five slaves as being three white men; you may be protected in the natural increase of your slaves; nay, more, as a matter of compromise you may increase their number if you choose, for twenty years, by importation; when these twenty years are out, you shall stop." The Supreme Court of the United States says, "well; is not this a recognition of slavery, of property in slaves?" "Oh, no," says the gentleman, "the rule must work both ways; there is a converse to the proposition." Now, sir, to an ordinary, uninstructed intellect, it would seem that the converse of the proposition was simply that at the end of twenty years you should not any longer increase your numbers by importation; but the gentleman says the converse of the proposition is that at the end of the twenty years, after you have, under the guarantee of the Constitution, been adding by importation to the previous number of your slaves, then all those that you had before, and all those that, under that Constitution, you have imported, cease to be recognized as property by the Constitution, and on this proposition he assails the Supreme Court of the United States — a proposition which he says will occur to anybody! . . .

I never heard this question disputed before; I never heard a suggestion that slaves were not protected as property by the Constitution of the

United States till I heard it from the Senator from Maine here the other day. In the sixteenth volume of Peters's Report there is the report of a case which occurred between the States of Maryland and Pennsylvania. It was elaborately argued. The Commonwealth of Pennsylvania sent her attorney general into the room below to affirm her right to the legislation which she had passed. Although the suit was in the name of an individual, really it was the rights of Maryland that were concerned, and it was the State of Maryland that was interested in the decision. The case is known by the title in the law books of Prigg *versus* the State of Pennsylvania. Every judge on the bench gave his decision in that case. Every judge on the bench concurred in the decision. Judge Story delivered the opinion of the court, the other judges delivering their individual opinions, where they did not precisely agree with the general language of the court. Amongst those judges was Judge McLean, one of the dissentient judges in the Dred Scott case. . . .

. . .[W]hen I find the entire court, man for man, concurring that the constitutional rights of the South are guarantied in slaves as property by this clause in the Constitution, I must express my intense surprise at hearing the Senator from Maine declare that the Dred Scott decision was not to be supported, because it rested as a corner-stone on the assumption that slaves were recognized by the Constitution as property, and that he denied that fact.

But, Mr. President, all these gentlemen who thus fail in the slightest degree to impugn the opinion of the court by argument, attempt to shake its authority by an assertion entirely destitute of the slightest foundation. Every Senator who has spoken on the subject of this decision has declared that the court said it was without jurisdiction to determine it, and then determined it. I say that all the judges declared that they had jurisdiction of the merits, and determined that point before they decided the merits; and I am prepared to prove it. There was not a judge on the bench who did not declare that he had jurisdiction of the merits. There were some of the judges who declared that they had jurisdiction of no other question; and Judge McLean was one of them. He said the question of jurisdiction was not before them at all, and so did Judge Catron; and both those judges said that the court had nothing before them but the merits. Every judge said that he had the merits before him. I will prove it.

When this decision was first published; when, as I am sorry to say, two of the judges of that court so far forgot the proprieties of their judicial station as to send forth a minority opinion, to forestall the public judgment, and to produce among the people of the country the impression that the integrity of their judiciary was no longer to be relied upon, and thus to subvert one of the foundations of our Government; when those opinions first went abroad, they were seized upon by the Republican presses through the land, and it was said everywhere, "this court is usurping power; it has no such power as that which it assumes; it first says it has no jurisdiction, and then, after declaring itself to be without power over the subject-matter, presumes to determine it." Every Senator on this side of the Chamber, who has spoken, has repeated this. I want to nail the assertion to the counter; the coin is false. . . .

The Supreme Court of the United States was the only tribunal to determine in the last resort whether it had jurisdiction or not over the question. It determined that it had. The Senator [Fessenden] says it began by determining that the plaintiff in the court below had no right to come into the court, and by reason thereof determined that the circuit court had no jurisdiction, and he puts in himself that consequently the Supreme Court had no jurisdiction. It is precisely his "consequently" that Chief Justice Taney says is a manifest mistake. . . .

The court said, "in our judgment, there are two points which settle the cause; one is the jurisdiction, the other the merits." The Senator says that by the time they had got through stating the first half of their opinion, he has a right to shut their mouths and say, "you shall not go on and give any other reason; the reason you have given is enough; you cannot say another word." This is a most curious proposition to maintain to anybody that has ever heard decrees or opinions rendered in courts of justice. . . .

Then, sir, the honorable Senator declares, point blank, that this question was not before the court. They consider that it was; the dissenting judges said it was; everybody there said it was; everybody but the Senator from Maine and his worthy colleagues, the Senator from New York and the Senator from Vermont. This notion was first started by some indecorous expressions in the opinions of the dissenting judges. They themselves, declaring that they had jurisdiction over the subject-matter, suggested that they would not consider the opinion of the other judges binding, because, in the opinion of other judges, the court below had no jurisdiction; "but," said Judge Taney, "this question is before me on its merits; I must decide it; it is my duty to decide it; I cannot avoid the duty." That is the language, if the gentleman will refer to it.

Now, Mr. President, I come to another point in my argument, which I approach with extreme pain, with unfeigned regret. From my earliest childhood, I have been taught to revere the judges of the highest court in the land, as men selected to render justice between litigants, not more by reason of their eminent legal acquirements, than because of a spotless purity of character, an undimmed luster of reputation which removed them far, far beyond even a doubt of their integrity. The long line of eminent judicial worthies which seemed to have culminated in a Marshall, has been continued in the person of one upon whom the highest eulogium that can be pronounced is to say that he was eminently worthy of being the successor of that illustrious judge. I know not, Mr. President, whether you, as I, have had the good fortune to see that magistrate in the administration of justice in his own circuit, or in the court sitting below us, of which he is the honored chief. I know not, sir, whether it has been your good fortune, as it has been mine, to hear the expressions of affectionate reverence with which he is spoken of by the people amongst whom he has passed his pure, his simple, and his spotless life. I know not, sir, whether you have listened, as I have, with interest to the expressions of respect and admiration that come from the members of his bar in their familiar intercourse with each other — spontaneous tributes, worth a thousand labored eulogies, to his eminent sagacity, to his vast legal learning, to the mild and serene dignity of his judicial deportment; above all, sir, above all, to the conscientious, earnest, almost painful sense of responsibility with which he holds the scale of justice in even and impartial hand between the litigants whose rights depend upon his judgment.

Mr. President, he is old, very old. The infirmities of age have bowed his venerable form. Earth has no further object of ambition for him; and when he shall sink into his grave after a long career of high office in our country, I trust that I do not rudely or improperly invade the sanctity of private life in saying that he will leave behind him, in the scanty heritage that shall be left for his family, the noblest evidence that he died, as he had lived, a being honorable to the earth from which he sprang, and worthy of the heaven to which he aspired.

This man, sir, thus beloved, thus revered, thus esteemed, has been compared upon this floor to the infamous Jeffreys, by the Senator from Maine, [Mr. HAMLIN.] This man has been charged by the Senator from New York [Mr. SEWARD] with a corrupt coalition with the Chief Magistrate of the Union. He charges in fact — not always in direct language, but partly by bold assertion and partly by insidious suggestions — that the Supreme Magistrate of the land and the judges of our highest court, and the parties to the Dred Scott case, got up a mock trial; that they were all in common collusion to cheat the country. . . .

Was this case got up? What are the facts? Men should be a little careful in making such accusations as these; unless, indeed, they care not whether they be true or false, being intended to answer some purpose, whether the one or the other. This case was got up, was it? By accident or design? In the exquisitely decorous and appropriate language of the Senator from New York, the Chief Justice of the United States and the Chief Magistrate of the Union were gambling at cards for the case, and Dred Scott was dummy in the imaginary game! What truth is there in these insinuations of design? Why, sir, Dred Scott had sought his freedom by the assertion of his rights in the State courts of Missouri years before the Kansas-Nebraska act was ever suggested, and years before the President of the United States was even a candidate for office; years before he was even Minister to England.

This case was determined in the supreme court of the State of Missouri,

in 1852, adversely to Dred Scott, and was remanded to the lower court
for further trial. Mr. Buchanan had, I believe, not then gone to England.
The Kansas bill had not been heard of, and was not in the imagination
of any man. When the case got back into the lower court, the counsel
for Dred Scott, finding that the opinion of the supreme court of the
State was adverse to his rights, withdrew his case from the State court,
and endeavored to better his client's chances by going into another jurisdiction. That is the way the case got into the Federal court; and when
was this? The case was carried into the Federal court in the city of St.
Louis, in November, 1853, before even the meeting of the Congress
which passed the Kansas-Nebraska act; . . .

> "Be it remembered that heretofore, to wit: on the second day of Novem-
> ber, in the year of our Lord 1853, came the abovenamed plaintiff, Dred
> Scott, by his attorney, and filed in the clerk's office of the circuit court of
> the United States for the Missouri district, the following declaration against
> the defendant, John F. A. Sandford."

Was that a case gotten up by design, between the President and the
court here? It was never carried there until they had lost all chance in
the State court; it was carried there as the last desperate resource of
defeated counsel; eager to maintain what he conceived to be the rights
of his client. Who was the counsel? The Senators from Missouri can
tell us who R. M. Field, of St. Louis, is, and probable they will verify
the assertion which I make here upon hear-say — I give it only upon
hear-say — that he is one of the most determined Free-Soilers in the
State of Missouri; has always declined to vote at elections until he was
able to cast his vote for a Free-Soil candidate, and until he aided in the
election of the Free-Soil Representative from the St. Louis district who
now sits in the other Chamber.

This case, thus brought up in November, 1853, was determined in the
court below, and a writ of error was taken to the Supreme Court of the
United States, before the Kansas bill was passed, and whilst Mr. Buchanan was in England! When it reached the Supreme Court of the
United States what became of it? . . .

I happen to know, however, whatever may be the fact with the other,
that one of the opposing counsel was not paid by any slaveholder at all;
that one of the opposing counsel volunteered as *amicus curiæ* by virtue
of his position as head of the bar of the Supreme Court of the United
States, by virtue of his position as ex-Attorney General of the United
States, by virtue of his position as a compeer of the honorable Senator,
and his former colleague on this floor from the State of Maryland, Mr.
Reverdy Johnson. That gentleman volunteered in the case as *amicus
curiæ*, because the whole section of the country to whose interests he
had been devoted from his birth had an interest in this great question
to be decided, and which, at the time of his volunteering in the case,

he did not yet know to be represented by counsel. The honorable Mr. Geyer, of Missouri, afterwards entered his name of record, and appeared for the defendant. . . .

Says the Senator from New York:

"The opposing counsel, paid by the defending slaveholder, had insisted, in reply, that that famous statute was unconstitutional. The mock debate had been heard in the chamber of the court in the basement of the Capitol, in the presence of the curious visitors at the seat of Government, whom the dullness of a judicial investigation could not disgust. The court did not hesitate to please the incoming President" —

Where are we, sir, that such language as this is used? Is this the Senate of the United States, and are we here, the ambassadors of coequal sovereignties, to be insulted by language like this? Is not this an insult to every one of us, direct and personal? . . .

Is there a solitary word of truth in this? Not one. Is a solitary fact alleged? Not one; but a broad and naked charge is made, which is intended to stamp infamy upon characters hitherto beyond the breath of reproach. Shame, shame upon the Senator that makes such charges as these and has no proof to support them. . . .

Does anybody find in the President's inaugural anything on this point, except that he learns the question is to be decided by the highest tribunal of the land, and that he, as every other good citizen is, is willing to render obedience to that tribunal? . . .

Now, does not the Senator from New York know, was it not published in every newspaper in the country, that the slave's master had died? Was it not known that the man who emancipated the slave was a Black-Republican compeer in the other House, of the Senator of New York, [Mr. CHAFFEE, of Massachusetts,] who was forced to give this emancipation after having long hesitated, by the indignant denunciations of the fellow-Republicans around him. Everybody knows that, and yet here we are told by the Senator that this gift of freedom to the slave was the *reward* granted by his master, the defendant, for playing the hand of dummy in a game of cards — a political game — with the venerable Chief Justice and Chief Magistrate of the Union. Shame, shame once more, upon the Senator who makes charges like these, without the shadow of ground for their support. . . .

4 *The Lincoln-Douglas Debates: 1858*

MR. LINCOLN: *Springfield,* June 17, 1858.

. . . While the opinion of the court, by Chief Justice Taney, in the Dred Scott case, and the separate opinions of all the concurring Judges, expressly declare that the Constitution of the United States neither permits Congress nor a Territorial Legislature to exclude slavery from any United States Territory, they all omit to declare whether or not the same Constitution permits a State, or the people of a State, to exclude it. *Possibly,* this is a mere omission; but who can be quite sure, if McLean or Curtis had sought to get into the opinion a declaration of unlimited power in the people of a State to exclude slavery from their limits, just as Chase and Mace sought to get such declaration, in behalf of the people of a Territory, into the Nebraska bill; — I ask, who can be quite sure that it would not have been voted down in the one case as it had been in the other? The nearest approach to the point of declaring the power of a State over slavery, is made by Judge Nelson. He approaches it more than once, using the precise idea, and almost the language, too, of the Nebraska act. On one occasion, his exact language is, "except in cases where the power is restrained by the Constitution of the United States, the law of the State is supreme over the subject of slavery within its jurisdiction." In what cases the power of the States is so restrained by the United States Constitution, is left an open question, precisely as the same question, as to the restraint on the power of the Territories, was left open in the Nebraska act. Put this and that together, and we have another nice little niche, which we may, ere long, see filled with another Supreme Court decision, declaring that the Constitution of the United States does not permit a *State* to exclude slavery from its limits. And this may especially be expected if the doctrine of "care not whether slavery be voted down or voted up," shall gain upon the public mind sufficiently to give promise that such a decision can be maintained when made.

Such a decision is all that slavery now lacks of being alike lawful in all the States. Welcome, or unwelcome, such decision is probably coming, and will soon be upon us, unless the power of the present political dynasty shall be met and overthrown. We shall lie down pleasantly dreaming that the people of Missouri are on the verge of making their State free, and we shall awake to the reality instead, that the Supreme Court

---

4 *Political Debates Between Hon. Abraham Lincoln and Hon. Stephen A. Douglas.* . . . (Columbus, Ohio, 1860), 4, 10–12, 20–21, 47–49, 95, 126–28, 204–06, 250–52.

has made Illinois a slave State. To meet and overthrow the power of that dynasty, is the work now before all those who would prevent that consummation. That is what we have to do. How can we best do it? . . .

Mr. Douglas: *Chicago,* July 9, 1858.

. . . The other proposition discussed by Mr. Lincoln in his speech consists in a crusade against the Supreme Court of the United States on account of the Dred Scott decision. On this question, . . . I desire to say to you unequivocally, that I take direct and distinct issue with him. I have no warfare to make on the Supreme Court of the United States, either on account of that or any other decision which they have pronounced from that bench. The Constitution of the United States has provided that the powers of government (and the Constitution of each State has the same provision) shall be divided into three departments — executive, legislative, and judicial. The right and the province of expounding the Constitution, and constructing the law, is vested in the judiciary established by the Constitution. As a lawyer, I feel at liberty to appear before the Court and controvert any principle of law while the question is pending before the tribunal; but when the decision is made, my private opinion, your opinion, all other opinions must yield to the majesty of that authoritative adjudication. I wish you to bear in mind that this involves a great principle, upon which our rights, our liberty and our property all depend. What security have you for your property, for your reputation, and for your personal rights, if the courts are not upheld, and their decisions respected when once fairly rendered by the highest tribunal known to the Constitution? I do not choose, therefore, to go into any argument with Mr. Lincoln in reviewing the various decisions which the Supreme Court has made, either upon the Dred Scott case or any other. I have no idea of appealing from the decision of the Supreme Court upon a Constitutional question to the decisions of a tumultuous town meeting. . . .

. . . I am opposed to this doctrine of Mr. Lincoln, by which he proposes to take an appeal from the decision of the Supreme Court of the United States, upon this high constitutional question, to a Republican caucus sitting in the country. Yes, or any other caucus or town meeting, whether it be Republican, American, or Democratic. I respect the decisions of that august tribunal; I shall always bow in deference to them. I am a law-abiding man. I will sustain the Constitution of my country as our fathers have made it. I will yield obedience to the laws, whether I like them or not, as I find them on the statute book. I will sustain the judicial tribunals and constituted authorities in all matters within the pale of their jurisdictions as defined by the Constitution.

But I am equally free to say that the reason assigned by Mr. Lincoln for resisting the decision of the Supreme Court in the Dred Scott case, does not in itself meet my approbation. He objects to it because that decision declared that a negro descended from African parents, who were brought here and sold as slaves, is not, and cannot be, a citizen of the United States. He says it is wrong, because it deprives the negro of the benefits of that clause of the Constitution which says that citizens of one State shall enjoy all the privileges and immunities of citizens of the several States; in other words, he thinks it wrong because it deprives the negro of the privileges, immunities and rights of citizenship, which pertain, according to that decision, only to the white man. I am free to say to you that in my opinion this government of ours is founded on the white basis. It was made by the white man, for the benefit of the white man, to be administered by white men, in such manner as they should determine. It is also true that a negro, an Indian, or any other man of inferior race to a white man, should be permitted to enjoy, and humanity requires that he should have all the rights, privileges and immunities which he is capable of exercising consistent with the safety of society. I would give him every right and every privilege which his capacity would enable him to enjoy, consistent with the good of the society in which he lived. But you may ask me, what are these rights and these privileges? My answer is, that each State must decide for itself the nature and extent of these rights. Illinois has decided for herself. We have decided that the negro shall not be a slave, and we have at the same time decided that he shall not vote, or serve on juries, or enjoy political privileges. I am content with that system of policy which we have adopted for ourselves. I deny the right of any other State to complain of our policy in that respect, or to interfere with it, or to attempt to change it. On the other hand, the State of Maine has decided that in that State a negro man may vote on an equality with the white man. The sovereign power of Maine had the right to prescribe that rule for herself. Illinois has no right to complain of Maine for conferring the right of negro suffrage, nor has Maine any right to interfere with, or complain of Illinois because she has denied negro suffrage.

. . . Kentucky, Virginia and other States have provided that negroes, or a certain class of them in those States, shall be slaves, having neither civil or political rights. Without indorsing the wisdom of that decision, I assert that Virginia has the same power by virtue of her sovereignty to protect slavery within her limits, as Illinois has to banish it forever from our own borders. I assert the right of each State to decide for itself on all these questions, and I do not subscribe to the doctrine of my friend, Mr. Lincoln, that uniformity is either desirable or possible. I do not acknowledge that the States must all be free or must all be slave.

. . . Mr. Lincoln goes for a warfare upon the Supreme Court of the United States, because of their judicial decision in the Dred Scott case. I yield obedience to the decisions in that court — to the final determination of the highest judicial tribunal known to our constitution. He objects

to the Dred Scott decision because it does not put the negro in the possession of the rights of citizenship on an equality with the white man. I am
opposed to negro equality. I repeat that this nation is a white people —
a people composed of European descendants — a people that have established this government for themselves and their posterity, and I am in
favor of preserving not only the purity of the blood, but the purity of the
government from any mixture or amalgamation with inferior races. I
have seen the effects of this mixture of superior and inferior races —
this amalgamation of white men and Indians and negroes; we have seen
it in Mexico, in Central America, in South America, and in all the Spanish-American States, and its result has been degeneration, demoralization,
and degradation below the capacity for self-government. . . .

MR. LINCOLN: *Chicago*, July 10, 1858.

. . . I have expressed heretofore, and I now repeat, my opposition to
the Dred Scott decision, but I should be allowed to state the nature of
that opposition, and I ask your indulgence while I do so. What is fairly
implied by the term Judge Douglas has used, "resistance to the decision?"
I do not resist it. If I wanted to take Dred Scott from his master, I would
be interfering with property, and that terrible difficulty that Judge
Douglas speaks of, of interfering with property would arise. But I am
doing no such thing as that, but all that I am doing is refusing to obey
it as a political rule. If I were in Congress, and a vote should come up
on a question whether slavery should be prohibited in a new Territory,
in spite of the Dred Scott decision, I would vote that it should.

. . . We let this property abide by the decision, but we will try to
reverse that decision. We will try to put it where Judge Douglas would
not object, for he says he will obey until it is reversed. Somebody has to
reverse that decision, since it is made, and we mean to reverse it, and
we mean to do it peaceably.

What are the uses of decisions of courts? They have two uses. As
rules of property they have two uses. First — they decide upon the
question before the court. They decide in this case that Dred Scott is
a slave. Nobody resists that. Not only that, but they say to everybody
else, that persons standing just as Dred Scott stands, is as he is. That
is, they say that when a question comes up upon another person, it will
be so decided again, unless the court decides in another way, unless the
court overrules its decision. Well, we mean to do what we can to have
the court decide the other way. That is one thing we mean to try to do.

The sacredness that Judge Douglas throws around this decision, is a
degree of sacredness that has never been before thrown around any other
decision. I have never heard of such a thing. Why, decisions apparently
contrary to that decision, or that good lawyers thought were contrary to
that decision, have been made by that very court before. It is the first

of its kind; it is an astonisher in legal history. It is a new wonder of the world. It is based upon falsehood in the main as to the facts — allegations of facts upon which it stands are not facts at all in many instances, and no decision made on any question — the first instance of a decision made under so many unfavorable circumstances — thus placed, has been held by the profession as law, and it has always needed confirmation before the lawyers regarded it as settled law. But Judge Douglas will have it that all hands must take this extraordinary decision, made under these extraordinary circumstances, and give their vote in Congress in accordance with it, yield to it and obey it in every possible sense. Circumstances alter cases. Do not gentlemen here remember the case of that same Supreme Court, some twenty-five or thirty years ago, deciding that a National Bank was constitutional? I ask, if somebody does not remember that a National Bank was declared to be constitutional? Such is the truth, whether it be remembered or not. The Bank charter ran out, and a re-charter was granted by Congress. That re-charter was laid before General Jackson. It was urged upon him, when he denied the constitutionality of the Bank, that the Supreme Court had decided that it was constitutional; and that General Jackson then said that the Supreme Court had no right to lay down a rule to govern a coördinate branch of the Government, the members of which had sworn to support the Constitution — that each member had sworn to support that Constitution as he understood it. I will venture here to say, that I have heard Judge Douglas say that he approved of General Jackson for that act. What has now become of all his tirade about "resistance to the Supreme Court?" . . .

MR. DOUGLAS: *Springfield,* July 17, 1858.

. . . [Mr. Lincoln] makes two points upon the Dred Scott decision. The first is that he objects to it because the court decided that negroes descended of slave parents are not citizens of the United States; and secondly, because they have decided that the act of Congress, passed 8th of March, 1820, prohibiting slavery in all of the Territories north of 36° 30', was unconstitutional and void, and hence did not have effect in emancipating a slave brought into that Territory. And he will not submit to that decision. He says that he will not fight the Judges or the United States Marshals in order to liberate Dred Scott, but that he will not respect that decision, as a rule of law binding on this country, in the future. Why not? Because, he says, it is unjust. How is he going to remedy it? Why, he says he is going to reverse it. How? He is going to take an appeal. To whom is he going to appeal? The Constitution of the United States provides that the Supreme Court is the ultimate tribunal, the highest judicial tribunal on earth, and Mr. Lincoln is going to appeal from that. To whom? I know he appealed to the Republican State Convention of Illinois, and I believe that Convention reversed the decision, but I am not aware that they have yet carried it into effect. How are they going to make that reversal effectual? Why, Mr. Lincoln tells us in his late Chicago speech. He explains it as clear as light. He says to the people of Illinois that if you elect him to the Senate he will introduce a bill to re-enact the law which the Court pronounced unconstitutional. [Shouts of laughter, and voices, "*Spot* the law."] Yes, he is going to spot the law. The court pronounces that law, prohibiting slavery, unconstitutional and void, and Mr. Lincoln is going to pass an act reversing that decision and making it valid. I never heard before of an appeal being taken from the Supreme Court to the Congress of the United States to reverse its decision. I have heard of appeals being taken from Congress to the Supreme Court to declare a statute void. That has been done from the earliest days of Chief Justice Marshall, down to the present time.

The Supreme Court of Illinois do not hesitate to pronounce an act of the Legislature void, as being repugnant to the Constitution, and the Supreme Court of the United States is vested by the Constitution with that very power. The Constitution says that the judicial power of the United States shall be vested in the Supreme Court, and such inferior courts as Congress shall, from time to time, ordain and establish. Hence it is the province and duty of the Supreme Court to pronounce judgment on the validity and constitutionality of an act of Congress. In this case they have done so, and Mr. Lincoln will not submit to it, and he is going to reverse it by another act of Congress of the same tenor. My opinion is that Mr. Lincoln ought to be on the supreme bench himself, when the Republicans get into power, if that kind of law knowledge qualifies a man for the bench. But Mr. Lincoln intimates that there is another mode by which he can reverse the Dred Scott decision. How is that? Why, he is going to appeal to the people to elect a President who will appoint judges who will reverse the Dred Scott decision. Well, let us see how that is going to be done. First, he has to carry on his sectional organization, a party confined to the free States, making war upon the slaveholding States until he gets a Republican President elected. ["He never will, sir."] I do not believe he ever will. But suppose he should; when that Republican President shall have taken his seat (Mr. Seward, for instance), will he then proceed to appoint judges? No! he will have to wait until the present judges die before he can do that, and perhaps his four years would be out before a majority of these judges found it agreeable to die; and it is very possible, too, that Mr. Lincoln's senatorial term would expire before these judges would be accommodating enough to die. If it should so happen I do not see a very great prospect for Mr. Lincoln to reverse the Dred Scott decision. But suppose they should die, then how are the new judges to be appointed? Why, the Republican President is to call upon the candidates and catechise them, and ask them, "How will you decide this case if I appoint you

judge?" Suppose, for instance, Mr. Lincoln to be a candidate for a va-
cancy on the supreme bench to fill Chief Justice Taney's place, and when
he applied to Seward, the latter would say, "Mr. Lincoln, I cannot appoint you until I know how you will decide the Dred Scott case?" Mr.
Lincoln tells him, and then asks him how he will decide Tom Jones's
case, and Bill Wilson's case, and thus catechises the judge as to how he
will decide any case which may arise before him. Suppose you get a
Supreme Court composed of such judges, who have been appointed by
a partisan President upon their giving pledges how they would decide
a case before it arose, what confidence would you have in such a court?

Would not your court be prostituted beneath the contempt of all mankind? What man would feel that his liberties were safe, his right of
person or property was secure, if the supreme bench, that august tribunal,
the highest on earth, was brought down to that low, dirty pool wherein
the judges are to give pledges in advance how they will decide all the
questions which may be brought before them? It is a proposition to
make that court the corrupt, unscrupulous tool of a political party.
But Mr. Lincoln cannot conscientiously submit, he thinks to the decision
of a court composed of a majority of Democrats. If he cannot, how
can he expect us to have confidence in a court composed of a majority
of Republicans, selected for the purpose of deciding against the Democracy, and in favor of the Republicans? The very proposition carries with
it the demoralization and degradation destructive of the judicial department of the Federal Government.

I say to you, fellow-citizens, that I have no warfare to make upon the
Supreme Court because of the Dred Scott decision. I have no complaints
to make against that court, because of that decision. My private opinions on some points of the case may have been one way and on other
points of the case another; in some things concurring with the court and
in others dissenting, but what have my private opinions in a question
of law to do with the decision after it has been pronounced by the highest judicial tribunal known to the Constitution? You, sir [addressing the
chairman], as an eminent lawyer, have a right to entertain your opinions
on any question that comes before the court and to appear before the
tribunal and maintain them boldly and with tenacity until the final decision shall have been pronounced, and then, sir, whether you are sustained or overruled your duty as a lawyer and a citizen is to bow in
deference to that decision. I intend to yield obedience to the decisions
of the highest tribunals in the land in all cases whether their opinions
are in conformity with my views as a lawyer or not. When we refuse
to abide by judicial decisions what protection is there left for life and
property? To whom shall you appeal? To mob law, to partisan caucuses,
to town meetings, to revolution? Where is the remedy when you refuse
obedience to the constituted authorities? I will not stop to inquire
whether I agree or disagree with all the opinions expressed by Judge

Taney or any other judge. It is enough for me to know that the decision has been made. It has been made by a tribunal appointed by the Constitution to make it; it was a point within their jurisdiction, and I am bound by it. . . .

Mr. Douglas: Freeport, August 27, 1858.

The next question propounded to me by Mr. Lincoln is, can the people of a Territory in any lawful way, against the wishes of any citizen of the United States, exclude slavery from their limits prior to the formation of a State Constitution? I answer emphatically, as Mr. Lincoln has heard me answer a hundred times from every stump in Illinois, that in my opinion the people of a Territory can, by lawful means, exclude slavery from their limits prior to the formation of a State Constitution. Mr. Lincoln knew that I had answered that question over and over again. He heard me argue the Nebraska bill on that principle all over the State in 1854, in 1855, and in 1856, and he has no excuse for pretending to be in doubt as to my position on that question. It matters not what way the Supreme Court may hereafter decide as to the abstract question whether slavery may or may not go into a Territory under the Constitution, the people have the lawful means to introduce it or exclude it as they please, for the reason that slavery cannot exist a day or an hour anywhere, unless it is supported by local police regulations. Those police regulations can only be established by the local legislature, and if the people are opposed to slavery they will elect representatives to that body who will by unfriendly legislation effectually prevent the introduction of it into their midst. If, on the contrary, they are for it, their legislation will favor its extension. Hence, no matter what the decision of the Supreme Court may be on that abstract question, still the right of the people to make a slave Territory or a free Territory is perfect and complete under the Nebraska bill. I hope Mr. Lincoln deems my answer satisfactory on that point. . . .

Mr. Lincoln: Jonesboro, September 15, 1858.

The second interrogatory that I propounded to him, was this:

"Question 2. Can the people of a United States Territory, in any lawful way, against the wish of any citizen of the United States, exclude slavery from its limits prior to the formation of a State Constitution?"

To this Judge Douglas answered that they can lawfully exclude slavery from the Territory prior to the formation of a Constitution. He goes on to tell us how it can be done. As I understand him, he holds that it can be done by the Territorial Legislature refusing to make any enactments for the protection of slavery in the Territory, and especially by adopting unfriendly legislation to it. For the sake of clearness I state it again; that they can exclude slavery from the Territory, 1st, by withholding what he assumes to be an indispensable assistance to it in the way of legislation; and, 2d, by unfriendly legislation. If I rightly understand him, I wish to ask your attention for a while to his position.

In the first place, the Supreme Court of the United States has decided that any Congressional prohibition of slavery in the Territories is unconstitutional — that they have reached this proposition as a conclusion from their former proposition, that the Constitution of the United States expressly recognizes property in slaves, and from that other Constitutional provision, that no person shall be deprived of property without due process of law. Hence they reach the conclusion that as the Constitution of the United States expressly recognizes property in slaves, and prohibits any person from being deprived of property without due process of law, to pass an act of Congress by which a man who owned a slave on one side of a line would be deprived of him if he took him on the other side, is depriving him of that property without due process of law. That I understand to be the decision of the Supreme Court. I understand also that Judge Douglas adheres most firmly to that decision; and the difficulty is, how is it possible for any power to exclude slavery from the Territory unless in violation of that decision? That is the difficulty.

In the Senate of the United States, in 1850, Judge Trumbull, in a speech, substantially, if not directly, put the same interrogatory to Judge Douglas, as to whether the people of a Territory had the lawful power to exclude slavery prior to the formation of a Constitution? Judge Douglas then answered at considerable length, and his answer will be found in the *Congressional Globe*, under date of June 9th, 1856. The Judge said that whether the people could exclude slavery prior to the formation of a Constitution or not *was a question to be decided by the Supreme Court.* He put that proposition, as will be seen by the *Congressional Globe*, in a variety of forms, all running to the same thing in substance — that it was a question for the Supreme Court. I maintain that when he says, after the Supreme Court have decided the question, that the people may yet exclude slavery by any means whatever, he does virtually say, that it is *not* a question for the Supreme Court. He shifts his ground. I appeal to you whether he did not say it was a question for the Supreme Court? Has not the Supreme Court decided that question? When he now says the people *may* exclude slavery, does he not make it a question for the people? Does he not virtually shift his ground and say that it is *not* a question for the court, but for the people? This is a very simple proposition — a very plain and naked one. It seems to me that there is no difficulty in deciding it. In a variety of ways he said that it was a question for the Supreme Court. He did not stop then to tell us that whatever the Supreme Court decides, the people can by withholding necessary "police regulations" keep slavery out. He did not make any such answer. I submit to you now, whether the new state of the case has not induced the Judge to sheer away from his original ground. Would not this be the impression of every fair-minded man?

I hold that the proposition that slavery cannot enter a new country without police regulations is historically false. It is not true at all. I hold that the history of this country shows that the institution of slavery was originally planted upon this continent *without* these "police regulations" which the Judge now thinks necessary for the actual establishment of it. Not only so, but is there not another fact — how came this Dred Scott decision to be made? It was made upon the case of a negro being taken and actually held in slavery in Minnesota Territory, claiming his freedom because the act of Congress prohibited his being so held there. *Will the Judge pretend that Dred Scott was not held there without police regulations?* There is at least one matter of record as to his having been held in slavery in the Territory, not only without police regulations, but in the teeth of Congressional legislation supposed to be valid at the time. This shows that there is vigor enough in slavery to plant itself in a new country even against unfriendly legislation. It takes not only law but the *enforcement* of law to keep it out. That is the history of this country upon the subject.

I wish to ask one other question. It being understood that the Constitution of the United States guaranties property in slaves in the Territories, if there is any infringement of the right of that property, would not the United States Courts, organized for the government of the Territory, apply such remedy as might be necessary in that case? It is a maxim held by the courts, that there is no wrong without its remedy; and the courts have a remedy for whatever is acknowledged and treated as a wrong.

Again: I will ask you, my friends, if you were elected members of the Legislature, what would be the first thing you would have to do before entering upon your duties? *Swear to support the Constitution of the United States.* Suppose you believe, as Judge Douglas does, that the Constitution of the United States guaranties to your neighbor the right to hold slaves in that Territory — that they are his property — how can you clear your oaths unless you give him such legislation as is necessary to enable him to enjoy that property? What do you understand by supporting the Constitution of a State, or of the United States? Is it not to give such Constitutional helps to the rights established by that Constitution as may be practically needed? Can you, if you swear to support the Constitution, and believe that the Constitution establishes a right, clear your oath, without giving it support? Do you support the Constitution if, knowing or believing there is a right established under it which needs specific legislation, you withhold that legislation? Do you not violate and disregard your oath? I can conceive of nothing plainer in the world. There can be nothing in the words "support the Constitution," if you may run counter to it by refusing support to any right established under the Constitution. And what I say here will hold with still more force against the Judge's doctrine of "unfriendly legislation." How could you, having sworn to support the Constitution, and believing it guarantied the right to hold slaves in the Territories, assist in legislation *intended to defeat that right?* That would be violating your own view of the Constitution. Not only so, but if you were to do so, how long would it take the courts to hold your votes unconstitutional and void? Not a moment. . . .

5 Senator Albert G. Brown

(Democrat-Mississippi)

Mr. President, the Supreme Court of the United States decided, in the celebrated Dred Scott case, that slaves were property, and that slaveholders had the same right to carry their slave property to the Territories that any other citizen from any other State, had to carry any other kind of property. The venerable Chief Justice declared further, that the whole duty of this Government towards slave property was to protect it. It therefore stands as the judicial exposition of the Constitution under which we live, that slaves are property; that we have the right to take them to the Territories, and have them protected after we get them there. If the decision means anything at all, it means that. Now, sir, by protection, if the word be not a cheat and delusion, we understand *adequate* protection, *sufficient* protection. . . .

I will show . . . that the mere naked Constitution does not afford that adequate protection which the nature and description of the property requires. The Constitution of itself, unaided by legislation, can no more protect slave property than it will protect any other species of property. Your ships upon the high seas are entitled to protection under the Constitution; but you aid your Constitution by statutory enactments, and, without that aid, the protection would not be efficient or effective. What I claim, and what the southern States will claim, upon this question, I will state in the spirit of the utmost frankness.

The judicial decision being such as I have described it, we shall claim for our slave property protection in the Territories. As I said before, by protection, we mean adequate protection — protection suited to the nature and description of property to be protected. We all know that a law which would protect inanimate property would not, in all cases, be sufficient to protect animate property; that is, a law which might give very adequate and sufficient protection to a wagon, might not give the

---

5 *Congressional Globe,* 35th Congress, 2nd Session, 1242–43 (February 23, 1859).

same sort of protection to a horse. Then, if you superadd to the animate property the power of reason, your law again must be adapted to that kind of property. Now, the slave partakes of all of these qualities, the inanimate, the animate, and, adding the power of reason, your law must be adapted to the nature of the thing. I mean to be understood on this question. The Constitution never gave us rights and denied us the means of protecting and defending those rights. The Supreme Court having decided that we have the right to carry our slaves into the Territories, and necessarily to have them protected after we get them there, they virtually decided that we have a right to call upon somebody to give us that protection, and to make it adequate, to suit it to the nature, character, and description of the property to be protected.

Now, sir, upon whom are we to call? According to the doctrine of non-intervention our first call is upon the Territorial Legislature. I should, therefore, go to the Territorial Legislature of Kansas, for instance, and say: "here is my slave property; I demand for it protection, adequate and sufficient protection; protection suited to the nature, character, and description of the property." If the Territorial Legislature refuse, then what am I to do? Am I, at that point, to abandon my rights, rights guarantied to me by the Constitution, by the Constitution as expounded by the Supreme Court? Am I, because Congress has chosen to adopt what it pleases to term a party compromise, to abandon my constitutional rights? No, sir; when that Territorial Legislature refuses protection for my slave property, I mean to come to Congress, and this will be my speech to you, "Senators: this Territorial Legislature is your creature. You breathed it into existence; it could not live an hour but under the sunshine of your approval; I come to tell you that your creature is not obeying the Constitution; that your creature is denying to me rights guarantied to me by the sacred charter of our liberties as expounded by the highest judicial tribunal in the land; your creature denies me protection for my slave property; I come to ask you, the master, whether you will grant me that protection;" and I am curious to know, in view of the approaching contest, what response I am to have to that speech. I know perfectly well that the Territorial Legislature of Kansas will deny protection for my property. However, or by what influence prompted to make the declaration, they will declare, as they have within the last three weeks, that they will not only afford no protection; but that they will withdraw protection, as far as they can, and substitute unfriendly legislation in its stead. Is it expected of me and my people that we are to fold this injustice to our bosoms, and cherish it, because it comes stamped, "accept this, or break up the Democratic party."

I ask northern gentlemen whether they would be quite content, under the same sort of compromise between conflicting elements in party, to have their right to call upon this Government to protect their mercantile marine frittered away. Your ships go out upon the high seas, they are assaulted by enemies, attacked by pirates, and what do you do? If the law be insufficient, you come to Congress and invoke its aid. When you ask that, would you be content, Senators from the North, to be told, "we have agreed to non-intervention on this question; we cannot give you any protection." You would say, as I say today, "Senators, the obligation is imposed upon you; not by a party compromise, but by the Constitution of your country, to protect this property, and you must do it." So I say in reference to slavery in the Territories: the obligation is upon Congress; the Supreme Court has already decided that we are entitled to protection. The Territorial Legislature, I repeat again, which denies it to us, is your creature; you made it, and you can unmake it. It lives upon your breath; it exists by your forbearance; and I, for one, am not content to be thus compromised out of my constitutional rights — rights secured to me by my forefathers, and guaranteed by the decision of the Supreme Court of the United States. I agreed to non-intervention; but I never agreed, after we had established rights by the decision of the Supreme Court, we were to be deprived of those rights by a congressional compromise. If, as the Supreme Court has decided, the obligation is upon you to protect my property, no agreement among politicians or parties can discharge you from that obligation.

I have heard it said, Mr. President, that when we come here with a bill asking protection for our slave property in the Territories, the dominant party of the North will take the other side of the proposition, and abolish slavery in the Territories. Impotent threat! Impotent appeal to cowardly fears! Have you any higher right to abolish slavery, because I ask protection for it, than you would have if I asked nothing? Does the mere fact of my coming and asking for my constitutional rights open the door to you to destroy my rights? Suppose the Senator from Massachusetts, who represents a very important commercial interest, a very important commercial marine, should come and ask you to amend and fortify your laws in reference to the coastwise trade; and should tell you that there were pirates in the Gulf, seizing his ships, plundering the cargo, and murdering the crews, scuttling the vessels; and suppose he came with a bill asking protection; I want to know if that would confer upon you any right to turn pirate yourselves, scuttle his ship, murder the crew, and steal the cargo? No, sir. If it were a case fairly stated and honestly fortified, you would say, "the obligation is upon us to give adequate and sufficient protection to this property, and we will do it by the naval and military power of the Government;" and have I, sir, less right to demand protection for my slave property in the Territories? and ought I to be content to take less? If I come and ask you to discharge your constitutional obligation, can you any more turn pirate in my case than you could turn pirate in the case of the Senator from Massachusetts? The obligation to protect is one thing; the power to destroy is altogether a different thing. I say, again, the threat that, if we come and demand protection for our slave property, you will take the converse of the proposition, and pass anti-slavery laws, passes me by as the idle wind. It is an impotent threat; and it appeals to cowardice and the meanest passions of the southern people.

I give you warning now, that if Kansas legislate in a spirit of hostility to slavery, the State which I represent, and, in my opinion, a vast majority of the southern people, will come to Congress, and demand of you, in obedience to the written Constitution as expounded by the illustrious men who adorn the Supreme Bench of the United States, that you annul their legislation, and substitute instead laws giving adequate and sufficient protection to slave property. When you have done that, you will have discharged your duty, and your whole duty; and, when you do less, you are derelict in your duty, under the Constitution of the United States. . . .

We ask nothing which we are not willing to give. We ask nothing that we are not willing to yield. Come and demand protection for your property, upon the high seas or in the Territories, and I shall be ready to give it; not with stinted measure, but I will give you that sort of protection which will secure you in the peaceable, quiet, and happy enjoyment of your property. When I come as an equal, and demand the same thing, I want to know whether you will measure to me that equal justice for which, I tell you, I have always been ready and am still ready and shall remain ready to mete out to you. . . .

I think I understand the position of the Senator from Illinois, [Mr. DOUGLAS,] and I dissent from it. If I understand him, he thinks that a Territorial Legislature may, by non-action or by unfriendly action, rightfully exclude slavery. I do not think so. But if territorial legislation is to be the end of legislation, he is right. If your doctrine of non-intervention shall be carried to the extent of allowing a Territorial Legislature, by non-action or unfriendly action, to annul a decision of the Supreme Court, then I say to the Senate and to the world that the Senator from Illinois is right; by non-action, by unfriendly action within the limitations of constitutional power, the Territorial Legislature can exclude slavery. But it is a question of power; not of right. What I want to know is, whether you will interpose against power and in favor of right; or whether you will stand by, dissenting in words from the Senator from Illinois, and yet, for all practical purposes, sustaining him by refusing to interpose your authority to overthrow the unconstitutional and tyrannical acts of your creature — the Territorial Legislature. The Senator thinks the Legislature has the right, by non-action or unfriendly action, to exclude me, with my slaves. You tell me you do not think so. But what matters it to me what you think, if you will do nothing to secure me in my rights? If the Territorial Legislature refuses to act, will you act? If it pass unfriendly acts, will you pass friendly? If it pass laws hostile to slavery, will you annul them, and substitute laws favoring slavery in their stead? If you cannot give affirmative answers to these questions, I care not a button for the difference between you and the Senator from Illinois. We have a right of protection for our slave property in the Territories. The Constitution, as expounded by the Supreme Court, awards it. We demand it; and we mean to have it.

I have already said that the Constitution, unaided by legislation, gives us the *right* to protection, but it does not give us the protection itself. It does not give us the power to punish those who trespass on our property. It does not give us the power to vindicate it in any manner, shape, or form. It gives us rights, but they are naked rights; and, until they are supported by legislation, they amount to nothing but naked rights. Non-action goes a great way to exclude slave property from a Territory — further, perhaps, than to exclude any other species of property; and yet it is true that no property can exist without laws to protect it. The Constitution may give the right, but the law must give the remedy. . . .

What I and my people shall ask is action; positive, unqualified action. Our understanding of the doctrine of non-intervention was, that you were not to intervene against us, but I never understood that we could have any compromise or understanding here which could release Congress from an obligation imposed on it by the Constitution of the United States. If the obligation is upon you, and that it is I appeal to the opinions of your illustrious judges, then how are you to escape? . . .

Mr. President, I may be asked what I would do in the event that my appeal for congressional protection turns out futile? I am prepared to tell you what I would do; but I am not prepared to tell you what the South would do. On this point I do not speak for the South; but I speak for that portion of the southern people who understand the question as I understand it. I will tell you what they and I will do. I will tell you more, what I will advise my people to do. At the very instant when you deny to us rights guaranteed by the Constitution, as expounded by the Supreme Court, and do it by the mere force of numbers, my mind will be forced irresistibly to the conclusion that the Constitution is a failure, and the Union a despotism. If I cannot obtain the rights guarantied to me and my people under the Constitution, as expounded by the Supreme Court, then, sir, I am prepared to retire from the concern. . . .

6 *Senator George E. Pugh*

(Democrat-Ohio)

I understood the Senator [Brown] to demand from the representatives of the northern States on this floor, whether they would agree to the passage of an act of Congress to protect slaves in the Territories taken there by the consent of their masters against the local legislation? I answer the Senator unhesitatingly, never; while I live, never. I consider it a monstrous demand, a violation of the plighted faith between the Democracy of the South and the Democracy of the North, again and again and again, in their legislation and in their platform; and if that be the price, as Senators say it is, the price will not be paid — certainly not, so far as I am concerned. Now, sir, I perfectly agree . . . [that] the Kansas-Nebraska act . . . was intended that, so far as the right of a slave-holder in the Territories was concerned, he should seek his remedy through the judicial department; and the Senator from Mississippi, who made this demand this morning, proclaimed that himself, in the year 1856, on the 2d day of July. . . .

I have to say this: if there be a citizen of any southern State, who thinks he has a right to take his slaves into a Territory and hold them in defiance of the territorial authorities, let him assert his right in a judicial court. If the court gives him the right, I submit to it. If the court denies his right, he must submit to it. There must be mutuality; you must not come here to Congress, asking from us that we shall take the local and domestic affairs of the Territory into our hands, when we have laid our authority aside, if we ever had any.

But the Senator from Virginia [Mason] says it is all decided. How decided? The Supreme Court has decided it. . . .

[F]orthwith we are told that the Supreme Court of the United States has become the appointed expounder of Democratic principles. Since when? Since they declared the Bank of the United States to be constitutional, which you repudiate in your platform? Since the judges of that court held the old sedition laws of John Adams to be constitutional, which you repudiate in your platform? Who constituted the judges of the Supreme Court the makers or expounders of Democratic principles? Certainly not Thomas Jefferson, who pronounced them the sappers and miners of the Constitution; certainly not Andrew Jackson, who told them he would interpret his own oath, as well as his own principles, accord-

---

6 *Congressional Globe*, 35th Congress, 2nd Session, 1249–51 (February 23, 1859).

ing to his views of the Constitution. No court shall make me a platform. When we get to going by courts, it seems to me we have departed from the whole spirit and principle of the Democratic party.

But, sir, the fact is that the court decided no such thing; there was no such question before them. In the whole Dred Scott case there was no act of a Territorial Legislature before them in any shape or form. No such question was argued, no such question was decided; nor is there the slightest allusion made to it in the opinion of any of the judges, so far as I recollect, but in that of the Chief Justice, and then it is made simply by way of making an illustration — what the lawyers call *arguendo*. This is the first time I ever heard, in a case where nine judges pronounce their opinions *seriatim*, that because one of them in illustration collaterally makes a reference, that becomes the decision of the court. I think it will take lawyers generally by surprise. The court did decide, and properly, that Congress has no power to exclude slavery from the Territories; and why? Because it is not conferred by the Constitution. That is properly decided. It was an act of Congress they had before them — the act of 1820, to prohibit slavery north of 36° 30′. That was the case, and that was the decision.

But the Senator . . . speaks of their rights under the Constitution; he says that the Constitution gives them the right to carry slaves into the Territories. Where? Will the Senator give me the article and the section? Where is it? There is no such provision. We are told that slavery is recognized in the Constitution. Certainly; and wherein? It is recognized as an institution established by the laws of the States, and it is even recognized as having no extra territorial force whatever; because, but for the provision for the redelivery of fugitives, it is evident that the moment a slave escaped out of the State the power of his master would be gone. You needed that in the Constitution, and it was put in the Constitution to supply a defect in that very form of property. I believe the Psalmist tells us that riches have wings. This form of property seems to have legs, if not wings; and that provision of the Constitution was put there for the express purpose of guarding the weakness of the disposition to emigrate of that species of property. That you shall have, to the last extent. Then the Constitution said, that inasmuch as, although this form of property was a man, you had robbed him of his manhood and condemned him to labor, it, too, would strip him of two fifths of his humanity when it came to estimate him either for purposes of taxation or representation. That is all within the States. Then it was provided that Congress might prohibit any more of that property being brought into this country after the year 1808, and might tax it *per capita* before that time. That is all.

I admit that it is recognized in all these relations as a form of property established by the laws of the States, to be protected within the States; to be protected on the high seas by the Federal Government; to be protected in the unoccupied Territories of the United States as against all foreign intervention. But, sir, I repeat the question of my colleague, does it carry it into those States which do not choose to admit that property? Has the Constitution that extent? Does its recognition of slaves as property to that extent carry them, not only upon the high seas and into the Territories, but does it carry them into the State of Illinois, which has undertaken to declare that she will not have them? If there be anything in this constitutional right which the Senator from Virginia has invoked, it is a right which extends over Illinois as well as over Kansas to-day, for the Constitution of the United States is as supreme in Illinois as it is in Kansas. There is no such right, and the court did not say so. The court said that Congress had no right to pass acts of legislation for the Territories beyond certain limits, and within those limits the right to prohibit any form of property was not granted. Therefore, when a citizen of South Carolina or Kentucky goes to one of the Territories, he meets the local law, whatever it be. The question may arise whether, in the absence of any legislation, he can hold his slave? That is a question to be decided by the judiciary. There may be a question whether this form of legislation or that form of legislation would deprive him of his title or injure his title. Let him go to the courts. Suppose the Dred Scott decision should be reversed about a year hence; that there should be a change in the court. . . .

I repeat my assertion; if the Constitution of the United States gives this form of property its peculiar protection, as gentlemen assert, and the right to carry it, it is carried into every State over the constitution and laws of the State; for the Constitution of the United States is supreme above the constitutions and laws of the States; and it means that, or it means nothing. There is no distinction; there can be none made; and my colleague put the very question which proved the fallacy of the whole proposition.

But Senators say there is no sovereignty in the Territories. I agree to that; but why do we deceive ourselves about words? There is no such language as sovereignty in the Constitution of the United States. Senators say it requires a power of sovereignty to exclude slavery, and the Senator from Mississippi has just now spoken of the sovereignty of the State which excludes slavery. He says it requires sovereign power to exclude slavery. Well, how is that sovereignty to be expressed? . . .

I understand . . . that the sovereignty can only speak through a constitution, and that it is in the constitution of a State only that the power to admit or exclude slavery is to be exercised. Why, sir, until the year 1820 not a State of this Union, in her constitution, either admitted or excluded slavery, and I do not believe Virginia did until 1850 or 1851. None of the States did it until Missouri when she came into the Union, and she put it into her constitution, not upon the idea that was peculiarly the place, but for the express purpose of disarming her Legislature. It was an ordinary legislative power, nothing else in the world; known and recognized as such and admitted as such by every State in the Union.

New York abolished slavery by law, Pennsylvania abolished slavery by law, and in the States where the institution continued, it was fostered, protected, and recognized by ordinary acts of legislation. . . .

Gentlemen speak of the rights of the South in the Territories? What are her rights, or the rights of the North, in the Territories? People who do not go to the Territories have no rights there at all, except to see that their land is not abused. The Senator from Mississippi says there are no people in the Territories; they are only inhabitants. Well, I should like to know what the people can be except inhabitants. He certainly does not mean to maintain that those who are not inhabitants are the people. No, sir; it is the right of self-government; you may cover it with nick-names as much as you please. Congress has said to these people, you are a community, with interests of your own, domestic rights of your own; for your own peace, liberty, and security, we relinquish you to your inherent right of self-government, subject only to these conditions which we specify in the organic act. Your organic act is not an enabling act to the Territories; it is a restraining act. We restrain you within these limits; but as for all the rest, so far from professing to confer on you any rights, take the right which the people have everywhere, unless restrained by tyrants, the right of self-government.

Now, sir, what is the mighty right that the Senator from Virginia says the southern Democracy are going to fight for? It is the right of one man in the State of Virginia to go into the Territory of Kansas, with her ninety-two or ninety thousand inhabitants, all of whom are of one opinion — their authorities, their Legislature, all consider that the presence of slaves is injurious to them; but in order that this one gentleman from the State of Virginia, who has not aided to reclaim the wilderness, who has undergone none of the perils of frontier life, may enjoy his sacred right of carrying his negro there against the will of everybody else, the Senator from Virginia, and both the Senators from Mississippi notify us that they intend to leave the Union, carrying flags and banners and music. Well, sir, if they choose to go, on so small a provocation as that, I do not think the Union is worth preserving any longer. Sir, it is an attempt to press upon the people of the Territories the laws of the States from which they come. Do they all carry the laws of their States? If the law of Virginia goes into Kansas with the citizens of Virginia in order to protect their slaves, does the law of my State go with the citizens of Ohio, and the law of Indiana with the citizens of Indiana, and the law of Oregon with the citizens of Oregon? How many laws will you have in your Territories? Why, sir, every man will literally be a law to himself. The laws of Virginia cannot go there unless the laws of every other State go, and thus you establish a kind of organized anarchy in every one of your Territories.

Sir, all this is a vast piece of special pleading, eked out by fictions of history, by propositions of law that cannot be maintained for an instant, by assertions as to what constitutions give, and by assertions as to what courts have decided, to build up a doctrine that is offensive to the pride and self-respect of every citizen of the non-slave-holding States. I will give you equality of rights, but I will have equality. You shall not carry the laws of your State into the Territories, unless you allow me to carry the laws of my State there. I agree that the laws of neither shall go there. Let the people of the Territories by themselves, through their own immediate representatives, chosen by the people, responsible to them, decide the whole question. I will agree that the Federal Government shall not interfere on either side by act or word, that it shall be left entirely to the people whose interest is concerned during their territorial form; and when they come to form their constitution and State government, whatever they say on that subject, be it to exclude or to tolerate slavery, they shall have my vote so long as I sit in this Chamber without any hesitation. But when you tell me that there is a negro sovereignty extending over all the Territories, that there is a peculiar species of property which no law can restrain, which no government can put down or regulate, but which goes by force of the Constitution — as if the Constitution, instead of being made for the benefit of the people, was made for the special aggrandizement of negro owners — and which is to prevail everywhere, and to overawe and strike down the right of self-government of white men, either in States or Territories, I tell you you have perverted the whole foundation of your Government.

Now, sir, I hope, at least for one, that the Senator from Mississippi understands my position distinctly. I tell him I will vote for no code, no act of Congress to interfere with the local legislation of the Territories excluding or admitting slavery — none. The Senators from Mississippi and Virginia, severally, have issued their proclamation as to what is to be the consequence. They hold the Democratic party in such very light esteem that, if that is the general sentiment of them in the northern States, they will not keep company with us any longer. Well, sir, they can keep company with us just as long as they please. I am very sure that I will trouble myself to no very great extent to restrain them. I am willing to agree with them upon the principles declared in the platform of our party. I will stand there; and I will have nothing more than the Constitution authorizes. Satisfy me that you have a right, under the Constitution of the United States, to carry your slaves into Territories and hold them there, or into the States and hold them there, and I will give you as many acts of Congress as you can desire. In my judgment, you have no such right. The assertion of it is offensive. The assertion of it violates the equality of the States. It puts the rights of the southern States far above the rights of the northern States. It degrades every non-slaveholder in the United States, and certainly every citizen of a non-slaveholding State. We are no longer your equals under such a doctrine; and whether it be in the Democratic party or anywhere else, for me, I intend to live on terms of equality, or I am content not to live at all.

D

Views from the Bench and Bar

Commentaries on the Dred Scott decision from the legal community notably lacked that element of vitriol and invective so common in political and editorial reactions. Among many northern lawyers, of course, there was obvious disappointment and dissatisfaction. But cooler, more dispassionate observers pointed out two other considerations arising from the decision. First, they expressed the fear that the Supreme Court had inflicted considerable damage to its prestige and power by alienating a powerful political constituency. One writer in the North American Review *suggested that the result would have little practical effect, but lamented that "the country will feel the consequences of the decision more deeply and more permanently, in the loss of confidence in the sound judicial integrity and strictly legal character of their tribunals, than in anything beside; and this perhaps may well be accounted the greatest political calamity which this country, under our forms of government, could sustain." More significant — and, unfortunately, more slighted — were several carefully-considered opinions that the decision's meaning had been greatly exaggerated by both its southern admirers and northern critics.*

1   THE SUPREME JUDICIAL COURT OF MAINE. In some quarters, the Dred Scott pronouncement created confusion and concern over the status of the free Negro. The Maine Legislature, for example, requested an advisory opinion from the State Supreme Court as to whether "free colored persons, of African descent," were authorized to vote for state and federal officers. Following the historical evidence mainly as presented in Justice Curtis's dissent, five of the seven state judges easily found grounds for an affirmative answer. Judge Woodbury Davis, however, emphatically insisted upon a state's right to determine such questions, irrespec-

1 44 *Maine Reports* 505, 581–589, 591–595; 517–521.

tive of any federal court ruling. Joshua W. Hathaway, dissenting from his colleagues, invoked the authority of John Marshall to stress the virtue and necessity of adhering to the superior commands of the United States Supreme Court.

Judge Woodbury Davis

. . . Every citizen of the states is a citizen of the United States; but what relation do the citizens of the several states sustain to each other? Congress has power to naturalize *foreigners*; but if a citizen of Massachusetts removes to South Carolina, who shall say whether he must be naturalized in order to become a citizen of the latter state? If each state might decide this for itself, there would be no reciprocity, and the Union, instead of being "more perfect," would be less perfect than it was under the confederation. For by that it was provided, in the fourth article, "that the free inhabitants of each state should be entitled to all the privileges and immunities of free citizens in the several states." Accordingly a similar provision was incorporated into the federal constitution. "The citizens of each state shall be entitled to all privileges and immunities of citizens in the several states." (Article four, section two.) This provision, *proprio vigore*, makes every citizen of the United States a citizen of the state in which he resides; and every citizen of each state of the United States. For it is clear that the states, when they entered into this compact, reserved no right to exclude from citizenship any class of free persons born in the United States. If otherwise, citizens of one state might be deprived of "the privileges and immunities of citizens" in another. So that every person born in the United States, or naturalized, or made a citizen by any treaty, has a right to citizenship in each state, of which that state cannot deprive him. If one state can dissolve the allegiance of any class of persons residing within its limits, and exclude them from citizenship, while the same class of persons are citizens of other states, we are still exposed to all the conflicts and troubles to which the states were liable in consequence of their separate power of naturalization under the confederation; and the evils are magnified and aggravated by their liability to fall upon native born, as well as naturalized citizens.

And as no state can exclude any class of persons from citizenship, so by granting the right of suffrage, and other franchises, to persons not citizens, they do not make them citizens. Every state may grant these franchises to *aliens*, but it does not thereby make them citizens of the state. Nor does the withholding of these franchises deprive any class of persons of any of the "privileges or immunities of citizens." The meaning of these terms, according to the highest authority, "is confined to such privileges and immunities as are fundamental, and belong of right to all free governments; such as the rights of protection of life and liberty; to acquire and enjoy property." (2 Kent's Com., 71.). . . .

And as no state, though it may withhold the elective franchise from citizens, can deprive them of their citizenship, so the federal government cannot deprive any class of persons of their citizenship. All free persons, native born, and all aliens, after they are naturalized, possess an *indefeasible* citizenship, of which no department of the federal government can divest them. The right of native born persons to citizenship is not within its jurisdiction. Not only is there no grant of any such power in the constitution; not only would the exercise of any such power be establishing privileged classes, in violation of its letter and spirit; but the existence of any such power would involve the total annihilation of the sovereignty of the states. Citizenship is indispensable to the security of other rights. If the federal government may deprive any class of persons of their citizenship, it may at any time reduce the population of any state, in whom the sovereignty resides, to the condition of aliens. The mere statement of the proposition is a sufficient refutation of it.

If the foregoing principles are sound, the following propositions seem to me conclusively to follow: *that* all free persons, born within the limits and jurisdiction of the United States, are citizens thereof, and, as such, are citizens of the several states where they reside; *that* the citizens of each state have the right to become citizens of any other state, simply by a change of residence, without any consent, or right of refusal, on the part of such state; *that* the right of suffrage is not an essential attribute to citizenship; *that* as states withhold this franchise from many classes of citizens, so they have power to confer it upon aliens; *but that* neither any state, *nor the federal government,* can deprive any class of free persons, born within the United States, of their citizenship.

I need not say that these propositions affirm the citizenship of free colored persons of African descent. That this class of persons, at the time when our independence was established, were regarded as citizens throughout the United States, and that in nearly all the states they exercised the most important franchises, are facts that cannot be controverted. That they owed allegiance to the government, both state and national, and would have been held guilty of treason for the same acts that would have constituted treason in other citizens, cannot be doubted. That they were able, without regard to special provisions of statute, to purchase and hold real estate, in every state, north and south, has never been questioned. The conclusion is irresistible, that they were, and are, citizens of the United States. . . .

Emancipated slaves, like other free persons of African descent, may hold and transfer real estate, may sue and be sued, and they are held as citizens, in distinction from *aliens,* in all the slave states. A few years before Mr TANEY was appointed Chief Justice of the United States Supreme Court, he was counsel for one who was sued by an emancipated slave, in the Circuit Court for the district of Maryland. Instead of pleading this fact *to the jurisdiction of the court,* he defended on other grounds, by a petition for an injunction; but the suit was sustained, on appeal, in the Supreme Court of the United States. *Legrand v. Darnall*, 2 Pet. R., 664. The question of jurisdiction was not raised; but the fact *that it was not*, indicates that the idea that such a person is not a citizen of the United States, has had its birth since that time. And as late as 1843, an emancipated slave was held by C. J. TANEY to be capable of suing in the Circuit Court, and his petition for his freedom was sustained in the Supreme Court of the United States. *Williams v. Ash*, 1 Howard R., 1. . . .

If it be said that history shows that at the time when the federal constitution was adopted, the white population of the country did not intend to admit colored persons of African descent to the privileges of citizenship, while the assertion is denied, it is also replied that we have no right to inquire what one class of persons intended, in derogation of the rights of any other class. It would be just as legitimate to inquire whether the African race intended to admit the whites to the privileges of citizenship. They all resided together, participants of that freedom which was the fruit of their common struggles and sacrifices. Whatever their disparity in numbers, or condition, neither had the right to eject the other from the common purchase, or make them aliens from the commonwealth. Such a right does not exist under any free government; certainly not under a government whose corner stone was laid upon the principle "that all governments derive their just powers from the consent of the governed."

But if the matter were pertinent, I affirm, as a historical fact, that at the time when our independence was established, the white population of this country did recognize the citizenship of colored persons of African descent, and did intend to secure to them the rights of citizens. That they at that time possessed the privileges and immunities of citizens in the states, and in nearly all of them enjoyed the right of suffrage as a constitutional right, is beyond all question. The members of the congresses, both before and during the confederation, were chosen, in part, by such persons. They were bound to represent these persons as a part of their constituents; and no evidence exists that they were not true to their trust. On the contrary, the evidence is indubitable that, during the whole period of our struggles, from the commencement of the agitation which resulted in the declaration of our independence, to the adoption of the federal constitution in 1789, the freedom and elevation of the African race was a prominent and cherished purpose with the leading statesmen of the country, both north and south.

On the 20th of October, 1774, the first continental congress passed the following resolution:

"We, for ourselves, and the inhabitants of the several colonies whom we represent, firmly agree and associate, under the sacred ties of virtue, honor, and love of country, as follows: we will neither import, nor purchase any slaves imported, after the first day of December next, after which time we will wholly discontinue the slave trade; and we will neither be concerned in it ourselves, nor will we hire our vessels, nor sell our commodities or manufactures to those who are concerned in it."

In 1775, the same congress solemnly denied that "the divine Author of our existence intended a part of the human race to hold an absolute property in, and an unbounded power over others."

In 1776, the declaration of our independence was unanimously adopted, declaring "liberty" to be an unalienable right of "all men."

On the 25th of June, 1778, an effort was made to amend the fourth article of the confederation, providing that "the free inhabitants of each of these states, shall be entitled to all the privileges and immunities of free citizens in the several states," by inserting the word "white" after the word "free," and before the word "inhabitants," so that colored persons should no longer have the right of general citizenship. But the amendment was defeated, only two states voting for it. That body could not have made a more explicit declaration, that colored persons, of African descent, were citizens of the United States.

In 1787, congress unanimously adopted the ordinance for the government of the territory north-west of the Ohio river, declaring that "there should be neither slavery, nor involuntary servitude therein, except as a punishment for crime." So far as slavery is a suspension or temporary extinction of citizenship, what measure could have been better adapted to secure to colored persons the right of citizenship? And yet there was not a single vote against it, from that portion of the United States where slavery now exists.

Does not this record prove, beyond any doubt, that during this formative period of our national institutions, the people of this country, instead of entertaining any design to deprive colored persons of their rights, and exclude them from citizenship, recognized them as citizens of the United States, and adopted effectual measures to protect them as such?

If we turn to the legislation of the several states during this period, we find abundant evidence of the same historical fact. Vermont abolished slavery in 1777; Massachusetts in 1780; New Hampshire in 1784. Pennsylvania passed an act of emancipation in 1780; and Connecticut and Rhode Island in 1784. All this was under the confederation: and all persons so emancipated thereby became, without any question, at that time citizens of the United States.

Nor was any change made, or attempted, when the federal constitution was formed. Nearly one half of the states had abolished slavery, either absolutely or prospectively; and the general expectation was that the others would do the same, at some future time; which was done afterwards by New York and New Jersey. The constitution was there-

fore, so framed, that while it should not interfere with slavery within
the states, so long as it should exist, it would need no change or amendment when slavery should be abolished. *It was adapted to a free country.*
Mr. Madison declared, in the convention that framed it, that it ought
to exclude "the idea that there could be property in man." That this
character was given to it by the deliberate purpose of the convention,
is evident from its action upon the clause for the rendition of fugitives.
(Article four, section two.) As originally reported, it was as follows:
"No person held to *servitude,* or labor, &c." On motion of Governor Ran-
dolph, of Virginia, the word "servitude" was stricken out, and the word
"service" inserted, by a unanimous vote; "the former being thought to
express the condition of slaves, and the latter the obligations of free
persons." (Madison papers.)

In whatever field the search is made, therefore, there is an entire failure
of any evidence, contemporaneous with the adoption of the constitution,
that the white population of the United States, if they had possessed the
right, had any desire, or intention, to exclude the African race and their
descendants from the benefits, privileges, and immunities of citizenship. . . .

I have thus far discussed this question as if it were new. I am aware,
however, that it has been raised, and opinions have been given, in the
courts of several of the southern states, and that it has recently been
discussed at great length in the case of *Scott* v. *Sandford,* by the Supreme
Court of the United States. And in this case I understand it to have
been distinctly decided, that colored persons of African descent, whose
ancestors were slaves, are not citizens of the United States. That such
is the opinion as promulgated by C. J. Taney, cannot be questioned. It
was announced by him as "the opinion of the court;" and I do not per-
ceive why the other members of the court should not be regarded as
concurring in it, except upon those points which they have expressly dis-
claimed. The mandate to the circuit court could not have issued, except
by order of a majority of the court. This mandate directed the case "to
be dismissed for want of jurisdiction, for the reason that the plantiff in
error is not a citizen of Missouri, in the sense in which that word is
used in the constitution." This was equivalent to an express denial that
he was a citizen of the United States. And the ground of the decision
was, that he belonged to a class of persons none of whom are citizens.

But though the Supreme Court of the United States have so decided,
I do not consider their opinion as binding upon us, upon the question
now presented to us. There may be cases in which we are bound to receive the decisions of that court as authority. How far this is the case
is a disputed question. But it cannot extend to cases in which the
powers of the state courts and of the United States courts are collateral,
co-extensive and independent. Cases respecting the right of suffrage,
though that right is limited by the constitution of this state to citizens

of the United States, are not cases arising under any law of the United States. (*Owings* v. *Norwood,* 5 Cranch R., 344.)

And if our court, upon claim of any colored person to be admitted to those privileges which are granted by our state constitution to citizens, sustain such claim, the case is not within the appellate jurisdiction of the Supreme Court of the United States. (12 Wheat. R., 117, 129.)

The opinion of the court, in the case of *Scott* v. *Sandford,* should therefore receive that consideration, and that only, to which its intrinsic merits entitle it.

I do not propose to examine this opinion at length. A few extracts will show its scope, and the consequences legitimately resulting from its adoption as the settled doctrine and policy of the country. . . .

It seems to me that [the majority's] . . . assertions and . . . doctrines need only to be stated, in order to be rejected. They are so clearly in conflict with the whole tone and spirit, both of the writings and the deeds of the great men of the revolution, that it is difficult to conceive how they can be credited by any intelligent, unprejudiced mind. The worst enemy of our institutions could hardly say anything better adapted to blacken the character of our ancestors, and cast reproach upon their memories.

If the Declaration of Independence "was not intended to include the enslaved African," but was a mere compact of their oppressors for their own advantage, while "the unhappy black race were never thought of or spoken of, except as property, and when the claims of the owner or the profit of the trader were supposed to need protection," then a decent respect for the opinions of mankind should have kept its authors silent. Such compacts had long been common enough, in limited monarchies, in aristocracies; even among brigands and pirates. Freedom of privileged classes, and equality among themselves, while trampling on the rights of others, was no new thing. The world did not need to be informed of it. As the manifesto of such a doctrine, the Declaration of Independence would not have merited the respect of mankind; it would not have justified a revolution; it would have given Washington and his compatriots no glory to fight for it, and their toil, and sacrifice, and blood, were offered in vain.

But it was not so. The Declaration of Independence was a heroic utterance of great truths, for all men; so understood by the world, so intended by its authors. They freely devoted fortune, honor, life, to sustain it. And they often avowed their purpose, as soon as the government should be established, to extend its blessings to the slaves. No man ever condemned slavery in stronger terms than Jefferson, Washington, and those who with them stood foremost in the revolutionary struggle. A resolution solemnly denying its right, was unanimously passed by the congress of 1775. The hope and the prophecy of general emancipation were the common theme of correspondence and public debate.

With this avowed purpose in view, the federal constitution was formed, and adopted by the people of the several states. It was designedly so made as to need no amendment when slavery should be abolished. Its privileges were granted to all, without distinction of race or color. Free colored persons have always been recognized as citizens under it, and they are entitled to the same privileges and immunities which the constitution guarantees to other citizens. I am, therefore, of opinion that free colored persons, of African descent, if born in this country, are citizens of the United States; and that, with the same restrictions which apply to white persons, they are authorized under the provisions of the constitution of this state, to be electors for governor, senators and representatives. . . .

JUDGE JOSHUA W. HATHAWAY

. . . In the case of *Dred Scott* v. *J. F. H. Sandford,* the Supreme Court of the United States has recently decided that negroes of African descent, whose ancestors were of pure African blood, and were brought into this country and sold as negro slaves, were not citizens of the United States.

In answering the question proposed to . . . [this] court, it is necessary to consider the legal effect of that decision.

By the federal constitution, article one, section two:

"No person shall be a representative who shall not have been seven years a citizen of the United States."

And by article one, section three:

"No person shall be a senator who shall not have been nine years a citizen of the United States."

By article one, section eight:

Congress has power "to establish an uniform rule of naturalization."

And by article four, section two:

"The citizens of each state shall be entitled to all privileges and immunities of citizens in the several states."

By these last two provisions of the constitution, and the laws of congress, upon the subject of naturalization, passed in pursuance of the power granted — the laws concerning citizenship in the United States, and in each state, were made entirely uniform; for it is certain, that in the sense in which the word *"citizen"* is used in the federal constitution, *"citizen of each state,"* and *"citizen of the United States,"* are convertible terms; they mean the same thing; for "the citizens of each state are entitled to all privileges and immunities of citizens in the several states," and "citizens of the United States" are, of course, citizens of *all* the United States.

But it is obvious that the uniformity of the laws concerning what constitutes a citizen of each and all the United States, cannot be authoritatively enforced, and the provisions of the federal constitution and laws upon that subject made effectual, unless there be some ultimate tribunal

— some final arbiter, whose decisions upon questions arising under the constitution and laws concerning it, shall be conclusive and binding upon all the states. By the laws of one state it may be provided that if a master come within its limits with his slave, the slave shall become, *ipso facto*, emancipated, and being once free, is always free, and that being native born in the United States, he is a citizen of the state, and therefore "entitled to all privileges and immunities of a citizen in the several states." While by the laws of the state from which he came it may be provided, that if he return there he shall not be entitled to the privileges and immunities of a citizen, but that he shall return to his former servitude. If each state has the power to determine, authoritatively, who are and who are not citizens of the state, and, consequently, who are and who are not citizens of the United States, any one state may effectually resist the laws of all the other states, and of congress, and create citizens of the United States who would be repudiated as such by every other state in the Union. There might be as many different classes of citizens as there are states, all citizens of some one state, and yet utterly powerless to enforce their constitutional rights to "all privileges and immunities of citizens in every other state." If such were the true interpretation of the constitutional powers of the federal government, and of the relations existing between it and the governments of the several states, and of their constitutional powers, the government of the United States would be imbecile and powerless for the most important purposes for which it was established. Indeed, it could not be, properly, denominated a *government*.

By the federal constitution, article six, section two:

"This constitution and the laws of the United States, which shall be made in pursuance thereof; and all treaties made, or which shall be made, under the authority of the United States, shall be the supreme law of the land, and the judges in every state shall be bound thereby, anything in the constitution or laws of any state to the contrary notwithstanding."

And by article three, section two:

"The judicial power shall extend to all cases in law and equity, arising under this constitution and the laws of the United States, [including among many enumerated subjects of jurisdiction] controversies between citizens of different states."

The general government, though limited as to its objects, is supreme with respect to those objects. This principle is part of the constitution, and if there be any who deny its necessity, none can deny its authority.

The necessity of uniformity as well as correctness in expounding the constitution and the laws of the United States, would itself suggest the propriety of vesting, in some single tribunal, the power of deciding in the last resort, all cases in which they are involved.

"The judicial power of every well constituted government must be co-extensive with the legislative, and must be capable of deciding every judicial question which grows out of the constitution and laws. If any proposition may be considered as a political axiom, this, we think, may be so considered."

[Per Mr. Chief Justice MARSHALL, in *Cohens* v. *Virginia*, 6 Wheaton's United States Reports, 264.]

The Supreme Court of the United States is a tribunal of ultimate jurisdiction; and its judicial power rightfully extending to cases arising under the constitution and laws, its judgment must become, "*ipso facto,* conclusive between the parties before it, in respect to the points decided," and "the case is not alone considered as decided and settled; but the principles of the decision are held, as precedents and authority, to bind future cases of the same nature." Story's Commentaries on the Constitution, pages 349, 350. . . .

From a careful consideration of the question proposed, I cannot avoid the conclusion that the decision of the Supreme Court of the United States in the case of *Scott* v. *Sandford,* before mentioned, so long as it shall stand as the final judgment of that tribunal, must be held as legally conclusive and binding upon the several states; and it is therefore my opinion, that "free colored persons of African descent, having a residence established in some town in this state for the term of three months next preceding any election," whose ancestors were of African blood, and were brought into this country and sold as negro slaves, not being citizens of the United States, are not authorized under the provisions of the constitution of this state to be electors for governor, senators and representatives. And it is also my opinion, that all other free colored persons of African descent, if there are any such in this state, who have the qualifications required by law to make free white persons electors for those officers, are authorized under the provisions of the constitution of this state to be electors for governor, senators and representatives.

As I could not concur in the opinion of the majority of the court upon the question presented, it became necessary for me to give my separate opinion, which is respectfully submitted. And I beg leave to refer to the opinion of the Supreme Court of the United States, delivered by Chief Justice MARSHALL, in *Cohens* v. *Virginia*, 6 Wheaton R., 264, and also to Story's Commentaries on the Constitution, vol. 1, book 3, ch. 4, entitled "Who is final judge or interpreter in constitutional controversies," in which authorities there is much valuable learning, and excellent reasoning, concerning the constitutional power of the Supreme Court, and the conclusiveness of its decisions.

2

GEORGE TICKNOR CURTIS a younger brother of the Supreme Court Justice, enjoyed great respect and prestige as a constitutional and legal authority. He served as counsel for the plaintiff in the Dred Scott case and vigorously defended the right of Congress to regulate slavery in the territories. Curtis hardly qualified as an abolitionist. As United States Commissioner in Boston in 1852, he had ordered the return of Thomas Sims, a runaway slave. Curtis's attitude toward the Fugitive Slave Act of 1850, his role in the Dred Scott case, and his analysis of the opinions, all testified that his primary concern remained the maintenance of national power and authority. In his careful dissection of the Dred Scott "decision," Curtis sought to clarify and explain the true "Opinion of the Court."

The decision of the Supreme Court of the United States in the Dred Scott case is so little understood, and its character as a judicial precedent is so generally misapprehended and so often misrepresented, that the following analysis of it may be useful.

The plaintiff, Dred Scott, brought an action of trespass in the Circuit Court of the United States for the District of Missouri, against the defendant, Sandford, for the purpose of establishing his freedom; and according to the requirements of law, in order to gain the jurisdiction of the Court, the plaintiff, in his writ, averred himself to be a "citizen" of the State of Missouri, and the defendant to be a "citizen" of the State of New York. The defendant filed a plea in abatement, alleging that the plaintiff is not a "citizen" of Missouri, because he is a negro of African descent, his ancestors having been of pure African blood, brought into this country and sold as slaves. To this plea the plaintiff demurred; and, as by his demurrer he admitted the *facts* alleged in the plea, the sole question on the demurrer was the question of law, whether a negro of African descent, whose *ancestors* were slaves, can be a citizen of the United States, for the purpose of suing a citizen of another State than his own in a Circuit Court. The Circuit Court gave judgment for the plaintiff on this question; and the defendant was ordered to plead to the merits of the action. He did so; and the substance of his plea in bar of the action was, that the plaintiff was his (the defendant's) slave, and that he had a right to restrain him as such. Upon the issue joined upon this allegation, the case went to trial upon the merits, under an agreed statement of facts, which ascertained, in substance, that the plaintiff, who was a slave in Missouri in 1834, was carried by his then master into

---

2 George Ticknor Curtis, "The Just Supremacy of Congress over the Territories." (Boston, 1859), 38–42.

the State of Illinois, and afterwards into that part of the Louisiana Territory in which slavery had been prohibited by the act of Congress called the Missouri Compromise, and was afterwards brought back to Missouri, and held and sold as a slave. The jury, under the instructions of the Court, found that the plaintiff, at the time of bringing his action, was a slave; and the defendant obtained judgment. The plaintiff then sued out a writ of error to the Supreme Court of the United States, which removed the whole record into that Court.

It will be observed that the record, as brought into the Supreme Court, presented two questions: —

1. The question arising on the plea to the jurisdiction of the Circuit Court, whether a negro of African descent, whose *ancestors* were *slaves,* can be a *citizen.*

2. The question involved in the verdict and judgment on the merits, whether the *plaintiff* was a *slave* at the time he brought his action. This question involved, among others, the inquiry whether the Missouri Compromise, which prohibited the existence of slavery in the Territory where the plaintiff was carried, was constitutional or not.

The importance and effect of the *Dred Scott decision* depend entirely upon the manner in which these questions were dealt with by the Supreme Court. If either of them was *judicially* decided by a majority of the Bench in the same way, the decision constitutes a judicial precedent, binding upon the Court hereafter, and upon all other persons and tribunals, until it is reversed in the same Court, to just the extent that such decision goes. If either of them was not judicially decided by a majority of the Bench in the same way, there is no precedent and no decision on the subject; and the case embraces only certain individual opinions of the judges. The following analysis will determine what has been judicially decided. The reader will observe, that, when the *plea in abatement* is spoken of, it means that part of the pleadings which raised the question whether a negro can be a citizen: the *merits of the action* comprehend the question whether the plaintiff was a *slave,* as affected by the operation of the Missouri Compromise, or otherwise. Keeping these points in view, every reader of the case should endeavor to ascertain the true answers to the following questions: —

I. How many of the judges, and which of them, held that the plea in abatement was rightfully before the Court, on the writ of error, so that they must pass upon the question whether a negro can be a citizen?

Answer. — Four: Chief-Justice, and Justice Wayne, Daniel, and Curtis.

II. Of the above four, how many expressed the opinion that a negro can *not* be a citizen?

Answer. — Three: Chief-Justice, and Justices Wayne and Daniel.

Judge Curtis, who agreed that the plea in abatement was rightfully before the Court, held that a negro *may* be a citizen, and that the Circuit Court, therefore, rightfully had jurisdiction of the case.

The opinions of these four judges on this question are to be regarded as *judicial;* they having held that the record authorized and required its decision. But as there are only three of them on one side of the question, and there is one on the other, and there were five other judges on the bench, there is no judicial majority upon this question, unless two at least of the other five concurred in the opinion that the question arising on the plea in abatement was to be decided by the Supreme Court, and *also* took the same view of that question with Judges Taney, Wayne, and Daniel.

But, in truth, there is not one of the other five judges who concurred with the Chief-Justice and Judges Wayne and Daniel on either of the above points.

Judge Nelson expressly avoided giving any opinion upon them. Indeed, he seems to have leaned to the opinion, that the plea in abatement was not before him: but, after saying there may be some question on this point in the Courts of the United States, he goes on to say, "In the view we [I] have taken of this case, it will not be necessary to pass upon this question; and we [I] shall therefore proceed at once to an examination of *the case upon its merits.*" He then proceeds to decide the case upon the merits, upon the ground, that, even if Scott was carried into a region where slavery did not exist, his return to Missouri, under the decisions of that State, is to be regarded as restoring the condition of servitude. Judge Nelson has never given the opinion that a negro cannot be a citizen, or that the Missouri Compromise was unconstitutional, or given the least countenance to either of these positions.

Judge Grier, after saying that he concurred with Judge Nelson on the question embraced by his opinion, also said that he concurred with the Chief-Justice that the Missouri-Compromise Act was unconstitutional. He neither expressed the opinion that a negro cannot be a citizen, nor did he intimate that he concurred in that part of the opinion of the Chief-Justice: on the contrary, he placed his concurrence in the *disposal of the case,* as ordered by the Court, expressly upon the ground that the plaintiff was a *slave,* as alleged in the pleas in bar.

Judge Campbell took great pains to avoid expressing the opinion that a free negro cannot be a citizen, and has given no countenance whatever to that dogma. He said, at the commencement of his opinion, after reciting the pleadings, "My opinion in this case is not affected by the plea to the jurisdiction, *and I shall not discuss the question it suggests.*" Accordingly, in an elaborate opinion of more than twenty-five pages 8vo, he confines himself exclusively to the question, whether the plaintiff was a *slave;* and he adopts or concurs in none of the reasoning of the Chief Justice, except so far as it bears upon the evidence which shows that the plaintiff was in that condition when he brought his suit. He concurred with the rest of the Court in nothing but the *judgment;* which was, that the case should be dismissed from the Court below for want of jurisdiction; and that want of jurisdiction, he takes good care to show, depends, in his view, on the fact that the plaintiff was a *slave,* and not on the fact that he was a free negro, of African descent, whose *ancestors* were slaves.

Thus there were only three of the judges who declared that a free negro, of African descent, whose ancestors were slaves, cannot be a "citizen," for the purpose of suing in the Courts of the United States, and whose opinions on this point are to be regarded as *judicial,* because they were given under the accompanying opinion, that the question was brought before them on the record. As *three* is not a majority of *nine,* the case of Dred Scott does not furnish a judicial precedent or judicial decision on this question.

With regard to the other question in the case, — that arising on what has been called the merits, — the reader will seek an answer to the following questions: —

I. Of the judges who held that the plea in abatement was rightly before them, and that it showed a want of jurisdiction in the Circuit Court, how many went on, notwithstanding their declared opinion that the case ought to have been dismissed by the Circuit Court for that want of jurisdiction, to consider and pass upon the merits which involved the question of the constitutional validity of the Missouri Compromise?

Answer. — Three: Chief-Justice, and Judges Wayne and Daniel.

II. Of the above three judges, how many held the Missouri-Compromise Act unconstitutional?

Answer. — Three: the same number and the same judges.

III. Of the judges who did not hold that the question of jurisdiction was to be examined and passed upon, and gave no opinion upon it, how many expressed the opinion on the merits that the Compromise Act was void?

Answer. — Three: Judges Grier, Catron, and Campbell.

IV. Of the remaining three judges, how many gave no opinion upon either of the two great questions, — that of citizenship, or that of the validity of the Compromise?

Answer. — One: Judge Nelson.

V. Of the remaining two judges, how many, who held that the question of citizenship was not open, still expressed an opinion upon it in favor of the plaintiff, and *also* sustained the validity of the Compromise?

Answer. — One: Judge McLean.

VI. The remaining judge (Curtis) held that the question of citizenship was open upon the record; that the plaintiff, for all that appeared in the plea in abatement, was a citizen; and, consequently, that the Circuit Court had jurisdiction. This brought him necessarily and judicially to a decision of the merits, on which he held that the Compromise Act was valid.

Thus it appears that six of the nine judges expressed the opinion that the Compromise Act was unconstitutional. But, in order to determine whether this concurrence of six in that opinion constitutes a judicial decision or precedent, it is necessary to see how the majority is formed. Three of these judges, as we have seen, held that the Circuit Court had no jurisdiction of the case, and ought to have dismissed it, because the plea in abatement showed that the plaintiff was not a citizen; and yet, when the Circuit Court had erroneously decided this question in favor of the plaintiff, and had ordered the defendant to plead to the merits, and, after such plea, judgment on the merits had been given against the plaintiff, and he had brought the record into the Supreme Court, these three judges appear to have held that they could not only decide *judicially* that the Circuit Court was entirely without jurisdiction in the case, but could also give a *judicial* decision on the merits. This presents a very grave question, which goes to the foundation of this case as a precedent or authoritative decision on the constitutional validity of the Missouri-Compromise Act, or any similar law.

If it be true, that a majority of the Judges of the Supreme Court can render a judgment ordering a case to be remanded to a Circuit Court, and there to be dismissed for a want of jurisdiction, which three of that majority declare was apparent on a plea in abatement, and these three can yet go on in the same breath to decide a question involved in a subsequent plea to the merits, then this case of Dred Scott is a judicial precedent against the validity of the Missouri Compromise. But if, on the other hand, the judicial function of each judge who held that the Circuit Court was without jurisdiction, for reasons appearing in a plea to the jurisdiction, was discharged as soon as he had announced that conclusion, and given his voice for a dismissal of the case on that ground, then all that he said on the question involved in the merits was extra-judicial, and the so-called "decision" is no precedent. Whenever, therefore, this case of Dred Scott is cited hereafter in the Supreme Court as a judicial decision of the point that Congress cannot prohibit slavery in a Territory, the first thing that the Court will have to do will be to consider and decide the serious question, whether they have made, or could make, a judicial decision that is to be treated as a precedent, by declaring opinions on a question involved in the merits of a judgment, after they had declared that the Court which gave the judgment had no jurisdiction in the case.

When it is claimed, therefore, in grave State-papers or elsewhere, whether in high or low places, that the Supreme Court of the United States, or a majority of its judges, has authoritatively decided that Congress cannot prohibit slavery in a Territory, it is forgotten or overlooked, that one thing more remains to be debated and determined; namely, whether the opinions that have been promulgated from that Bench adverse to the power of Congress do, in truth and in law, constitute, under the circumstances of this record, an actual, authoritative, judicial decision.

These observations respecting the Dred Scott case are submitted to the public, and especially to the legal profession, with the most entire respect for the several judges; with every one of whom, the writer believes he may say, he has the honor to sustain friendly relations, as he certainly reverences their exalted functions. In perfect consistency with these sentiments, he may be permitted to say, that whatever may be thought of the expediency of expressing opinions on every question brought up by a record, or argued at the bar, there must always be a subsequent inquiry how far such opinions, in the technical posture of the case, as it was presented and disposed of, make a *judicial decision*.

3

EDWARD BATES served as Lincoln's Attorney General from 1861 to 1863. In this capacity he confronted the application of the principles implied by Dred Scott. Although historians since have disputed whether parts of Taney's opinion were *obiter dicta* or not, Bates decidedly thought so at the time. A congressional act regulating coastal trade required that masters of American vessels be American citizens. A number of free Negroes commanded such schooners and accordingly had been halted by Treasury Department revenue cutters. In 1862 Secretary of the Treasury Salmon P. Chase inquired of Bates whether free men of color were citizens of the United States and, if qualified, could serve as ships' captains. In his reply, Bates relied primarily on Justice Curtis's presentation of legislative and judicial evidence sustaining Negro citizenship and, in effect, dismissed Taney's remarks as irrelevant and not binding.

Some time ago I had the honor to receive your letter submitting, for my opinion, the question whether or not *colored men* can be citizens of the United States. . . .

Your letter states that "the schooner Elizabeth and Margaret, of New Brunswick, is detained by the revenue cutter Tiger, at South Amboy, New Jersey, because commanded by a 'colored man,' and so by a person not a citizen of the United States. As colored masters are numerous in our coasting trade, I submit, for your opinion, the question suggested by Captain Martin of the Tiger: *Are colored men citizens* of the United States, and therefore competent to command American vessels?"

3 *Official Opinions of the Attorneys General of the United States*, X (Washington, 1868), 382–383, 409–413.

The question would have been more clearly stated if, instead of saving *are colored men citizens,* it had been said, *can colored men be citizens of the United States;* for within our borders and upon our ships, both of war and commerce, there may be *colored* men, and *white* men, also, who are not citizens of the United States. In treating the subject, I shall endeavor to answer your question as if it imported only this: Is a man legally incapacitated to be a citizen of the United States by the sole fact that he is a *colored,* and not a white man?

Who is a citizen? What constitutes a citizen of the United States? I have often been pained by the fruitless search in our law books and the records of our courts, for a clear and satisfactory definition of the phrase *citizen of the United States.* I find no such definition, no authoritative establishment of the meaning of the phrase, neither by a course of judicial decisions in our courts, nor by the continued and consentaneous action of the different branches of our political government. For aught I see to the contrary, the subject is now as little understood in its details and elements, and the question as open to argument and to speculative criticism, as it was at the beginning of the Government. Eighty years of practical enjoyment of citizenship, under the Constitution, have not sufficed to teach us either the exact meaning of the word, or the constituent elements of the thing we prize so highly. . . .

. . . [T]he celebrated case of Scott *vs.* Sandford, (19 Howard's Reports, 393,) is sometimes cited as a direct authority against the capacity of free persons of color to be citizens of the United States. That is an entire mistake. The case, as it stands of record, does not determine, nor purport to determine, that question. It was an ordinary suit for freedom, very common in our jurisprudence, and especially provided for in the legislation in most of the slaveholding States, as it is in Missouri. For convenience the form of the action usually is, and is in this case, *trespass,* alleging an assault and battery and false imprisonment, so as to enable the defendant, (the master,) if he choose, to make a direct issue upon the freedom or slavery of the plaintiff, which is the real point and object of the action, by pleading, in justification of the alleged trespass, that the plaintiff is a slave — his own or another man's.

Such an action Dred Scott, if entitled to freedom, might have brought in the State court, without any allegation of citizenship, and without being, in fact, a citizen. But it seems he desired to bring his action in the circuit court of the United States in Missouri; and, to enable him to do that, he had to allege citizenship, because Mr. Sanford, the defendant, was a citizen of New York, and unless the plaintiff were a citizen of Missouri (or some other State,) the national court had no jurisdiction of the case.

The plaintiff having made his election to sue in the United States court, the defendant might if he would, have pleaded *in bar* to the merits of the action, but he exercised his election to plead *in abatement* to the jurisdiction of the court; thus, that the action, if any, "accrued to the said Dred Scott out of the jurisdiction of this court, and exclusively within the jurisdiction of the courts of the State of Missouri, for that, to wit, the said plaintiff, Dred Scott, is not a citizen of the State of Missouri, as alleged in his declaration, [not because he was not born there, and born free, but] *because he is a negro* of African descent; his ancestors were of pure African blood, and were brought to this country and sold as negro slaves, and this the said Sandford is ready to verify. Wherefore he prays judgment whether this court can or will take further cognizance of the action aforesaid." To this plea the plaintiff demurred, and the circuit court sustained the demurrer, thereby declaring that the facts stated in the plea, and confessed by the demurrer, did not disqualify Scott for being a citizen of Missouri, and so that the United States circuit court had jurisdiction of the cause.

The circuit court having taken jurisdiction, the defendant had, of course, to *plead over* to the merits of the action. He did so, and issues were joined, and there was an elaborate trial of the facts, which resulted in a verdict and judgment in favor of the defendant. And thereupon the plaintiff brought the case up to the Supreme Court by writ of error.

The power of the Supreme Court over the proceedings and judgments of the circuit court is appellate only, and this for the sole purpose of enabling the court above to affirm what has been rightly done, and reverse what has been wrongly done, in the court below. If the error of the court below consist in the illegal asumption of power to hear and determine the merits of a case not within its jurisdiction, of course, the court above will correct that error by setting aside whatever may have been done by usurped authority. And, in doing this, the court above has no more power than the court below had to hear and determine the merits of the case. And to assume the power to determine a case not within the jurisdiction is as great an error in the court above as in the court below; for it is equally true, in all courts, that the jurisdiction must first be ascertained before proceeding to judgment.

In this particular case the Supreme Court did first examine and consider the plea in abatement, and did adjudge that it was a good plea, sufficient to oust the jurisdiction of the circuit court. And hence it follows, as a necessary legal consequence, that whatever was done in the circuit court after the plea in abatement, and touching the merits of the case, was simply void, because done *coram non judice.*

Pleas in abatement were never favorites with the courts in England or America. Lord Coke tells us that they must be "certain to a certain intent, in every particular," and in practice they are always dealt with very strictly. When, therefore, the Supreme Court affirmed the plea in abatement in this case, I assume that it is affirmed, in manner and form, as written, and not otherwise. And this not merely because pleas in abatement are always considered *stricti legis,* but, also, and chiefly, because the decision tends to abridge the valuable rights of persons natural born in the country, which rights ought not to be impaired except upon the clearest evidence of fact and law.

Taking the plea, then, strictly as it is written, the persons who are excluded by this judgment from being citizens of Missouri must be negroes, not mulattoes, nor mestizos, nor quadroons. They must be of *African* descent, not Asiatic, even though they come of the blackest Malays in southeastern Asia. They must have had *ancestors*, (yet that may be doubtful if born in slavery, of putative parents, who were slaves, and, being slaves, incapable of contracting matrimony; and therefore every child must needs be a bastard, and so, by the common law, *nullius filius*, and incapable of ancestors.) His ancestors, if he had any, must have been of *pure* African blood, not mixed with the tawny Moor of Morrocco, or the dusky Arab of the desert, both of whom had their origin in Asia. They must have been *brought* to this country, not come voluntarily; and *sold*, not kept by the importer for his own use, nor given to his friends.

In this argument I raise no question upon the legal validity of the judgment in Scott *vs.* Sandford. I only insist that the judgment in that case is limited in law, as it is, in fact, limited on the face of the record, to the plea in abatement; and, consequently, that whatever was said in the long course of the case, as reported, (240 pages,) respecting the legal merits of the case, and respecting any supposed legal disability resulting from the mere fact of color, though entitled to all the respect which is due to the learned and upright sources from which the opinions come, was *"dehors the record,"* and of no authority as a judicial decision. . . .

And now, upon the whole matter, I give it as my opinion that the *free man of color*, mentioned in your letter, if born in the United States, is a citizen of the United States; and, if otherwise qualified, is competent, according to the acts of Congress, to be master of a vessel engaged in the coasting trade. . . .

E

Epilogue

In his debates with Douglas, Lincoln repeatedly stated that the Republican party intended to reverse the Dred Scott decision. That promise was fulfilled by the first Republican-controlled Congress in 1862, which ignored the now mild protests of the subdued Democracy. But bitterness and enmity toward Chief Justice Taney lingered in influential quarters. In February 1865 a routine proposal to appropriate congressional funds for a commemorative bust of Taney — as had been done for all of his predecessors in this high office — stimulated the latent hostility. Charles Sumner, with the assistance of key congressmen, blocked the effort at the time, and for the next nine years. Sumner's remarks have served — perhaps exaggeratedly — as representative of contemporary Republican opinion of the Chief Justice.

1 *The Republican Congress Replies: 1862*

An act to secure Freedom to all Persons within the Territories of the United States

Be it enacted by the Senate and House of Representatives of the United States of America in Congress assembled, That from and after the passage of this act there shall be neither slavery nor involuntary servitude in any of the Territories of the United States now existing, or which may at any time hereafter be formed or acquired by the United States, otherwise than in punishment of crimes whereof the party shall have been duly convicted.

---

1 *Statutes at Large XII*, 432 (June 19, 1862).

2 Charles Sumner on

Chief Justice Taney: 1865

"Nothing but good of the dead." This is a familiar saying, which, to a certain extent, may be acknowledged. But it is entirely inapplicable when statues and busts are proposed in honor of the dead. Then, at least, truth must prevail.

If a man has done evil during life he must not be complimented in marble. And if indiscreetly it is proposed to decree such a signal honor, then the evil he has done must be exposed; nor shall any false delicacy seal my lips. It is not enough that he held high place, that he enjoyed worldly honors, or was endowed with intellectual gifts.

> "Who wickedly is wise, or madly brave,
> Is but the more a fool, the more a knave."

What is the office of Chief Justice, if it has been used to betray Human Rights? The crime is great according to the position of the criminal.

If you were asked, sir, to mention the incident of our history previous to the rebellion which was in all respects most worthy of condemnation, most calculated to cause the blush of shame, and most deadly in its consequences, I do not doubt that you would say the Dred Scott decision, and especially the wicked opinion of the Chief Justice on that occasion. I say this with pain. I do not seek this debate. But when a proposition is made to honor the author of this wickedness with a commemorative bust, at the expense of the country, I am obliged to speak plainly.

I am not aware that the English judges who decided contrary to Liberty in the case of ship-money, and thus sustained the king in those pretensions which ended in civil war, have ever been commemorated in marble. I am not aware that Jeffreys, Chief Justice and Chancellor of England, famous for his talents as for his crimes, has found any niche in Westminster Hall. No, sir. They have been left to the judgment of history, and there I insist that Taney shall be left in sympathetic companionship. Each was the tool of unjust power. But the Power which Taney served was none other than that Slave Power which has involved the country in war.

I speak what cannot be denied when I declare that the opinion of the Chief Justice in the case of Dred Scott was more thoroughly abominable

---

2 *Congressional Globe*, 38th Congress, 1st Session, 1012–13 (February 23, 1865).

than anything of the kind in the history of courts. Judicial baseness reached its lowest point on that occasion. You have not forgotten that terrible decision where a most unrighteous judgment was sustained by a falsification of history. Of course the Constitution of the United States and every principle of Liberty was falsified, but historical truth was falsified also. . . .

In these words, solemnly and authoritatively uttered by the Chief Justice of the United States, humanity and truth were set at naught, and the whole country was humbled. "Then you and I and all of us fell down while bloody *slavery* flourished over us."

I quote his words fully so that there can be no mistake. Here then is his expressed assertion, that at the Declaration of Independence in 1776, and the adoption of the national Constitution in 1789, in Europe as well as in our own country, "colored men had no rights which white men were bound to respect." Now, sir, this is false — atrociously false. It is notorious that there were States of the Union where, at the adoption of the Constitution, colored persons were free, and even in the enjoyment of the electoral franchise, while in England the *Somersett* case had already decided that there could be no distinction of persons on account of color, and Scotland, Holland, and France had all declared the same rule. On this point there can be no question. And yet this Chief Justice, whom you propose to honor with a marble bust, had the unblushing effrontery to declare that at that time, as well abroad as at home, "colored men had no rights which white men were bound to respect;" and this he said in order to justify a wicked interpretation of the Constitution. Search the judicial annals and you will find no perversion of truth more flagrant.

Sir, it is not fit, it is not decent, that such a person should be commemorated by a vote of Congress; especially at this time when liberty is at last recognized. If you have money to appropriate in this way, let it be in honor of the defenders of liberty now gathered to their fathers. There was John Quincy Adams. There also was Joshua R. Giddings. Let their busts be placed in the court-room, if you please, where with marble lips they can plead always for human rights and teach[,] judge and advocate the glory and the beauty of justice. Then will you do something not entirely unworthy of a regenerated land; something which will be an example for future times; something which will help to fix the standard of history.

I know that in the court-room there are busts of the other Chief Justices. Very well. So in the hall of the doges, at Venice, there are pictures of all who filled that high office in unbroken succession, with the exception of Marino Faliero, who, although as venerable from years as Taney, was deemed unworthy of a place in that line. Where his picture should have been there was a vacant space which testified always to the justice of the republic. Let such a vacant space in our court-room testify to the justice of our Republic. Let it speak in warning to all who would betray liberty.

Let me . . . [say] that the name of Taney is to be hooted down the page of history. Judgment is beginning now; and an emancipated country will fasten upon him the stigma which he deserves. The Senator says that he for twenty-five years administered justice. He administered justice at last wickedly, and degraded the judiciary of the country, and degraded the age. . . .

4

★ DRED SCOTT
AT THE
BAR OF HISTORY

1   JAMES FORD RHODES (1848–1927), after a successful industrial and business career, used his fortune to pursue an avocation of historical writing. Rhodes lacked formal education, but mastered the techniques of scholarship and produced highly-regarded narratives of American history that won him a wide audience. In 1898 he served as President of the American Historical Association. His most noteworthy work was the *History of the United States from the Compromise of 1850 to 1877* (7 vols., 1893–1906). Rhodes's interpretation of the Dred Scott case closely followed his general view that slavery and the clash of abstract ideals were the chief causes of the Civil War.

. . . [There were] many attempts of the national legislature and the executive to settle the slavery question. We have now to consider a grave attempt in the same line by the United States Supreme Court. The reverence for this unique and most powerful judicial tribunal of the world was profound. It is possible that from the time of the decision of the Dartmouth College case to the death of Chief Justice Marshall, the court held a loftier place in public opinion than in 1857; for Marshall was one of the world's great judges, and he had forcibly impressed his wonderful legal mind upon the country's jurisprudence. At that time De Tocqueville had written: In the hands of the Supreme Court "repose unceasingly the peace, the prosperity, the existence even, of the Union." But in 1857 the reverence for the Supreme Court was greater than now. In much of the political literature of the day it is regarded almost as a fetich; it was looked upon as something beyond the pale of ordinary human institutions. When men became Supreme Court judges, they were believed to be no longer actuated by the prejudices and passions of common humanity. During the slavery agitation there had been propositions of various kinds to refer disputed questions to this court, on the theory that there a wholly impartial and severely just decision might be had. The Democrats who disagreed about the construction of the Kansas-Nebraska act concurred in the proposal to leave the question to the highest judicial tribunal.

In 1857, the Supreme Court was composed of Chief Justice Taney, Justices Wayne, Daniel, Catron, Campbell, Democrats from the slave States; Grier and Nelson, Democrats, and McLean, a Republican, and Curtis, a Whig, from the free States. From the importance of their personality, two of these judges deserved special notice.

---

1 James Ford Rhodes, *History of the United States From the Compromise of 1850.* (New York, 1900), II, 249–61. Footnotes omitted.

Chief Justice Taney belonged to one of the old Roman Catholic families of Maryland, and was himself a devout adherent of that religion. A good student of law, he devoted much time to history and letters; and the thoughts, words, and style of great writers had for him a powerful charm. He especially loved Shakespeare and Macaulay. He rose to eminence at the Maryland bar; he was an untiring worker, and allowed nothing to distract him from his professional duties and domestic life. Of a passionate nature, he had very decided political opinions. President Jackson appointed him Attorney-General, and he soon became the President's trusted and confidential adviser. When Duane, the Secretary of the Treasury, refused to withdraw the government deposits from the United States Bank, Jackson removed him and put Taney in his place. Taney understood banking and finance, and, being a man after Jackson's own heart, supported the President unreservedly in his war against the bank. The Senate refused to confirm Taney as Secretary of the Treasury, and Jackson appointed him Justice of the Supreme Court. Chief Justice Marshall, though disliking the President and his policy, had a good opinion of Taney's legal ability, and made an effort to secure his confirmation; but action on his nomination was indefinitely postponed. In July, 1835, Marshall died, and Jackson appointed Taney Chief Justice. As the political complexion of the Senate had changed, he did not fail of confirmation, although he had for opponents Webster and Clay.

To fill the place of Chief Justice Marshall was a difficult task, and Taney suffered continually by comparison with his great predecessor; yet as the years went on, he gained solid reputation by accurate knowledge of law, clearness of thought, and absolute purity of life. His written opinions are characterized by vigor of style, reflecting the hours he passed with the masters of our literature.

Curtis had the rich New England culture. By nature a lawyer, he had received at the Harvard law school, sitting at the feet of Judge Story, the training which those who thirsted for legal knowledge could acquire from the instructions of such a teacher. He was thoroughly read in English history. He owed his appointment as justice to Webster, who, when Secretary of State, recommended him most highly to President Fillmore. Curtis was an absolutely impartial judge. His reasoning was clear to laymen and a delight to lawyers. Though his style was a model of compression, he never forgot a point nor failed to be perspicuous. His course on the bench was a fine testimonial to the choice of Webster, whom New England lawyers regarded as the master of their profession.

In the Dred Scott case the opposing principles of slavery and freedom came sharply into conflict in the judicial opinions of Taney and Curtis. The negro Dred Scott had several years previously sued for the freedom of himself and family, and the case came up to the Supreme Court in a regular way. The detailed history of the affair has for our purpose no importance; it went through various stages, and many collateral points were involved. While the freedom or slavery of four negroes was at stake, the interest in their fate is completely overshadowed by the importance of the questions to which the suit gave rise. As a matter of fact, Dred Scott, after being remanded to slavery by the Supreme Court, was emancipated by his master; but he had served as a text for weighty constitutional and political arguments.

Standing out beyond the merits of the case and all other points involved. two questions of vast importance were suggested by the facts. Could a negro whose ancestors had been sold as slaves become a citizen of one of the States of the Union? For if Dred Scott were not a citizen of Missouri, where he had mostly lived, he had no standing in the United States Court.

The second question, Was the Missouri Compromise constitutional? came up in this manner. Dred Scott had been taken by his master, an army surgeon, to Fort Snelling, which was in the northern part of the Louisiana territory, now Minnesota, and had remained there for a period of about two years. In this territory slavery was forever prohibited by the Missouri Compromise, and the counsel for Dred Scott maintained. that by virtue of the restriction, residence there conferred freedom on the slave. Thus might arise the question, Was the Missouri Compromise constitutional? and this carried with it the more practical question, Had Congress the power to prohibit slavery in the territories? On the basis of the assertion of this power, the Republican party was builded; and if this power did not inhere in Congress, the Republican party had constitutionally no reason for existence.

The case was first argued in the spring of 1856. Justice Curtis wrote Ticknor, April 8th, the result of the conferences of the judges: "The court will not decide the question of the Missouri-Compromise line — a majority of the judges being of opinion that it is not necessary to do so. (This is confidential.) The one engrossing subject in both houses of Congress, and with all the members, is the presidency; and upon this everything done and omitted, except the most ordinary necessities of the country, depends."

At the term of court, December, 1856, the case was re-argued, and the counsel discussed all the questions involved. Still, the judges decided to view the matter only in its narrow aspect, and in its particular bearing on the status of Dred Scott and his family. To Justice Nelson, of New York, was assigned the duty of writing the opinion of the court. He astutely evaded the determination whether the Missouri Compromise act was constitutional; nor did he consider it necessary to pass upon the citizenship of the negro, but in arguing the case on its merits the decision was reached that Dred Scott was still a slave. Had this been the conclusion of the matter, the Dred Scott case would have excited little interest at the time, and would hardly have demanded more than the briefest notice from the historian.

But there now began a pressure on the southern judges, who constituted a majority of the court, to decide the weighty constitutional question involved in the case. The unceasing inculcation of Calhoun's doctrine regarding slavery in the territories had now brought southern Democrats, and among them the five southern judges, round to that notion. Of course the pressure was adroit and considerate, for the judges were honest men impressed with the dignity of their position. The aim was simply to induce them to promulgate officially what they privately thought. It is a tradition that Justice Campbell held back. This is to a certain degree confirmed by a letter of his written long after the event; but if three southern judges were decidedly in favor of pronouncing a judgment on the constitutional question, it needed only to gain the chief justice to carry along with them Campbell, and perhaps the two Democratic judges from the North. Before the Dred Scott decision was pronounced, Taney, both in character and ability, stood much higher than any other member of the court.

The chief justice was gained. The bait held out to his patriotic soul was that the court had the power and opportunity of settling the slavery question. He had now nearly reached the age of eighty, and, had he been younger, he might have detected the flaws in the reasoning which led him to so decided a position. "Our aged chief justice," wrote Curtis, February 27th, 1857, in a private letter, "grows more feeble in body, but retains his alacrity and force of mind wonderfully," though he "is not able to write much." Certainly the Dred Scott opinion of Taney shows no weakness of memory or abated power of reasoning; but it may have been that age had enfeebled the will and made him more susceptible to influences that were brought to bear upon him.

Before Justice Nelson read his opinion in conference, Justice Wayne, of Georgia, at a meeting of the judges, stated that the case had excited public interest, and that it was expected that the points discussed by counsel would be considered by the court. He therefore moved that the chief justice should "write an opinion on all of the questions as the opinion of the court." This was agreed to, but some of the judges reserved the privilege of qualifying their assent. Justice Wayne had worked industriously to bring this about, and his efforts had an important influence in persuading the chief justice, and Judges Grier, of Pennsylvania, and Catron, of Tennessee, of the expediency of such a course. This determination, though shrouded in the secrecy of Supreme Court consultations, leaked out. Reverdy Johnson, whose constitutional argument had a profound influence on Taney, made his plea December 18th, 1856, and on New Year's Day of 1857, Alexander Stephens wrote to his brother: "The decision [of the Dred Scott case] will be a marked epoch in our history. I feel a deep solicitude as to how it will be. From what I hear, *sub rosa,* it will be according to my own opinion on every point, as abstract political questions. The restriction of 1820 will be held to be unconstitutional. The judges are all writing out their opinions, I believe, seriatim. The chief justice will give an elaborate one." On the 5th of January, Pike wrote the New York *Tribune* that the rumor was current in Washington that the Supreme Court had decided that Congress had no constitutional power to prohibit slavery in the territories.

Two days after the inauguration of Buchanan, Chief Justice Taney delivered the opinion of the court. He stated that one of the questions to be decided was: "Can a negro whose ancestors were imported into this country and sold as slaves become a member of the political community formed and brought into existence by the Constitution of the United States, and as such become entitled to all the rights and privileges and immunities guaranteed by that instrument to the citizen?" The answer is no. Negroes "were not intended to be included under the word 'citizens' in the Constitution, and therefore can claim none of the rights and privileges which that instrument provides for and secures to the citizens of the United States." Moreover, "In the opinion of the court, the legislation and histories of the times, and the language used in the Declaration of Independence, show that neither the class of persons who had been imported as slaves, nor their descendants, whether they had become free or not, were then acknowledged as a part of the people, nor intended to be included in the general words used in that memorable instrument.

"It is difficult, at this day, to realize the state of public opinion in relation to that unfortunate race which prevailed in the civilized and enlightened portions of the world at the time of the Declaration of Independence, and when the Constitution was framed and adopted. But the public history of every European nation displays it in a manner too plain to be mistaken.

"They had for more than a century before been regarded as beings of an inferior order, and altogether unfit to associate with the white race, either in social or political relations; and so far inferior that they had no rights which the white man was bound to respect, and that the negro might justly and lawfully be reduced to slavery for his benefit. He was bought and sold, and treated as an ordinary article of mechandise and traffic, whenever a profit could be made by it. The opinion was at that time fixed and universal in the civilized portion of the white race. It was regarded as an axiom in morals as well as in politics, which no one thought of disputing, or supposed to be open to dispute; and men in every grade and position in society daily and habitually acted upon it in their private pursuits, as well as in matters of public concern, without doubting for a moment the correctness of this opinion."

Citing the famous clause of the Declaration of Independence which asserted "that all men are created equal," the chief justice said: "The general words above quoted would seem to embrace the whole human family, and if they were used in a similar instrument at this day would be so understood. But it is too clear for dispute that the enslaved African race were not intended to be included, and formed no part of the people who framed and adopted this declaration."

The chief justice put the other constitutional question plainly: Was Congress authorized to pass the Missouri Compromise act "under any of the powers granted to it by the Constitution?" The Louisiana territory "was acquired by the general government, as the representative and trustee of the people of the United States, and it must therefore be held in that character for their common and equal benefit. . . . It seems, however, to be supposed that there is a difference between property in a slave and other property, and that different rules may be applied to it in expounding the Constitution of the United States." But "the right of property in a slave is distinctly and expressly affirmed in the Constitution. . . . And no word can be found in the Constitution which gives Congress a greater power over slave property, or which entitles property of that kind to less protection than property of any other description." It is the opinion of the court, therefore, that the Missouri Compromise act "is not warranted by the Constitution, and is therefore void."

All of the judges read opinions. The four southern judges and Grier distinctly agreed with the chief justice that the Missouri Compromise was unconstitutional; and they concurred sufficiently in the other points to constitute his conclusions the opinion of the court, as it was officially called. It thus received the assent of two-thirds of the judges. Justice Nelson read the opinion he had prepared when it was decided to confine the judgment of the court to the merits of the case, while Justices McLean and Curtis dissented from the determination of the court. As Curtis covered more fully and cogently the ground, we have now to consider his opinion.

"I dissent," he began, "from the opinion pronounced by the chief justice. . . . The question is, whether any person of African descent whose ancestors were sold as slaves in the United States can be a citizen of the United States. . . . One mode of approaching this question is to inquire who were citizens of the United States at the time of the adoption of the Constitution.

"Citizens of the United States at the time of the adoption of the Constitution can have been no other than citizens of the United States under the confederation. . . . It may safely be said that the citizens of the several States were citizens of the United States under the confederation. . . . To determine whether any free persons descended from Africans held in slavery were citizens of the United States under the confederation, and consequently at the time of the adoption of the Constitution of the United States, it is only necessary to know whether any such persons were citizens of either of the States under the confederation at the time of the adoption of the Constitution.

"Of this there can be no doubt. At the time of the ratification of the

Articles of Confederation, all free native-born inhabitants of the States of New Hampshire, Massachusetts, New York, New Jersey, and North Carolina, though descended from African slaves, were not only citizens of those States, but such of them as had the other necessary qualifications possessed the franchise of electors, on equal terms with other citizens. . . . I shall not enter into an examination of the existing opinions of that period respecting the African race, nor into any discussion concerning the meaning of those who asserted in the Declaration of Independence that all men are created equal; that they are endowed by their Creator with certain inalienable rights; that among these are life, liberty, and the pursuit of happiness. My own opinion is that a calm comparison of these assertions of universal abstract truths, and of their own individual opinions and acts, would not leave these men under any reproach of inconsistency; that the great truths they asserted on that solemn occasion they were ready and anxious to make effectual whenever a necessary regard to circumstances, which no statesman can disregard without producing more evil than good, would allow; and that it would not be just to them, nor true in itself, to allege that they intended to say that the Creator of all men had endowed the white race exclusively with the great natural rights which the Declaration of Independence asserts. But this is not the place to vindicate their memory. As I conceive, we should deal here . . . with those substantial facts evinced by the written constitutions of States, and by notorious practice under them. And they show, in a manner which no argument can obscure, that in some of the original thirteen States free colored persons, before and at the time of the formation of the Constitution, were citizens of those States." Therefore, "my opinion is that under the Constitution of the United States every free person born on the soil of a State, who is a citizen of that State by force of its constitution or laws, is also a citizen of the United States."

In considering the power of Congress to prohibit slavery in the territories, Justice Curtis cited "eight distinct instances, beginning with the first Congress, and coming down to the year 1848, in which Congress has excluded slavery from the territory of the United States; and six distinct instances in which Congress organized governments of territories by which slavery was recognized and continued, beginning also with the first Congress and coming down to the year 1822. These acts were severally signed by seven Presidents of the United States, beginning with General Washington and coming regularly down as far as John Quincy Adams, thus including all who were in public life when the Constitution was adopted.

"If the practical construction of the Constitution, contemporaneously with its going into effect, by men intimately acquainted with its history from their personal participation in framing and adopting it, and continued by them through a long series of acts of the gravest importance, be entitled to weight in the judicial mind on a question of construction, it would seem to be difficult to resist the force of the acts above adverted to."

Furthermore, "Slavery, being contrary to natural right, is created only by municipal law." Then, "Is it conceivable that the Constitution has conferred the right on every citizen to become a resident on the territory of the United States with his slaves, and there to hold them as such, but has neither made nor provided for any municipal regulations which are essential to the existence of slavery? . . . Whatever theoretical importance may be now supposed to belong to the maintenance of such a right, I feel a perfect conviction that it would, if ever tried, prove to be as impracticable in fact as it is, in my judgment, monstrous in theory."

Every possible phase of this question was considered by Justice Curtis, and the conclusion arrived at was that the acts of Congress which had prohibited slavery in the territories, including of course the Missouri Compromise, "were constitutional and valid laws."

That a man of the years of Taney could construct so vigorous and so plausible an argument was less remarkable than that a humane Christian man could assert publicly such a monstrous theory. Yet such work was demanded by slavery of her votaries. The opinion of Taney was but the doctrine of Calhoun, announced for the first time in 1847, and now embodied in a judicial decision. As the North grew faster than the South, as freedom was stronger than slavery, it was the only tenable theory on which slavery could be extended. It is a striking historical fact that in but thirteen years of our history, from 1847 to 1860, could such an opinion have been delivered from the Supreme bench. Only by the conviction that slavery was being pushed to the wall, in conjunction with subtle reasoning like that of Calhoun, who tried to obstruct the onward march of the century by a fine-spun theory, could a sentiment have been created which found expression in this opinion of Taney, outraging as it did precedent, history, and justice.

That Taney committed a grievous fault is certain. He is not to be blamed for embracing the political notions of John C. Calhoun; his environment gave that shape to his thoughts; but he does deserve censure because he allowed himself to make a political argument, when only a judicial decision was called for. The history of the case shows that there was no necessity for passing upon the two questions we have considered at length. Nothing but an imperative need should have led judges, by their training and position presumably conservative, to unsettle a question that had so long been acquiesced in. The strength of a constitutional government lies in the respect paid to settled questions. For the judiciary to weaken that respect undermines the very foundations of the State. As [Senator Stephen A.] Douglas sinned as a statesman, so Taney sinned as judge; and while patriotism and not self-seeking impelled him, the better motive does not excuse the chief justice; for much is demanded from the man who holds that high office. Posterity must condemn Taney as unqualifiedly as Douglas.

2

EDWARD S. CORWIN (1878–1963), long regarded as one
of the foremost commentators on American constitutional development, wrote more than two hundred books, articles, and reviews
over a half-century span. After receiving his Ph. D. from the University of Pennsylvania, he was one of Woodrow Wilson's early
choices for the preceptorial system at Princeton, where he remained
for his entire academic career. Some of his most important and
enduring writings are *The Doctrine of Judicial Review and Other
Essays* (1914), *Court Over Constitution* (1938), *The President:
Office and Powers* (1940, 1958), and *Liberty Against Government*
(1948). During the New Deal he served as an advisor to several
agencies, and from 1949 to 1952, he edited *The Constitution Anno-
tated: Analysis and Interpretation* for the Legislative Reference
Section of the Library of Congress. Corwin's essay on Dred Scott
marked the first scholarly foray into the legal merits and context
of the case since the Civil War period.[1]

Having had occasion recently to renew my acquaintance with the case
of Scott *v.* Sandford,[2] I have become persuaded that the usual historical
verdict with reference to it needs revision in three important particulars:
first, as to the legal value of the pronouncement in that case of unconstitutionality with reference to the Missouri Compromise; secondly, as
to the basis of that pronouncement; thirdly, as to the nature of the issue
between Chief Justice Taney and Justice Curtis upon the question of
citizenship that was raised by Dred Scott's attempt to sue in the federal
courts.[3]

The main facts leading up to and attending this famous litigation may
be summarized as follows:[4] Dred Scott, a slave belonging to an army
officer named Emerson, was taken by his master from the home state,
Missouri, first into the free state of Illinois and thence into that portion of
the national territory from which, by the eighth section of the Missouri
Compromise, slavery was "forever" excluded. Here master and slave remained two years before returning to Missouri, the latter in the meantime having married with his master's consent. In 1852 Dred sued his

---

[1] In substance this paper was read before the American Historical Association at its
annual meeting, December 29, 1910.

[2] 19 Howard 393–633 (cited below as "Rep").

[3] See James Ford Rhodes, *History of the United States,* II. 251 *et seq.;* James
Schouler, *History of the United States,* V. 377 *et seq.;* Nicolay and Hay, *Abraham
Lincoln,* II., ch. 4; Theodore Clarke Smith, *Parties and Slavery,* ch. 14.

[4] The agreed statement of facts is to be found, Rep. 397–399.

---

2 Edward S. Corwin, "The Dred Scott Decision in the Light of Contemporary Legal
Doctrines," *The American Historical Review,* XVII (October 1911), 52–69. Reprinted by permission of the American Historical Association.

master for freedom in one of the lower state courts and won the action, but upon appeal the decision was reversed by the supreme court of the state, upon the ground that Dred's status at home was fixed by state law regardless of what it was abroad — a decision which plainly ran counter to the whole trend of decision by the same court for the previous generation. Thereupon the case was remanded to the inferior court for retrial but Dred, having in the meantime upon the death of Emerson passed by bequest to Sandford, a citizen of New York, now decided to bring a totally new action in the United States circuit court for the Missouri district, under section 11 of the Act of 1789. In order to bring this action Dred had of course to aver his citizenship of Missouri, which averment was traversed by his adversary in what is known as a plea in abatement, which denied the judisdiction of the court upon the ground that Dred was the descendant of African slaves and was born in slavery. The plea in abatement the circuit court overruled, but then proceeded to find the law on the merits of the case for the defendant Sandford; and from this decision Dred appealed to the United States Supreme Court.

Scott *v.* Sandford was first argued before the Supreme Court in the December term of 1855. From a letter of Justice Curtis we learn that in the view the court took of the case, it would find it unnecessary to canvass the question of the constitutionality of the Missouri Compromise.[5] And indeed it was evidently of a mind to evade even the question of jurisdiction, as raised by the plea in abatement, had it not been for the fact, as it presently transpired, that Justice McLean, a candidate for the Republican presidential nomination, had determined to make political capital of the controversy by writing a dissenting opinion, reviewing at length the history of African slavery in the United States from the Free Soil point of view. McLean's intention naturally produced some uneasiness among his brethren and particularly such as came from slave states, three of whom now began demanding reargument of the questions raised in connection with the plea in abatement.[6] This demand being acceded to, the case came on for reargument in the December term of 1856, that is, after the presidential election was over. Yet even now it was originally the purpose of the court to confine its attention to the question of law raised by the circuit court's decision, which rested upon the same ground as the state supreme court's earlier decision, and Justice Nelson was commissioned to write an opinion sustaining the circuit

[5] Curtis to Ticknor, April 8, 1856. George Ticknor Curtis, *Life of Benjamin Robbins Curtis,* I. 80.

[6] Ashley of Ohio's positive testimony on the basis of report current at the time Scott *v.* Sandford was pending, supplies the explanation needed of the demand for reargument, since the final disposition of the case would be precisely the same whether the circuit court were held to have erred in taking jurisdiction or, having rightfully taken jurisdiction, to have properly decided the case on its merits. *Congressional Globe,* 40th Cong., 3d sess., App., p. 211. See also McLean's opinion, Rep. 529–564, and Curtis's animadversions on the same, *ibid.,* 620.

court.[7] Since the defeat of Fremont, however, and Buchanan's election, the advantage of position lay all with the pro-slavery membership of the court. Some of the latter contingent, therefore, but chiefly Justice Wayne of Georgia, who had on another occasion displayed a rather naïve view of the judicial function, now began bringing forward the notion that, as expressed in Wayne's very frank opinion, "the peace and harmony of the country required the settlement . . . by judicial decision" of the "constitutional principles" involved in the case.[8] Yielding at last to this pressure, Chief Justice Taney consented to prepare "the opinion of the Court," as it is labelled, covering all issues that had been raised in argument before the court in support of the defendant's contentions. What was to be the scope of the court's decision was known to Alexander H. Stephens, as early as January, 1857,[9] and undoubtedly to Buchanan when he delivered his inaugural address. And to know what scope the decision was to take was equivalent practically to knowing its tenor, since it was extremely improbable that a majority of the court would have allowed so broad a range to inquiry had they not been substantially assured beforehand of its outcome. When, therefore, Buchanan in his inaugural address bespoke the country's acquiescence in the verdict of the court, "whatever it might be," his very solicitude betrayed that, as Lincoln inferred, he was talking from the card.

For obvious reasons, hostile criticism of the Dred Scott decision has always found its principal target in the Chief Justice's opinion, and the gravamen of such criticism has always been that the great part of it, particularly the portion dealing with the Missouri Compromise, was *obiter dictum*. I do not, however, concur with this criticism, for reasons which I shall now endeavor to make plain. And in the first place, it ought to be clearly apprehended what difficulty attaches to a charge of this sort against a deliberate utterance of the Supreme Court of the United States, evidently intended by it to have the force and operation of law, and for the reason that the ultimate test of what *is* law for the United States is, and at the time of the Dred Scott decision was, the opinion of the Supreme Court. On the other hand, the Supreme Court is not theoretically an irresponsible body: by the very theory that makes it final judge of the laws and the Constitution it is subject to these; as by virtue of its character as court it is subject to the *lex curiae*, that is to say, is bound to make consistent application of the results of its own reasoning and to honor the precedents of its own creation. What the charge of *obiter dictum* amounts to therefore is this: first, that the action of the Chief Justice in passing upon the constitutionality of the eighth

[7] Rep. 529–564. The fact that Nelson was commissioned to write an opinion *sustaining* the lower court again shows that intrinsically the question of the lower court's jurisdiction was regarded as unimportant.

[8] Rep. 454–455.

[9] See Rhodes, p. 253, and references.

section of the Missouri Compromise was illogical, as being inconsistent with the earlier part of his opinion, the purport of which, it is alleged, was to remove from the court's consideration the record of the case in the lower court and, with it, any basis for a pronouncement upon the constitutional question; and secondly, that the action of the Chief Justice was also in disregard of precedent, which, it is contended, exacted that the court should not pass upon issues other than those the decision of which was strictly necessary to the determination of the case before it, and particularly that it should not unnecessarily pronounce a legislative enactment unconstitutional. Let us consider these two points in order.

As already indicated, the primary question before the court upon the reargument was what disposition to make of the plea in abatement which the circuit court had overruled, thereby taking jurisdiction of the case,[10] and upon this point a majority of the court, including both Chief Justice Taney and Justice Curtis, ruled decisively both that the plea in abatement was before it and that the decision of the circuit court as to its jurisdiction was subject to review by the Supreme Court.[11] Evidently the charge of illogicality lies against only those judges of the above mentioned majority who, after overruling the plea in abatement and so pronouncing against the jurisdiction of the circuit court upon the grounds therein set forth, passed to consider the further record of the case, by which the constitutional issue was raised. But was such proceeding necessarily illogical? Upon this point obviously the pertinent thing is to consider Taney's own theory of what he was doing, which he states in substantially the following language at the conclusion of his argument on the question of the plaintiff's citizenship: but waiving, he says, the question as to whether the plea in abatement is before the court on the writ of error, yet the question of jurisdiction still remains on the face of the bill of exceptions taken by the plaintiff in which he admits that he was born a slave but contends that he has since become free; for if he has not become free then certainly he cannot sue as a citizen.[12] In other words, the Chief Justice's theory was, not that he was canvassing the case on its merits, which he could have done with propriety only had he chosen to ignore the question of jurisdiction, but that he was fortifying his decision upon this matter of jurisdiction by reviewing the issues raised in the bill of exceptions, *as well as* those raised by the plea in abatement; in other words that he was canvassing the question of jurisdiction afresh.

The matter of the validity of the Chief Justice's mode of proceeding

[10] *Supreme Court Reports, Lawyer's Edition*, bk. xv., 694, 697.

[11] This majority consisted of the Chief Justice and Justices Wayne, Daniel, Campbell, and Curtis. Grier considered it sufficient to canvas the question of the lower court's jurisdiction on the basis of the facts stated in the bill of exceptions. Nelson did not consider the question of jurisdiction. Catron and McLean did not deem the question of jurisdiction to be before the court.

[12] Rep. 427. Note also the Chief Justice's statement of the issue at the opening of his opinion, Rep. 400.

then comes down to this question: Is it allowable for a court to base a decision upon more than one ground and if it does so, does the auxiliary part of the decision become *obiter dictum?* Upon the general question of what constitutes *dictum* we find the writer in the *American and English Encyclopedia of Law* indicating the existence of two views among common-law courts. By one of these views none of a judicial opinion is decision save only such part as was necessary to the determination of the rights of the parties to the action. By the other view, on the contrary, all of an opinion is decision which represents a deliberate application of the judicial mind to questions legitimately raised in argument.[13] On the precise question above stated the writer speaks as follows:

> Where the record presents two or more points, any one of which, if sustained, would determine the case, and the court decide them all, the decision upon any one of the points cannot be regarded as *obiter*. Nor can it be said that a case is not authority on a point because, though that point was properly presented and decided in the regular course of the consideration of the case, another point was found in the end which disposed of the whole matter. The decision on such a question is as much a part of the judgment of the court as is that on any other of the matters on which the case as a whole depends. The fact that the decision might have been placed upon a different ground existing in the case does not render a question expressly decided by the Court a dictum.[14]

True, this exact statement of the matter is of comparatively recent date, but it is supported by judicial utterances some of which antedate the Dred Scott decision and others of which, conspicuously one by Chief Justice Waite in Railroad Companies *v.* Schutte, plainly purport to set forth long standing and settled doctrine.[15] It is apparent moreover that this is the only doctrine tenable, for, were the opposite view taken, the law would remain unsettled precisely in proportion as the court presumed to settle it, since with a decision resting upon more than a single ground it would be always open to those so disposed to challenge the validity of all but one of such grounds, and that one selected at whim. Thus granting — what indeed is evident — that Taney was under no necessity of canvassing both the question of Dred's citizenship and that of his servitude, yet since he did canvass both questions with equal deliberation, who is to say which part of his opinion was decision and which *obiter?*

However, it is urged that an exception must be made in the case of constitutional questions, which should be left undecided if possible. To

---

[13] *Encyc.* (2d ed.), "Dictum", IX. 452–453: "Stare Decisis". XXVI. 168–169. *Cf.* Carroll *v.* Carroll's Lessee, 16 How. 275, 287, and Alexander *v.* Worthington. 5 Md. 471, 487.

[14] *Ibid.,* 171. I am indebted for this reference to Elbert W. R. Ewing's *Legal and Historical Status of the Dred Scott Decision* (Washington, 1909). I may add that this is the sum total of my indebtedness to the work mentioned.

[15] 103 U.S. 118, cited with approval in Union Pacific R. R. Co. *v.* Mason City etc., R. R. Co., 199 U.S. 160.

quote Justice Curtis's protest against the Chief Justice's opinion: "a great
question of constitutional law, deeply affecting the peace and welfare
of the country, is not . . . a fit subject to be thus reached;" such is the
argument.[16] So far however is this alleged exception from being justified
by the history of the matter, that it would be far nearer the truth to say
that, if constitutional cases comprise a class by themselves in this reference, they warrant an exceptionally broad view of the legal value of
judicial opinion. Let us consider for example some of Chief Justice Marshall's decisions in this connection, but particularly his decision in
Cohens v. Virginia.[17]

In that case the plaintiff in error had been indicted and subjected to
trial and penalty under a Virginia statute for selling tickets for a lottery
which Congress had chartered for the District of Columbia. As in the
Dred Scott case, the primary question before the court was one of jurisdiction, though in this case the Supreme Court's own jurisdiction, which
counsel for Virginia denied upon four grounds: first, that a state was
defendant, contrary to the Eleventh Amendment; secondly, that no writ
of error lay from a state court to the Supreme Court; thirdly, that if the
act in question was meant to extend to Virginia it was unconstitutional;
and fourthly, that it was not meant so to extend. Ultimately Marshall
dismissed the case for want of jurisdiction upon the last ground, which
involves no constitutional question, but before he did so he not only invited argument upon the other points, but in the greatest of his opinions
he met and refuted every argument advanced by counsel for Virginia
thereupon. Yet by the test set for Taney's opinion in the Dred Scott
case, all the valuable part of this great decision is *obiter dictum*, and
that of the most gratuitous kind, since its purport was not in support of
but counter to the final disposition of the immediate issue before the
court.[18] And in truth Cohens v. Virginia was criticized by Jefferson[19]
upon grounds quite similar to those taken by the critics of Chief Justice
Taney's opinion in Scott v. Sandford, notwithstanding which, however,
it has always been regarded as good law in all its parts and indeed was

16 Rep. 590.
17 6 Wheat. 264.
18 The portion of Marshall's opinion in Cohens v. Virginia which comprises the
leading decision on the point with which it deals runs as follows: "It is, then, the
opinion of the court, that the defendant who removes a judgment rendered against
him by a state court into this court, for the purpose of re-examining the question
whether that judgment be in violation of the constitution or laws of the United
States, does not commence or prosecute a suit against the State." By the test set
by the critics of C. J. Taney's opinion in Scott v. Sandford, however, the above
quoted utterance is not decision; for its author continues thus: ". . . But should we
in this be mistaken, the error does not affect the case now before the court," the
reason being that since Cohens was not a citizen of "another State," the Eleventh
Amendment did not apply.
19 *Writings* (Memorial Edition), XV. 297–298, 326, 389, 421, 444–452.

so treated and enforced, once and again, by the court over which Taney himself presided.[20]

The fact of the matter is that the critics of Chief Justice Taney take their view of the proper scope of judicial decision from the common law rather than from American constitutional law. Altogether, the only feasible definition, historically, of *obiter dictum* in the field of American constitutional law would seem to be, a more or less casual utterance by a court or members thereof upon some point not deemed by the court itself to be strictly before it and not necessary to decide, as preliminary to the determination of the controversy before it. Such an utterance, for example, is that of Chief Justice Marshall at the close of his decision in Brown *v.* Maryland, where he says that he "supposes" that the principles he has just applied to a case arising in connection with foreign commerce would also apply in a case of commerce among the states.[21] This pronouncement is obviously an aside upon a point not argued before the court and it is quite justifiably ignored by Chief Justice Taney in his opinion in the License cases,[22] whereas the rest of Marshall's opinion in Brown *v.* Maryland Taney treats as law, though the entire second portion of it, dealing with the commerce clause, was unnecessary, as the immediate issue before the court had already been disposed of under Article I., Section 10 of the Constitution.

Chief Justice Taney had therefore, it appears, an undeniable right to canvass the question of Scott's servitude in support of his decision that Scott was not a citizen of the United States, and he had the same right to canvass the question of the constitutionality of the Missouri Compromise in support of his decision that Scott was a slave. To all these points his attention was invited by arguments of counsel and to all of them he might cast it with propriety by a well-established view of the scope of judicial inquiry in such cases. If then the decision rendered by six of the nine judges on the bench, that the Missouri Compromise was unconstitutional, is to be stigmatized as unwarrantable, which is all that the court of history can do with it, it is not by pronouncing it to have been *obiter dictum* but by discrediting, from the standpoint of the history of constitutional law antedating the decision, the principles upon which it was rested.

Turning then to consider the constitutional decision directly, we find our task simplified to this extent: that the entire court, majority and dissenting minority alike, are in unanimous agreement upon the proposition that, whatever the source of its power, whether Article IV, Section 3 of the Constitution or the right to acquire territory and therefore to

[20] R. I. *v.* Mass., 12 Pet. 744 (1838), and Prigg *v.* Pa., 16 Pet. 539 (1842). See also Taney's own opinion in United States *v.* Booth, 21 How. 506 (1858).

[21] 12 Wheat. 419, 449.

[22] 5 How. 504, 574–578; see also J. McLean, *ibid.*, 594.

govern it, Congress in governing territory is bound by the Constitution — a proposition to which the court has always adhered, though there has been latterly some alteration of opinion as to what provisions of the Constitution control Congress in this connection. And this was the question that troubled the majority in the Dred Scott case. The Missouri Compromise was unconstitutional, that was certain; but just why — that was immensely uncertain. The extremist position of all was taken by Justice Campbell, whose doctrine was that the only power Congress had in the territories, in addition to its powers as the legislature of the United States, was the power to make rules and regulations of a conservatory character "for the preservation of the public domain, and its preparation for sale or disposition." From this it was held to follow that whatever the Constitution and laws of the states "validly determine to be property, it is the duty of the Federal Government, through the domain of jurisdiction merely Federal, to recognise to be property."[23] This of course is the extremest Calhounism, from which it came later to be deduced, with perfect logic, that it was the duty of the federal government, not only to admit slavery into the territory, but to protect it there. But, as Benton showed in his famous *Examination of the Dred Scott Case*, this particular phase of Calhounism was, at the date of the Dred Scott decision, less than ten years old.

And it is at this point that we come upon the second error I had in mind at the outset of this paper, an error traceable to Benton, but ever since repeated by historians of the Dred Scott decision, namely, the assumption that that decision rested exclusively upon Calhounist premises. Nothing however could be farther from the fact, for though Justice Daniel of Virginia seems to go almost as far as Campbell in representing the power of Congress in governing the territories as a mere proprietary power of supervision, yet even he rejects Campbell's notion that Congress was the mere trustee of the states; while Justices Catron of Tennessee, an old Jacksonian Democrat, Grier of Pennsylvania and of similar traditions, Wayne, a southern Whig, and the Chief Justice himself, could by no means consent thus to read the Constitution through the spectacles of the prophet of nullification. Upon what grounds then were these judges to rest their pronouncement of the unconstitutionality of the Missouri Compromise? Let us first take up the case of Catron and then turn to that of the Chief Justice, who spoke upon this point for himself, for Grier and Wayne, and to a great extent, for Daniel.

Catron paid his respects to the Calhounist point of view in the following words: "It is due to myself to say, that it is asking much of a judge, who has for nearly twenty years been exercising jurisdiction, from the western Missouri line to the Rocky Mountains, and on this under-

---

[23] Rep. 509–517; the quotations are from pp. 514 and 515.

standing of the Constitution," namely that Congress has power really to govern the territories, "inflicting the extreme penalty of death for crimes committed where the direct legislation of Congress was the only rule, to agree that he had been all the while acting in mistake, and as an usurper." Setting out from this extremely personal point of view, Catron found that Congress possessed *sovereignty* over its territory, limited however in this case by the treaty with France, with which the anti-slavery article of the Missouri Compromise was, he held, incompatible, and always by the spirit of the Constitution, which stipulates for the citizens of each state the rights and privileges of citizens of the several states and demands that the citizens of all states be treated alike in the national territory. It is true that Catron draws the idea of the equality of the states to his support, but his concern is plainly for the rights of citizenship rather than the prerogatives of statehood.[24] And in this connection it is worth recalling that almost exactly thirty years before, as Chief Justice of Tennessee, Catron had rendered the decision in Van Zant *v.* Waddell,[25] which is the first decision in which the concept of class legislation is distinctly formulated as a constitutional limitation, and which is a landmark in the history of American constitutional law.

But the most strongly nationalistic, or more precisely *federalistic*, of all the opinions upon the constitutional question was that of the Chief Justice, who again followed Marshall in tracing the power of Congress to govern territories to its power to acquire them. Upon what ground then was he to rest his condemnation of the Missouri Compromise? In one or two passages Taney speaks of Congress as "trustee," but it is as trustee of the "whole *people* of the Union" and for *all* its powers. The limitations upon the power of Congress must therefore, in this case as in all cases, be sought in the Constitution, "from which it derives its own existence, and by virtue of which alone it continues to exist and act as a Government and sovereignty."[26] From this it follows that when Congress enters a territory of the United States it cannot "put off its character and assume discretionary or despotic powers which the Constitution had denied to it": it is still bound by the Constitution. Therefore Congress can make no law for the territories with respect to establishing a religion, nor deny trial by jury therein, nor compel anyone to be a witness against himself in a criminal proceeding. "And," the Chief Justice continues, "the rights of private property have been guarded with equal care." They "are united with the rights of person, and placed on the same ground by the fifth amendment to the Constitution, which provides that no person shall be deprived of life, liberty, and property, without due process of law. And an act of Congress which deprives a citizen of the

[24] Rep. 522–527.
[25] 2 Yerg (Tenn.) 260.
[26] Rep. 448–449. The italics are mine.

United States of his liberty or property, merely because he came himself or brought his property into a particular Territory of the United States, and who had committed no offence against the laws, could hardly be dignified with the name of due process of law."[27]

Such then is the basis of the Chief Justice's decision: the "due process of law" clause of the Fifth Amendment. The striking feature of this objection to the prohibitory clause of the Missouri Compromise is its baffling irrelevancy. It is true that the Supreme Court had in 1855, in Murray v. the Hoboken Company,[28] laid down the doctrine that all legal process was not necessarily due process, that in providing procedure for the enforcement of its laws Congress was limited in its choice to the methods in vogue at the time of the adoption of the Constitution. But in the Dred Scott case no matter of procedure was involved, the antagonists of the law in question being opposed not to the *method* of its enforcement, but to its enforcement at all; not to the mode of its operation, but to its substance. If lack of due process therefore was chargeable in such a case, it was chargeable in the case of any enactment, penal or of other sort, no matter by what machinery it was designed to be carried out, if the general result of its enforcement would be to diminish someone's liberty or property for no fault of his own, save as determined by the law in question. In a word, legislation would be practically at an end.

Naturally, the amazing character of this doctrine did not escape the attention of Justice Curtis, who had been spokesman for the court in the Hoboken case. If the Missouri Compromise did indeed comprise one of a class of enactments proscribed by the Fifth Amendment, what then, Justice Curtis inquired, was to be said of the Ordinance of 1787, which Virginia and other states had ratified notwithstanding the presence of similar clauses in their constitutions? What again was to be said upon that hypothesis of the act of Virginia herself, passed in 1778, which prohibited the further importation of slaves? What was to be said of numerous decisions in which this and analogous laws had been upheld and enforced by the courts of Maryland and Virginia, against their own citizens who had purchased slaves abroad, and that without anyone's thinking to question the validity of such laws upon the ground that they were not law of the land or due process of law? What was to be said of the act of Congress of 1808 prohibiting the slave trade and the assumption of the Constitution that Congress would have that power without its being specifically bestowed, but simply as an item of its power to regulate commerce? What finally, if the scope of congressional authority to legislate was thus limited by the Fifth Amendment, was to be said of the Embargo Act, which had borne with peculiar severity upon the

27 *Ibid.*, p. 450.
28 18 How. 272.

people of the New England States, but the constitutionality of which had been recently asserted by the court in argument in the roundest terms.[29]

The plain implication of this apparently crushing counter-argument of Justice Curtis is that the Chief Justice was, at this point, making up his constitutional law out of whole cloth. Was this implication quite fair? The answer is that it was not, as a brief examination of the legal history involved will show.[30] What Taney was attempting to do in the section of his opinion above quoted was to engraft the doctrine of "vested rights" upon the national constitution as a limitation upon national power by casting round it the "due process of law" clause of the Fifth Amendment. But neither the doctrine of "vested rights" nor yet such use of "due process of law" was novel, and indeed the former was, in 1857, comparatively ancient. The doctrine of "vested rights" signified this: that property rights were sacred by the law of nature and the social compact, that any legislative enactment affecting such rights was always to be judged of from the point of view of their operation upon such rights, and that when an enactment affected such rights detrimentally without making compensation to the owner, it was to be viewed as inflicting upon such owner a penalty *ex post facto* and therefore as void. The foundation for the doctrine of "vested rights" was laid in 1795 by Justice Patterson in his charge to the jury in Van Horn *v.* Dorrance,[31] but more securely still by Justice Chase in his much cited dictum in Calder *v.* Bull,[32] in which he propounds what may be regarded as the leavening principle of American constitutional law, the doctrine, namely, that entirely independent of the written Constitution, legislative power is limited by its own nature, the principles of republican government, natural law and social compact.

Reposing upon this foundation, as well as upon the principle of the separation of the powers of government, the doctrine of "vested rights" soon found wide acceptance, being infused by Marshall in 1810 into the "obligation of contracts" clause of the national Constitution[33] and receiving from Chancellor Kent in 1811 its classic formulation in Dash *v.* Van Kleeck.[34] Presently, however, principles hostile to the doctrine began to appear, particularly the doctrine of "popular sovereignty," which insisted in the first place upon tracing the sanctity of the written Constitution, not to a supposed relation to fundamental rights but to its character as the immediate enactment of the sovereign people, and in the

[29] Rep. 626–627; the Virginia cases cited are 5 Call 425 and 1 Leigh 172, and the Maryland case is 5 Harr. and J. 107. He might have added 2 Munf. (Va.) 393.
[30] See the writer on "The Doctrine of Due Process of Law before the Civil War," *Harvard Law Review*, XXIV. 366 *et seq.;* 460 *et seq.*
[31] 2 Dall. 309 (1795).
[32] 3 Dall. 386 (1798).
[33] 6 Cr. 87, Fletcher *v.* Peck.
[34] 7 Johns. (N. Y.) 498.

second place upon the natural predominance of the legislature in government as comprising the immediate representatives of the people.
From 1830 on, the doctrine of the "police power," that is, the power of
the legislature to regulate all rights in the furtherance of its own view of
the public interest, began to supersede the doctrine of "vested rights" as
the controlling maxim of American constitutional law, receiving indeed
from Taney himself, in his opinions in the Charles River Bridge case and
License cases, a distinct impetus.[35] In this situation obviously the problem before those judges who wished to adhere to the older doctrine was
to discover some phrase of the written Constitution capable of subserving
the purposes of the doctrine of "vested rights." The discovery was made
by the North Carolina supreme court, in 1832, in the case of Hoke v.
Henderson,[36] in which the use made of the phrase "law of the land" of
the North Carolina constitution affords an exact counterpart to Taney's
use of "due process of law" in Scott v. Sandford. From North Carolina the
notion spread to New York, where it was utilized by Justice Bronson in
1843 in Taylor v. Porter.[37] The immediate source of Taney's inspiration,
however, was probably — though there is no hint of the matter in the
briefs filed by Sandford's attorneys — the decision of the New York court
of appeals in the case of Wynehamer v. the People in which, in the
interval between the first and second arguments of the Dred Scott case,
an anti-liquor law was pronounced unconstitutional under the "due
process of law" clause of the New York constitution, as comprising, with
reference to existing stocks of liquor, an act of destruction which it was
not within the power of government to perform, "even by the forms
which belong to due process of law."[38]

So much by way of justification of Chief Justice Taney. There is however another side to the matter. In the first place, as above hinted, Taney
was performing in Scott v. Sandford what for him was a distinct *volte
face* toward the doctrine of "vested rights." In the second place, he was
availing himself of what at the time was decidedly the weaker
tradition of the law. For not only had the doctrine of "vested rights," in
1857, generally gone by the board in its original form, but save in North
Carolina and New York it had, in its new disguise, practically no hold
anywhere. Essentially contemporaneous with the Wynehamer case were
similar cases in an even dozen states. In all save one the law was
upheld, and in that case it was overturned upon the basis of the doctrine
of natural rights.[39] Furthermore, in only one court, that of Rhode Island,

[35] 11 Pet. 420 (1837); 5 How. 504 (1846).
[36] 2 Dev. 1, preceded by Univ. of N. C. v. Foy, 2 Hayw. 310 (1807). See also
Webster's argument in the Dartmouth College case, 4 Wheat. 518, 575 *et seq.*
[37] 4 Hill (N. Y.) 140, preceded by the matter of John and Cherry Sts., 19 Wend.
676, and followed by White v. White, 5 Barb. 474, Powers v. Bergen, 6 N. Y. 358,
and Westervelt v. Gregg, 12 N. Y. 209 (1854).
[38] 13 N. Y. 378, 420 (through Justice A. S. Johnson).
[39] *Harv. Law Rev.*, XXIV. 471–474.

and that subsequently to the New York decision, was the "due process of law" or "law of the land" clause adduced as a limitation upon substantive legislation. Said the Rhode Island court on that occasion: "It is obvious that the objection confounds the power of the assembly to create and define an offense, with the rights of the accused to trial by jury and due process of law . . . before he can be convicted of it."[40]

This utterance may be taken, without hesitation, as decisive of the established interpretation of the "due process of law" clause in 1857. But all this is upon the assumption of a parity between Congress and the state legislature with reference to the doctrine of vested rights. In the third place, however, no such parity could, upon fundamental principles, have been justifiably conceived to exist at the date of Scott *v.* Sandford. The doctrine of "vested rights" rested upon the hypothesis of the recognition by the common law of certain fundamental rights which the people of the respective states possessed from the outset and which they could not be supposed to have parted with by mere implication in establishing the legislative branch of the government.[41] But these considerations were entirely irrelevant to the case of the legislative powers of Congress for two distinct, but equally powerful, reasons. In the first place it was a fundamental maxim in Taney's day that there was no such thing as a common law of the United States.[42] In the second place the power of Congress is not a loosely granted general power of legislation but a group of specifically granted powers. While, therefore, the federal courts from the very outset — though very sparingly in Taney's day — in cases which fell to their jurisdiction because of the character of the parties involved and in which therefore state law was to be enforced, repeatedly passed upon the validity of state laws under "general principles of constitutional law,"[43] the United States was always conceived strictly as a government of delegated powers, neither deriving competence from, nor yet finding limitation in, principles external to the Constitution. It was therefore always a fundamental principle of constitutional construction with Marshall that within the sphere of its delegated powers the national government was sovereign, not merely as against the rights of the states but also against the rights of individuals, a point of view which he sets forth with great explicitness in his opinion in Gibbons *v.* Ogden[44] with reference to the commercial power of Congress and

[40] St. *v.* Keeran, 5 R. I. 497; see also 5 R. I. 185, and 3 R. I. 64 and 289.

[41] See J. Patterson in Van Horne *v.* Dorrance, cited above; J. Story in Terrett *v.* Taylor, 9 Gr. 43 (1815), and in Wilkinson *v.* Leland, 2 Pet. 627 (1829).

[42] The leading case on this point is that of Wheaton and Donaldson *v.* Peters and Grigg, 8 Pet. 591, 658.

[43] See note 40, *supra;* see also J. Miller in Loan Association *v.* Topeka, 20 Wall. 655 (1874) and in Davidson *v.* New Orleans, 96 U. S. 97 (1877).

[44] 9 Wheat. 1, 196–197. The doctrine here stated is that the only limitations upon the power of Congress in the regulation of foreign and interstate commerce are the purely political limitations which arise from the responsibility of Congress to its constituents.

which Justice Daniel reiterates, so far as the rights of persons are concerned, as late as 1850 in United States *v.* Marigold.[45] True, Taney does
find the restriction which he is applying in the Constitution itself, namely,
in the "due process of law" clause of the Fifth Amendment, but what
this admission signifies is simply this: that his use of the clause in question can draw no valid support from the earlier history of the doctrine
of "vested rights," which upon fundamental principles was applicable
only as a limitation upon the legislative power of the states, and that
therefore its only justification is to be found in what, in 1857, was a
relatively novel doctrine peculiar to the courts of two states.

But though Taney's invocation of the "due process of law" clause of
the Fifth Amendment had so little to warrant it in the constitutional law
of the day, it has received subsequently not a few tokens of ratification.
Particularly is it noteworthy that the Republican opponents of the Dred
Scott decision, instead of utilizing Curtis's very effective dissent at this
point, now pounced upon the same clause of the Constitution and by
emphasizing the word "liberty" in it, instead of the word "property,"
based upon it the dogma that Congress could not *allow* slavery in the
territories.[46] After the Civil War Taney's Republican successor, Chase,
used the "due process of law" clause of the Fifth Amendment in his
opinion in Hepburn *v.* Griswold in the same sense in which Taney used
it in Scott *v.* Sandford, but only as a limitation upon the implied powers
of Congress.[47] This doctrine was flatly rejected by the Supreme Court,
speaking through Justice Strong, in Knox *v.* Lee.[48] Yet a few years later,
Justice Strong himself was elaborating the Taney-Chase point of view
in his dissenting opinion in the Sinking Fund cases, and connecting it
with Hoke *v.* Henderson.[49] Of late years too the same doctrine has shown
a disposition to crop up repeatedly, though it is uncertain whether it has
ever attained the dignity of formal decision.[50] Meantime of course, since
the middle nineties, when the Supreme Court began to regard itself as
the last defense of the country against socialism, it has been applying
steadily in modified form the North Carolina-New York doctrine in

[45] 9 How. 560.

[46] See the Republican Platform of 1860, para. 8. At this point the Republicans
followed McLean's opinion rather than Curtis's. Note the significance in this connection of the discussion as to whether slaves were recognized by the Constitution;
and also of the discussion as to whether slavery was recognized by natural law.

[47] 8 Wall. 603, 624; *cf.* J. Miller's cogent answer, *ibid.*, 637–638. Also, *cf.* the
Chief Justice's own decision in Veazie Bank *v.* Fenno. in the same volume of reports, 533 *et seq.*

[48] 12 Wall. 457, 551. C. J. Chase elaborates upon his earlier argument under the
Fifth Amendment at 580–582; he quotes the old dictum in Calder *v.* Bull to support
his position.

[49] 99 U. S. 700, 737–739.

[50] See the various justices in the Northern Securities Company case, 193 U. S. 197,
332, 362, 397–400. See also J. Harlan in Adair *v.* United States, 208 U. S. 161,
172–174; *cf.* J. McKenna, *ibid.*, 180–190, and J. Holmes, 191.

limitation of state legislative power under the Fourteenth Amendment.[51]

Turning finally to the consideration of our third main topic, namely the character of the issue between Chief Justice Taney and Justice Curtis upon the question of citizenship raised by Dred's attempt to sue in the federal courts, we find that it can be disposed of rather briefly. The usual view of the issue referred to is that it resolved itself into a dispute as to the relative weight to be given to the two conflicting sets of facts bearing upon the question whether negroes were in any case capable of citizenship at the time of the adoption of the Constitution, a dispute in which it is generally agreed that Justice Curtis had the weight of evidence on his side. This account of the matter is inaccurate. A careful comparison of Chief Justice Taney's opinion with that of Justice Curtis reveals the fact that the fundamental issue between the two judges, though it is not very specifically joined, is not whether there may not have been negro citizens of states in 1787 who upon the adoption of the Constitution became citizens of the United States, but from what source citizenship within the recognition of the Constitution was supposed to flow thenceforth. Upon this point, Curtis's view was that citizenship within the recognition of the Constitution in the case of persons born within the United States was through the states, while Taney's view was that a "citizen of the United States," to use his frequent phrase, always, unless descended from those who became citizens at the time of the adoption of the Constitution, owed his character as such to some intervention of national authority — was, in short, a product of the national government.[52] Curtis's theory, it can hardly be doubted, was that of the framers of the Constitution, wherefore Taney's pretense of carrying out not only the spirit but the very letter of the Constitution as it came from the framers, becomes at this point particularly hollow.[53] On the other hand, Taney's view is a very logical, and indeed inevitable, deduction from his whole body of doctrine with reference to the federal system. This doctrine, which came from the "Virginia School" after its disappointment at the failure of the Virginia and Kentucky Resolutions to establish the primacy of the states in the federal system, was the theory of the dual nature of that system: the states independent and sovereign within their sphere and the national government within its. This theory Taney had voiced from the beginning of his judicial career, so that, at this point at

[51] See the writer on "The Supreme Court and the Fourteenth Amendment," *Michigan Law Review*, VII. 642–672. See also Holden *v.* Hardy, 169 U. S. 366, and Lochner *v.* the People of the State of New York, 198 U. S. 45.

[52] Taney states his position on this point at pp. 404–406 and 417–418 of the Report, and Curtis states his at p. 581.

[53] Taney translates the "citizens of each State" clause of the Constitution as "citizens of the United States," but the derivation of this clause from the Articles of Confederation forbids any such notion. See also *Federalist,* no. XLII.

least, he was acting consistently with his past. Also, without doubt, the doctrine in question was pretty well established by 1857, both in judicial decision and in political thinking.[54]

To summarize: I conclude, first, that the Dred Scott decision was not *obiter dictum* within any definition of *obiter dictum* obtainable from a fair review of the practice of the Supreme Court, particularly under Marshall, in constitutional cases; secondly, that it was not based by the majority of those entering into it upon Calhounist premises; and thirdly, that Justice Curtis's supposed refutation of Taney's argument upon the question of Dred Scott's title to a *prima facie* citizenship within the recognition of the Constitution is a fiction. None of these results, however, goes far to relieve that decision of its discreditable character as a judicial utterance. When, as in this case, the student finds six judges arriving at precisely the same result by three distinct processes of reasoning, he is naturally disposed to surmise that the result may possibly have induced the processes rather than that the processes compelled the result, though of course such surmise is not necessarily sound; but when he discovers further that the processes themselves were most deficient in that regard for history and precedent in which judicial reasoning is supposed to abound his surmise becomes suspicion; and finally when he finds that beyond reasoning defectively upon the matter before them, the same judges deliberately gloss over material distinctions (as for example, in this case, the distinction between sojourn and domicile) and ignore precedents that they have themselves created (as for example, in this case, the decisions regarding the operation of state decisions upon questions of comity) his suspicion becomes conviction. The Dred Scott decision cannot be, with accuracy, written down as usurpation, but it can and must be written down as a gross abuse of trust by the body which rendered it. The results from that abuse of trust were moreover momentous. During neither the Civil War nor the period of Reconstruction did the Supreme Court play anything like its due role of supervision, with the result that during the one period the military powers of the President underwent undue expansion, and during the other the legislative powers of Congress. The court itself was conscious of its weakness, yet notwithstanding its prudent disposition to remain in the background, at no time since Jefferson's first administration has its independence been in greater jeopardy than in the decade between 1860 and 1870; so slow and laborious was its task of recuperating its shattered reputation.

---

[54] For a statement of this doctrine, see Taney's opinion in the United States *v.* Booth, cited above, note 19. It should be noted in passing that this elucidation of the real issue between Taney and Curtis on the citizenship question throws additional light on the close relation existing in Taney's mind between the question of Dred's servitude and that of his citizenship.

3

FRANK H. HODDER (1860–1935) taught for over four decades at the University of Kansas. He was a founding member of
the Mississippi Valley Historical Association and its president in
1924–1925. He wrote extensively on Kansas history and the pre-
Civil War era, particularly concentrating on Stephen A. Douglas
and the legislative and political history of the 1850's. While
Hodder's analysis of the Court's internal politics since has been refuted quite effectively, it nevertheless proved useful to many historians. In particular, his emphasis on personal motives, especially
those of Justice Curtis, and on the political machinations of the
other justices, served to buttress the ideas of the "repressible" and
"needless" war theories of Civil War interpretation that were dominant in Hodder's day.

It has come to be realized in recent years that the written history of
the United States during the decades preceding the Civil War, has been
based largely upon anti-slavery propaganda. With respect to no single
topic is this true in so high a degree as it is of the Dred Scott case. The
reason for this is clear. The dissenting opinions of McLean and Curtis,
especially that of Curtis, were immediately accepted by the Anti-Slavery
party as a final statement of the law of slavery, and in the South the
opinion of Taney was accepted in the same way. No party ever subjects
its platform to careful analysis or pays much attention to the criticism
of the opposing party. The histories, written largely in the North and in
New England, have followed the traditions of their section. . . .

Scott's case in the state courts dragged through six years.[1] In the first
trial in the Circuit Court of St. Louis County, judgment was against
Scott, but a new trial was granted, and in the second trial judgment was
given for Scott. The case was then taken on writ of error to the State
Supreme Court. It was in this court that the case first assumed a political
complexion. The struggle over the territory acquired from Mexico and
the Compromise of 1850 had revived the slavery controversy and in particular had raised the question of the power of Congress over slavery in
the territories. In March, 1852, the Supreme Court of Missouri decided
against Scott by a vote of two judges against one.[2] The majority of the

[1] Record of local cases reprinted in John D. Lawson, American State Trials (St.
Louis, 1914–23), XIII, 220–41. These records were missing for many years, having
been withdrawn by a local attorney who removed to California and found among
his papers after his death.
[2] 15 Missouri, 577–92.

3 Frank H. Hodder, "Some Phases of the Dred Scott Case." *Mississippi Valley Historical Review*, XLI (June 1929), 3–22. Reprinted by permission of the Organization of American Historians. Some introductory material and footnotes omitted.

Court based their opinion upon the ground that the laws of other states and territories had no extra-territorial effect in Missouri, except such as Missouri saw fit to give them. They repudiated the eight Missouri precedents in Scott's favor upon the ground that "times had changed" and that the free states, by obstructing the return of fugitive slaves, refused to recognize the law of slave states. The dissenting judge, Justice Gamble, thought that the earlier precedents ought to be followed.

At this juncture, it was agreed between the parties, at the suggestion of Roswell M. Field, who now appeared in the case as attorney for Scott, that the case be taken to the federal courts by bringing a new suit in the United States Circuit Court for the District of Missouri. The normal procedure would have been to take the case directly to the United States Supreme Court upon writ of error, but the Supreme Court had, in 1850, in the similar case of Strader v. Graham, refused to assume jurisdiction by this process. Moreover, the parties on both sides were desirous of securing the opinion of the Supreme Court on all the issues involved and, if the case had been taken up on writ of error, the Court, even if it had assumed jurisdiction, would have given judgment only on the points to which exception had been taken.

It is usually stated that Mr. Field was a radical opponent of slavery. That such was not the case is proved by his own letters and the testimony of Montgomery Blair. Mr. Field was opposed to slavery, but in common with many moderate men, both opposed and favorable to slavery, he thought that the question of the power of Congress over slavery in the territories was a legal question and that an authoritative decision of it by the highest court in the land would bring peace to a distracted people. For this reason, as he wrote Blair, he welcomed a decision of the question even though it should be against him. . . .

Suit was therefore brought in the United States Circuit Court for Missouri by Scott as a citizen of Missouri against Sanford as a citizen of New York. Sanford, in his first plea, denied the jurisdiction of the Court on the ground that Scott was a negro and therefore could not be a citizen of Missouri and entitled, thereby, to sue in a federal court. This is the celebrated plea in abatement, repeated reference to which in the opinions tends to confuse the non-professional reader of the case. The Court overruled the plea and the suit went to trial on the merits of the case. March 15, 1854, Judge Wells ruled that the facts were with Sanford, and the jury found accordingly. Scott then excepted to this instruction and the case was taken to the United States Supreme Court on writ of error. Ten days later, the Kansas-Nebraska Act was passed and the question of the power of Congress over slavery in the territories became more acute than ever.

On the very day that the Kansas-Nebraska Act was passed, it seems that Field wrote to Montgomery Blair to induce him to try the case in the Supreme Court.[3] Field was well acquainted with Blair who had lived fifteen years in St. Louis, but had recently removed to Washington to practice in the courts of the District of Columbia. Blair did not receive the letter at this time as he had gone to California to settle the affairs of his brother James who had died in San Francisco. December 24, 1854, Field again wrote Blair, without referring to his former letter, in regard to taking the case. The case was docketed, December 30, 1854, and upon this date Blair, having returned from California, wrote Field that he would take the case. Field replied, January 7, 1855, in a long letter suggesting the mode of procedure.[4] It was too late to prepare for trial before the adjournment of the Court for the spring recess, February 28, and the case necessarily went over until the next term of court. Blair made strenuous efforts to secure the assistance of other counsel but without success.[5] The case was argued for the first time from the 11th to the 14th of February, 1856. Blair alone appeared for Scott. H. S. Guyer, United States senator from Missouri, and Reverdy Johnson appeared for Sanford.

The case was taken up for conference on the 12th of May. Its disposition turned upon the point whether the question of the jurisdiction of the lower court could be raised, after Sanford had accepted its jurisdiction by pleading over to the facts and the case had come to the Supreme Court upon an exception taken to the instruction of the lower court on the facts. Upon this point, the Court divided sharply without reference to the judges' attitude toward slavery. Four of them — Taney, Wayne, Daniel, and Curtis — thought that the question of jurisdiction could be considered and four — McLean, Catron, Grier, and Campbell — thought that it could not. Nelson was inclined to the former view but, being uncertain, suggested that the case be re-argued upon the question whether or not the jurisdiction of the lower court was subject to review and, if so, whether or not Scott was a citizen of Missouri. This suggestion was accepted without objection.

Years afterward, James M. Ashley, member of Congress from Ohio, charged that the real reason for postponing the case was to prevent McLean, by a dissenting opinion, from making political capital in support of his candidacy for the presidential nomination at the approach-

[3] Bernard C. Steiner, *Life of Roger Brooke Taney* (Baltimore, 1922), 331.

[4] I am indebted to Miss Stella M. Drumm, librarian of the Mo. Hist. Soc., for copies of the Field letters.

[5] Blair in *Nat. Intel.*, Dec. 25, 1856. A part of this letter is printed in Charles Warren, *The Supreme Court in United States History* (rev. ed., Boston, 1926), II, 282, where the date is given as December 24.

One of the curiosities of the case is a long letter (ms.) from Judge Wells, dated, Feb. 12, 1856, advising Blair how to secure a reversal of his own decision in the Circuit Court. Wells's idea was that the Circuit Court was bound by the local law, but that the Supreme Court was not. The letter did not reach Blair until after his argument in the Supreme Court.

ing Republican convention.[6] Ashley was such a strong partisan that the charge is open to suspicion. In any event, there is no contemporary evidence to support it. Nelson could have had no interest in McLean's candidacy one way or the other, but he might have preferred to postpone the decision of the case until after the presidential election. In November, Buchanan was elected President.

From December 15, to December 18, 1856, the case was argued before the Supreme Court for the second time. Guyer and Johnson appeared for Sanford as before. George Ticknor Curtis assisted Blair in arguing the question of the power of Congress over slavery in the territories. After the second argument, Nelson reached the conclusion that the jurisdiction of the lower court was not subject to review. With the accession of Nelson, a majority of the Court held this view. February 14, 1857, the Court agreed to dispose of the case without raising the question of jurisdiction and without discussing the territorial question, and Nelson was asked to prepare the opinion of the Court on that basis.

It immediately appeared that McLean and Curtis intended to submit dissenting opinions covering the territorial question. Under these circumstances, Wayne thought it incumbent upon the southern judges to set forth their views of the territorial question, and finally convinced the reluctant Chief Justice of the necessity of so doing. At a subsequent conference, in the absence of Nelson, a majority of the judges requested Taney to prepare the opinion of the Court covering all the issues involved. When informed of this, Nelson insisted upon adhering to the opinion that he had prepared at the request of the Court, and Grier was inclined to concur with him.

When Buchanan began the preparation of his inaugural address, he was at a loss to know what to say about the Dred Scott case. Accordingly, February 3, he wrote to Judge Catron, with whom he was on intimate terms, asking whether the opinions would be delivered before the 4th of March. Catron replied on the 6th and 10th of February that the case had not yet come up in conference. On the 19th, after the conferences that began on the 14th, Catron wrote that the *Court had been forced to pass upon the constitutionality of the Missouri Compromise by the determination of two of their members to present dissenting opinions.* "A majority of my brethren will be forced up to this point by two dissentients," he said. In addition, he remarked how important it was that the majority should present a united front and asked Buchanan to "drop Grier a line" to that effect. Buchanan wrote immediately, as requested, and Grier replied on February 23, setting forth at considerable length the status of the case before the Court, remarking that the question of constitutionality would be forced upon them by the dissent of McLean and Curtis and adding that on account of "the weak state of the Chief

6 *Congressional Globe,* 40 Cong., 3 Sess., Ap. 211, Feb. 13, 1869.

Justice's health" the opinions would not be delivered until the 6th of March. It is thus clear that the primary responsibility for the discussion of the territorial question rests upon McLean and Curtis. It is eighteen years since the two letters of McLean and Curtis were published by John Bassett Moore in his edition of Buchanan's *Works*.[7] Their publication created a sensation at the time, but their import has not yet been embodied in our histories or our historical thinking.[8]

The opinion of Nelson, which but for the dissent of McLean and Curtis would have been the opinion of the Court, held that when a slave returns to a slave state his status is determinable by the courts of that state. That question had been decided by unanimous opinion of the Court, in 1850, in the case of Strader *v*. Graham. The Ordinance of 1787 and the Compromise of 1820, whatever their validity, had no extra-territorial force. Scott was a slave because the Supreme Court of Missouri had decided that he was a slave. The judgment of the lower court should therefore be affirmed. This was the only respectable opinion delivered by the Court.[9] It was not only correct in law, but it was best for the free states. It relieved them from any obligation to give effect to the laws of slave states except as they were bound by the fugitive-slave clause of the Constitution. Immediately thereafter, the courts of New York, in the case of Lemmon *v*. People, by giving freedom to eight slaves who were temporarily landed in New York City, en route from Virginia to Texas, affirmed the principle that every state has the right to determine the status of all persons within its jurisdiction.[10] Since that time the principle has been accepted as a matter of course and innumerable decisions have been

[7] Catron's letter of February 10 and Grier's of February 23 are in John Bassett Moore, *The Works of James Buchanan*. . . . (Philadelphia, 1910), X, 106–108. The earlier letters were discovered by Philip G. Auchampaugh and published in "James Buchanan, the Court and the Dred Scott Case," *Tennessee Historical Magazine*, X, 234–38. I am greatly indebted to Dr. Auchampaugh for calling my attention to them.

[8] Edward Channing, *A History of the United States* (New York, 1925), VI, 179, says that Moore adds, "apparently as a contribution of his own," that the action seems to have been brought about by the minority rather than by the majority of the Court. This was not a contribution of Judge Moore's but the distinct assertion of both letters.

Professor Channing gives the erroneous impression that the consideration of the case was unduly delayed by the Supreme Court. In view of the fact that the plaintiff was not prepared for trial at the term at which the case was docketed and that the case was twice argued, its disposition was unusually prompt. When the case was decided, there were six cases of earlier date that were still before the Court. Among them was the famous case of Ableman *v*. Booth which was not decided until more than a year later. Plaintiff's fees were billed to Blair and promptly paid. Defendant's fees were billed to Guyer and never paid. As a result the mandate was never issued. *Supreme Court Docket for 1856*. Scott's costs amounted to $154.68. Gamaliel Bailey raised this sum by asking Republican members of Congress to contribute $2 each. Horace White, *Life of Lyman Trumbull* (Boston, 1913), 83.

Scott and his family were transferred by Dr. Chaffee to Henry Taylor Blow, by whom they were emancipated.

[9] Cf. John Lowell and Horace Gray, *A Legal Review of the Case of Dred Scott* (Boston, 1857), 51, 57, reprinted from the *Law Reporter*, June, 1857.

[10] 20 New York, 562–644.

based upon it.[11] It is easy today to see that there should have been no other opinion in the Dred Scott case. Nelson is entitled to the credit of being the only member of the Supreme Court who thought clearly in the midst of seething political controversy. McLean, the first of the two judges whose dissent forced the consideration of the merits of the case, was the only Republican member of the Court. He was a perennial candidate for the presidency. He had been a candidate in the Anti-Masonic convention of 1831, was nominated by the legislature of Ohio in 1836, was mentioned in the Whig convention of 1848, received 196 votes in the Republican convention of 1856, and, although seventy-five years of age, still hoped for the nomination in 1860.[12] He took the unusual ground that a judge was under no obligation to refrain from political discussion and stoutly defended the propriety of his candidacy for the presidency. He wrote frequent letters on political questions to personal friends, and to the press for publication. He had long opposed slavery. In 1841, he had invoked the "higher law" against the interstate slave trade,[13] but in 1850 acquiesced in the opinion of the Supreme Court in the case of Strader v. Graham that the Court had no jurisdiction in the case of negroes claiming freedom in a slave state by reason of a temporary sojourn in a free state. Nevertheless, his dissent in the Dred Scott case was not unexpected. Even before the case had come to trial, he had written a newspaper editor in Ohio stating the ground that he intended to take.[14]

Quite otherwise was it in the case of Judge Curtis. Curtis was an old-line Whig. As a lawyer, before his appointment to the Supreme Court, he had been identified with the slave interest. In 1836, in the case of the slave Med, he had maintained that an owner might bring a slave to Massachusetts and hold her there in slavery until returning to a slave state.[15] It was surely a far cry from the contention that a slave could be held in a free state to the ground that Curtis took in the Dred Scott case, that temporary residence in a free state had the effect of emanci-

[11] See cases based upon this principle cited by Morris M. Cohn, "The Dred Scott Case in the Light of Later Events," *American Law Review*, XLVI, 548–57. The most famous are the New York cases refusing to give effect to divorces granted outside the state without jurisdiction of both the parties.

[12] McLean to Thaddeus Stevens, May 12, 1860. McLean Papers, Library of Congress.

[13] Groves v. Slaughter, 15 Peters, 508.

[14] McLean to Teesdale, Nov. 2, 1855. *Bibliotheca Sacra*, LVI, 737–38. Charles A. and Mary Beard's *Rise of American Civilization* (New York, 1927) II, 19 says that the McLean Papers show that McLean notified the Court of his intention to dissent. A careful examination failed to locate any such notification. Among the Papers are many letters congratulating McLean upon his opinion. Both McLean and Curtis violated the tradition of the Court by giving their opinions to the press in advance of official publication. 19 Howard, containing the opinions, was issued, May 28, and the *National Intelligencer* began reprinting them on the following day.

[15] Benjamin R. Curtis (ed.) *A Memoir of Benjamin R. Curtis* (Boston, 1879), 85–89. The *Memoir* was written by George Ticknor Curtis. Commonwealth v. Aves, 18 Pickering, 195–225.

pating a slave after return to a slave state. In 1850, Curtis defended the fugitive slave law in a speech in Faneuil Hall.[16] He was doubtless right in so doing, but his course was very unpopular in Massachusetts. Immediately after his appointment to the Supreme Court, while sitting as circuit judge, he committed himself, in a charge to a grand jury, to the extreme doctrine that any combination to resist by force the operation of any law constituted treason, and that all persons in any way connected with such combinations were guilty of treason, whether or not they were present at the time of the commission of an overt act.[17] In 1854, he procured the indictment of Theodore Parker and Wendell Phillips for obstructing legal process on account of speeches they had made on the Burns case at a public meeting, but subsequently quashed the indictment on a technicality.[18] The northern press denounced him savagely. The New York *Tribune* said: "He is not a Massachusetts judge — He is a slave catching judge, appointed to office as a reward for his professional support given to the fugitive slave bill."[19]

After the first argument in the Dred Scott case, Curtis wrote George Ticknor confidentially: "The Court will not decide the question of the Missouri Compromise line — a majority of the judges being of the opinion that it is not necessary to do so."[20] Apparently at that time he had no thought of dissenting from this opinion.[21] In 1854, before the Dred Scott case had come to the Supreme Court, Curtis had written Ticknor complaining of the salaries paid to the Court. "They are so poor," he wrote, "that not one judge on the bench can live on what the Government pays him."[22] Soon after the decision was rendered in the Dred Scott case, Curtis resigned from the bench, at the same time writing ex-President Fillmore that he had done so on account of the inadequacy of the salary.[23] Obviously if he were to return to Boston to practice law,

---

[16] *Ibid.*, 123–36.

[17] 2 Curtis, 630–36.

[18] Curtis *op. cit.*, 173–74, 177–78. Parker's *Trial of Theodore Parker for the Misdemeanor of a Speech in Faneuil Hall* (Boston, 1855) is violently partisan but there is no reason to doubt the correctness of his statement of Curtis' agency in procuring the indictment. The indictment was quashed in Stowell's case and nolle prossed in the others. U. S. *v.* Stowell, *Federal Cases*, 16409.

[19] Quoted in Warren, *op. cit.*, II, 262.

[20] Curtis, *op. cit.*, 180.

[21] After the first argument of the case, a correspondent of the New York *Tribune*, writing, April 10, 1856, reported that McLean, Curtis, and Grier would dissent from the majority of the Court. Quoted in Warren, *op. cit.*, II, 284. The guesses of the correspondents are so wide of the mark that they are not to be taken seriously. Certainly Grier had no thought of dissenting. C. H. Hill wrote George Ticknor Curtis, August 25, 1878: "Judge McLean and Judge Curtis were to dissent in a brief opinion to be drawn up I think by Judge McLean." Curtis, *op. cit.*, 235. This is Mr. Hill's recollection of a statement made by Judge Curtis in conversation nearly five years before, and the next sentence implies that he is uncertain about it. McLean and Curtis differed so widely on the subject of jurisdiction that they could scarcely have joined in one opinion.

[22] Curtis, *op. cit.*, 175.

[23] *Ibid.*, 250.

it was necessary to rehabilitate his reputation in Massachusetts. How far that consideration may have influenced him in deciding to dissent from the opinion that it was originally intended should be given by Judge Nelson is an interesting subject for speculation. Whether or not that was the purpose, it had that effect. Within a week after his resignation, he received seven retainers in important cases. His receipts from fees during the succeeding years amounted to $650,000 which was much better financially than being a justice of the Supreme Court.[24]

During the years that followed his retirement from the Court, Judge Curtis was strangely reticent in regard to the Dred Scott case. As he and his brother were both involved in the case, the one as judge and the other as attorney, it would have been natural for them to discuss it at some time, but they seem never to have done so. Upon one occasion Judge Curtis did discuss the case quite freely with a Mr. Clement H. Hill, and when George Ticknor Curtis wrote the *Memoir* of his brother, in 1879, he utilized the points that Mr. Hill could recall of this conversation five years after it took place.[25]

McLean and Curtis would have been justified in refusing to concur in the opinion of Nelson had they been able to present good reasons for doing so, but this they did not do. It is not necessary to summarize the whole of the two opinions. They followed different lines. McLean denied that the jurisdiction of the lower court was in question and refused to discuss it. In this way, he avoided his record in the case of Strader *v.* Graham. Curtis claimed that the question of the jurisdiction of the lower court was before the Supreme Court. He did not show that the lower court had jurisdiction, but he did show that the plea to the jurisdiction was insufficient and was improperly overruled. Then he showed that free negroes had been regarded as citizens in some states and unwarrantedly concluded that, if they were citizens in some states, they had a right to sue as citizens in any state. This might be true of free negroes, whose home was in a state in which free negroes were regarded as citizens, who happened to be sojourning in another state, but was not true of any other negroes and was not true of Scott. Even if Scott had claimed his freedom in Illinois, he could not have sued in the federal courts as a citizen of Illinois because Illinois did not recognize free negroes as citizens and Lincoln, in debate with Douglas, said that he would never be in favor of doing so.

Waiving the question of jurisdiction, both opinions came to the same point, viz. the effect upon Scott of his return to Missouri. That was the vital point in their view of the case. McLean said that a proper respect for the laws of Illinois, which is interstate comity, required that Missouri give effect to them. Curtis said that the rules of international law required that Missouri give effect to the laws of Illinois. The rules of inter-

[24] *Ibid.*, 264, 268.
[25] *Ibid.*, 234.

national law applied to the states of the Union constitute inter-state comity. Thus both opinions, stripped of extraneous issues and superfluous verbiage, come to this: that inter-state comity required Missouri to recognize Scott as a free man because he might have claimed freedom in Illinois and Wisconsin Territory.

For this assumption there was no foundation whatever. In the first place inter-state comity is dependent upon reciprocity. As Nelson pointed out, if a proper respect for the laws of Illinois required Missouri to give effect to them, then a proper respect for Missouri required that Illinois give effect to her laws and Scott would not have been free in Illinois. Not only did the free states not give effect to the slave laws of slave states, but it was notorious that many people in free states were assisting slaves in slave states to escape from their masters. In the second place, no state ever gives effect to the laws of other states when they are considered against public policy. Most of the southern states prohibited free negroes from coming to and settling within their limits. This had been the subject of violent controversy at the time of the admission of Missouri. Ever since the Vesey plot in Charleston, in 1822, the South had felt that free negroes were likely to foment slave insurrection and were, therefore, an element of danger. No state admits any person or class of persons whose presence is regarded as dangerous. This is so obvious that it would never have been questioned had the public mind not been warped by the controversy over slavery. As no chain is stronger than its weakest link, the arguments of both McLean and Curtis failed because untenable at the vital point, and did not justify their refusal to concur in the opinion of Nelson.

Before taking up the opinion of the Chief Justice, it should be said that Taney was opposed to slavery. In his early life, he incurred great odium by defending a Methodist minister, indicted for inciting a slave insurrection by condemning slavery in a sermon.[26] He manumitted the slaves he inherited except two, who were too old to take care of themselves and these he supported until their death. The position that he took in the Dred Scott case was the result of a mistaken sense of duty and not of any partiality for slavery. His opinion was designated by the *Reporter* as the opinion of the Court and properly so designated, since a majority of the Court concurred in the conclusions stated although not in the reasoning upon which they were based.[27] In recent years, his opinion has been extravagantly praised,[28] but like the opinions of McLean and Curtis, it was a political opinion, and like them, it failed at the crucial point.

[26] Tyler, *op. cit.*, 125–31. Gruber case in Lawson, *op. cit.*, I, 69–106.
[27] E. W. R. Ewing, *Legal and Historical Status of the Dred Scott Decision* (Washington, 1909) chap. v.
[28] *Ibid.* Also Cohn, "The Dred Scott Case," *Am. Law Rev.*, XLVI, 548–57. Lawson, *op. cit.*, XIII, xx.

In the first part, Taney undertook to prove that no negro could be a citizen. He did this in order to show that the plea to the jurisdiction of the lower court, that Scott was a negro, was sufficient and ought not to have been overruled. In order to maintain this thesis he took the untenable ground that citizenship was derived from the federal government. The framers of the Constitution, in order to secure its ratification, left many things to the states that they might have liked to regulate. Among other things they expressly provided that the qualifications for suffrage should be prescribed by the states. Inferentially, they left it to the states to determine who should be citizens, except in the matter of aliens, and there it remained until the adoption of the Fourteenth Amendment. The question whether any negro could be a citizen was not properly before the Court, but only the question whether this particular negro was a citizen, and that had already been decided by the proper authority — the Supreme Court of his own state. Curtis, by way of rebuttal, showed that in some states free negroes were regarded as citizens although, as a matter of fact, there was a distinct judicial opinion to that effect in only one state — the state of North Carolina.[29] It was this part of Curtis' opinion that gave it the appearance of weight. Taney undertook to distinguish between citizenship in a state and citizenship in the United States. Even if the distinction had been tenable, it was immaterial, since the right to sue in a federal court on the ground of diverse citizenship depended solely upon state citizenship. The phrase "citizen of the United States" was used in the Constitution only in prescribing the qualifications for the presidency and for members of Congress and was in no way involved in the case. At its close, Taney himself admitted that the discussion was unnecessary, since it appeared from the record that Scott was a slave and upon that ground final judgment was rendered. As it was unnecessary, it ought not to have been presented.

The second part of Taney's opinion was an argument to prove that the Court had a right to discuss the merits of the case after deciding that it had no jurisdiction. It is now conceded that technically Taney acted in accordance with what at that time was the practice of the Court.[30] Nevertheless, as Taney knew that the opinion he was about to give would create great public excitement and would be popularly regarded as *obiter dicta,* he ought to have acted with more discretion.

The third part of Taney's opinion was a discussion of the merits of the case. In this part he took the ground that the power of Congress to

[29] Reversed as far as voting was concerned, in 1854, by constitutional amendment. On negro citizenship, see Report on Citizenship, 62–66, *House Document* 326, 59 Cong., 2 Sess., Serial 5175. Also, Gordon E. Sherman, "Emancipation and Citizenship," *Yale Law Journal,* XV, 263–83.

[30] Ewing, *op. cit.,* chap. vi. E. S. Corwin, "The Dred Scott Decision," *The Doctrine of Judicial Review* (Princeton, 1914), 133–40.

govern acquired territory was derived from the treaty-making power rather than from the power of Congress to "make needful rules and regulations respecting the territory and other property of the United States." One view was as good as the other, and the source of the power was immaterial as long as the power was conceded. Taney then contended that the power must be exercised subject to the restrictions of the Constitution, among others the prohibition to take "life, liberty or property without due process of law." Taney claimed that slaves were property nationally. In support of this claim, he could point only to the clauses of the Constitution postponing the prohibition of the slave trade until 1808 and providing for the return of fugitives. Neither furnished any basis for the contention. The provision respecting the slave trade was a distinct recognition of the fact that the trade was objectionable and should be prohibited at the earliest possible time. As pointed out by both McLean and Curtis, the fugitive-slave clause expressly recognized the fact that slaves were property by state law. "Any person held to service in any state, *under the laws thereof*," escaping into another state shall be delivered up.

Property is whatever the law protects as such. All private property is based upon local law. As a matter of comity, every state recognizes whatever is property in other states, provided it be not objectionable in character, but every state refuses to recognize as property anything that is objectionable. The fugitive-slave clause of the Constitution, instead of being a general recognition of slaves as property, was precisely the reverse, the recognition of slaves as property in a particular case, viz. in the event of their escape to a place where they might not otherwise be so recognized. The prohibition to take property without due process of law, applied to slaves only where they were property, i.e., in slave states and in the event of their escape to free states. Upon this point the whole of Taney's argument falls to the ground. Moreover, an act of Congress, within the scope of its powers, would be due process of law and on this score, also, Taney's argument would fail.

It is not necessary to analyze the remaining opinions in detail. Grier concurred with Nelson but agreed with Taney in believing that the Missouri Compromise was unconstitutional. This attempt to take both sides was apparently the only effect of Buchanan's letter. Wayne and Daniel concurred absolutely with Taney. Campbell and Catron agreed with the principal opinions of Taney but reached their conclusions by different processes of reasoning. Both assumed that slavery was national but did not state the grounds of their belief. Both agreed that Congress must protect it in the territories because otherwise it would create inequality among the states. Campbell claimed that the power of Congress over the territories was limited to external regulation, while Catron claimed that it was plenary but inconsistently denied the power of Congress to prohibit slavery in them.[31] The consensus of the majority opinions was that slavery was national and that Congress could not prohibit it in the territories but must protect it there. In this way the Court sustained the so-called doctrine of non-intervention. The only point decided by the judgment of the Court was that the status of a slave, leaving a slave state and subsequently returning to it, was determinable by the courts of that state. The case was resented, not for what it decided, but for what the opinions portended.

All the territory acquired from Mexico, outside of the state of California, had been organized into the two territories of Utah and New Mexico, upon the condition that the status of slavery therein should be determined by the local courts subject to appeal to the Supreme Court of the United States. All of the territory acquired from France, north of the state of Missouri and extending from the Missouri River to the Rocky Mountains, had been organized as the territories of Kansas and Nebraska upon the same condition. It was clear that as soon as a case involving the status of slavery in any of these territories, aggregating approximately one third of the total area of the United States, should reach the Supreme Court, a majority of the Court would say that Congress could neither prohibit slavery nor authorize the people of the territory to do so, but must protect it. Most people believed that this decision had already been made. Buchanan in submitting the Lecompton constitution to Congress said in his message: "It has been solemnly adjudged by the highest judicial tribunal known to our laws that slavery exists in Kansas by virtue of the Constitution of the United States. Kansas is therefore as much a slave state as Georgia or South Carolina." When the President of the United States did not understand any better than that what had been done, it was not to be expected that the people would.

It is impossible to exaggerate the effect of the Dred Scott decision. It destroyed Douglas. Upon this question the issue was immediately joined between Lincoln and Douglas. Douglas was forced to fall back upon the doctrine of unfriendly legislation which he had originally promulgated in 1850. This enabled Lincoln to reply: "Judge Douglas says that a thing may be lawfully driven away from a place where it has a lawful right to be." Upon this issue the South deserted Douglas and the Democratic party divided. The Dred Scott decision revived the Republican party.[32] The party was nearly bankrupt for the lack of an issue. The Kansas issue

[31] Catron claimed that the Missouri Compromise was "void" because in conflict with the Louisiana Treaty, but also said that "it violates the most leading feature of the Constitution." He was very emphatic in his opinion that the question of jurisdiction was not before the Court. He feared that the Court might impugn the jurisdiction that he had exercised for nearly twenty years in the territory west of Missouri. Writing to Judge Samuel Treat (May 31, 1857), he expressed the fear that his view of the case would not reach the public through the publication of his opinion in the press. Ms.

[32] Albert J. Beveridge, *Life of Abraham Lincoln, 1809–1858* (Boston, 1928), II, 450, 453.

was worn out. People were tired of hearing of "bloody Kansas." Just at the right moment, the Dred Scott case provided a new issue and upon this issue Lincoln was nominated for the presidency and elected. The Civil War might not have been averted, but the only chance of averting it lay in the election of Douglas by a united party and the adoption of a new compromise which could have tided over the crisis until a larger degree of intercommunication and a better understanding between the sections had rendered possible a peaceful solution of the problem of slavery.

The most important recent discussion of the Dred Scott case is Professor Corwin's, but unhappily, at its close, he harks back to the old anti-slavery cry that Taney was "guilty of a gross breach of trust."[33] It was rather a fatal error of judgment. But obviously, whatever measure of condemnation is meted out to Taney attaches in even greater degree to McLean and Curtis, whose dissenting opinions caused Taney to abandon the original decision to dispose of the case without discussing the political questions involved. Of the three, the most blame falls upon Curtis. Taney had been brought up in the tradition that slavery was national, and at his advanced age it was doubtless difficult for him to change his opinions. McLean had long been associated with the anti-slavery movement and was blinded by political ambition. Curtis had no strong prepossessions or party affiliations, and it is difficult to explain his course except on private grounds. Had Curtis concurred with Nelson, there would have been no majority opinion of the Court that slavery was national and that Congress must protect it in the territories. In that event the Dred Scott case would never have been heard of and the whole course of American history would have been changed.

---

[33] Corwin, *op. cit.*, 157.

4

WALLACE MENDELSON was born in 1911 and received his doctorate in Political Science from The University of Wisconsin and his law degree from Harvard. He is Professor of Government at The University of Texas and has been Editor-in-Chief for the reports of the United States Commission on Civil Rights. His numerous writings on the Supreme Court, including this essay, reflect a deep belief in the wisdom and virtue of judicial restraint. In a recent book, *Conflict in the Court: Justices Black and Frankfurter* (1961), Mendelson offered a succinct and timely analysis of the modern clash over judicial philosophy in the Supreme Court. Professor Mendelson's collection of essays, *Capitalism, Democracy, and The Supreme Court* (1960), contains a fuller view of the Dred Scott case in the perspective of Chief Justice Taney's entire judicial career.

The *Dred Scott* decision[1] is not, as our folklore would have it, the classically worst, or even a typical, assertion of judicial supremacy. To be sure, earlier abolitionist-inspired interpretations have given way to a rather general acceptance of it as a "sincere" judicial effort to solve a nation-wrecking problem.[2] But even this latter view obscures the fact that the most criticized decision in American jurisprudence was undertaken only upon explicit invitation of Congress and did no more than give constitutional sanction to a position held long and persistently by most contemporary voters. This view — the present thesis — obviates an otherwise tantalizing paradox: that Chief Justice Taney should suddenly in 1857 abandon that Jacksonian respect for popular sovereignty and the democratic processes which for twenty years had been the hallmark of his philosophy upon the bench.[3]

Acquisition of the Mexican and Oregon territories during the administration of President Polk (1845–1849) revived the old problem of the extension of slavery — the problem which in the case of the Louisiana Purchase had been settled by the Missouri Compromise of 1820. After

---

[1] Scott v. Sandford, 19 How. 393 (U.S. 1857), holding the Missouri Compromise unconstitutional on the ground, *inter alia*, that the Fifth Amendment prohibited Congress from interfering with slavery in the territories.

[2] See, for example, Charles Evans Hughes, *Roger Brooke Taney*, 17 A. B. A. J. 785, 787 (1931).

[3] See Mendelson, *Chief Justice Taney — Jacksonian Judge*, 12 U. of Pitt. L. Rev. 381 (1951).

---

4 Wallace Mendelson, "Dred Scott's Case — Reconsidered." *Minnesota Law Review,* XXXVIII (December 1953), 16–28. Reprinted by permission. Copyright 1953 by the Minnesota Law Review Foundation.

full discussion, President Polk and the members of his Cabinet unanimously agreed that the principle of the old compromise should be adapted to current needs.[4] That is, the 36° 30′ parallel should be recognized as the boundary between freedom and slavery from the Louisiana territory to the Pacific. But that simple solution was no longer acceptable in the North. The Wilmot Proviso, supported by resolutions of all but one of the northern state legislatures, would have prohibited by act of Congress the introduction of slavery into any of the newly acquired domain.[5] After its adoption by the House of Representatives in February, 1847, southern leaders abandoned their willingness to compromise on the old Missouri basis and took the line that Congress had no power to proscribe slavery anywhere.[6] Thus in typical American fashion a vexing problem of social policy was translated into constitutional jargon and became a "legal question." Supporters of Wilmot's Proviso, of course, assumed Congressional power to outlaw slavery in the territories, while the Northern ultras held that the Constitution itself prohibited slavery in the territories. Southerners found constitutional denial of national power to interfere with their peculiar proprietary interests.[7] Upon the issue so joined Congress was unable to make a decision, for while the Northern view prevailed in the House, it was blocked in the Senate. Accordingly settlers in the new territory had to do without government because Congress could not decide whether they must do without slaves.[8]

This impasse is the background of the attempted Clayton Compromise[9] of mid-1848 whereby Congress in organizing the California and New Mexico territories was to remain silent on the subject of slavery, leaving its introduction or prohibition to rest

". . . on the Constitution, as the same should be expounded by the [territorial] judges, with a right to appeal to the Supreme Court of the United States."[10]

In this manner, according to Senator Clayton of Maine, Congress would "avoid the decision of this distracting question, leaving it to be settled by the silent operation of the Constitution itself. . . ."[11] After elaborate debate the Clayton Compromise was passed in the Senate and defeated in the House (the latter still intent upon the Wilmot Proviso). But the essence of Clayton's proposal lived on to be incorporated in the great

[4] The Diary of James K. Polk, entries for Jan. 5, 16, 1847 (Quaife ed. 1910).
[5] 1 Morrison and Commager, The Growth of the American Republic 598 (1942).
[6] Id: at 599–600; McLaughlin, A Constitutional History of the United States 512–513 (1936).
[7] For a review of the opposing constitutional theories, see *id.* at 514 *et seq.*
[8] 1 Morrison and Commager, *op. cit. supra* note 5, at 599.
[9] Cong. Globe, 30th Cong., 1st Sess. 950, 1002 (1848).
[10] *Ibid.*
[11] *Ibid.*

Compromise of 1850[12] and the Kansas-Nebraska Act of 1854[13] and to reach fruition in the *Dred Scott* decision.

In January, 1850, Henry Clay of Kentucky introduced in the Senate the famous resolutions which were the foundation of the Compromise of 1850. His second resolution, recognizing the incompatibility of the northern and southern views as to the power of Congress, proposed that

> ". . . it is inexpedient for Congress to provide by law either for its [slavery's] introduction into, or exclusion from, any part of the said territory; and that appropriate territorial governments ought to be established by Congress in all of the said territory . . . without the adoption of any restriction or condition on the subject of slavery."[14]

This was the doctrine of Congressional non-intervention with slavery in the territories which Lewis Cass, presidential candidate of the Democratic Party, had sponsored in his famous Nicholson Letter[15] of December, 1847 — and which Stephen Douglas was later to adopt and make famous under the banner of "popular [read territorial] sovereignty." But it was perfectly clear that Congressional silence would leave uncertain the legal status of slavery in the new domain. To obviate this, amendments to Clay's non-intervention provisions (in the bills embodying his resolutions) were offered by both northern and southern ultras to embody their respective constitutional views. Thus, for example, Senator Baldwin of Connecticut, offering one such amendment, observed:

> "I agree entirely in the sentiment which was advanced the other day by the Senator from Louisiana [Mr. Soule] that we ought not to pass a law which shall be understood in a different sense by those who cooperate in its passage. . . . The people demand a law, a rule for their conduct clear and intelligible. They do not ask us to give them a Delphic response, which may be interpreted in one way or another, according to the wishes of every inquirer. . . . The object of my amendment is simply to declare what we mean."[16]

But Senator Clay knew the futility of such "clarifying" amendments. It was in exactly those rapids that settlement of the territorial problem had been floundering since 1846. Congressional avoidance of the disputed issue and reference of it, as a constitutional question, to the judiciary, was precisely the essence of his compromise. As Clay put it, in answer to Baldwin:

---

[12] Embodied in four separate measures as follows: The Texas and New Mexico Act, 9 Stat. 446 (1850); The Utah Act, 9 Stat. 453 (1850); The Fugitive Slave Act, 9 Stat. 462 (1850); Act Abolishing the Slave Trade in the District of Columbia, 9 Stat. 467 (1850).

[13] 10 Stat. 277 (1854).

[14] Sen. J., 31st Cong., 1st Sess. 118 (1850); Cong. Globe, 31st Cong., 1st Sess. 245 (1850).

[15] McLaughlin, *op. cit. supra* note 6, at 512–513.

[16] Cong. Globe, 31st Cong., 1st Sess. 1146 (1850).

"The bill leaves in full force the paramount authority of the Constitution. . . . Now what ought to be done more satisfactory to both sides of the question, to the free States and to the slaveholding States, than to apply the principle of [Congressional] non-intervention to the state of the law in New Mexico, and to leave the question of slavery or no slavery to be decided by the only competent authority that can definitely settle it forever, the authority of the Supreme Court of the United States.

"The honorable Senator from Connecticut [Mr. Baldwin] on yesterday wanted the law settled. Suppose, then, we were to make a declaration of the law pleasing to the learned Senator . . . how if we were to attempt to settle this question could it be settled? In the first place we can not settle it, because of the great diversity of opinion which exists; and yet the Senator will ask those who differ with him in opinion to surrender their opinion, and, after they have made this sacrifice of opinion, can they declare what the law is? When the question comes up before the Supreme Court of the United States, that tribunal will declare what the law is."[17]

On this basis the slavery extension aspects of the Compromise of 1850 were settled. Congress simply delegated to the territorial legislatures of Utah and New Mexico all power over slavery which Congress itself might have, the extent of that power being the subject of vigorous dispute:

". . . the legislative power of the territory shall extend to all rightful subjects of legislation consistent with the Constitution of the United States [with certain exceptions not here relevant]."[18]

Then to facilitate settlement of the constitutional question, special liberalizing provisions were made in regard to federal court jurisdiction in slavery litigation. Thus after providing that "writs of error and appeals [to the Supreme Court of the United States] from the final decisions of said [territorial] supreme court shall be allowed, and may be taken in the same manner and under the same regulations as from the circuit courts of the United States, where the value of the property or amount in controversy . . . shall exceed one thousand dollars . . . ," special exception was made "in all cases involving title to slaves" where it was provided, "the said writs of error or appeals shall be allowed . . . without regard to the value of the matter, property, or title in controversy. . . ." Similarly "a writ of error or appeal shall be allowed to the Supreme Court of the United States . . . upon any writ of habeas corpus involving the question of personal freedom. . . ."[19]

---

[17] *Id.* at 1155. See the following for typical expressions of willingness to accept judicial settlement of the slavery extension problem: Yulee of Florida, Cong. Globe, 31st Cong., 1st Sess., appendix, 95–96 (1850); Phelps of Vermont, *id.* at 95; Clay of Kentucky, *id.* at 916; Davis of Mississippi, *id.* at 154; Turney of Tennessee, *id.* at 297.

[18] The Texas and New Mexico Act, 9 Stat. 446 (1850); The Utah Act, 9 Stat. 453 (1850).

[19] *Ibid.*

These provisions are a verbatim copy of parts of the Clayton Compromise which had been added to Senator Clayton's original bill after Senators Hamlin and Corwin had raised the point that the normal federal jurisdictional amount of one thousand dollars would prevent effective operation of Clayton's proposal to shunt the slavery extension issue over to the courts.[20] It is, of course, significant that both provisions liberalizing the right of appeal to the Supreme Court (that relating to habeas corpus as well as the eliminating the "jurisdictional amount") were new in federal law. Senator Corwin's comment on the scheme is apposite — Congress had enacted a law suit, not a law.[21]

This interpretation was adopted by Senator Stephen A. Douglas' Committee on Territories which reported out on January 4, 1854, the Dodge Bill for the organization of the Nebraska Territory:

"In the judgment of your committee, those measures [the acts constituting the Compromise of 1850] were intended to have a far more comprehensive and enduring effect than the mere adjustment of the difficulties arising out of the recent acquisition of Mexican territory. They were designed to establish certain great principles, which would . . . in all time to come, avoid the perils of a similar agitation, by withdrawing the question of slavery from the halls of Congress and the political arena, and committing it to the arbitrament of those who were immediately interested in, and alone responsible for its consequences. [There follows recital of some of the arguments as to the constitutionality of slavery in the territories and of the power of Congress with respect to slavery.] Your committee do not feel themselves called upon to enter into the discussion of these controverted questions. They involve the same grave issues which produced the agitation, the sectional strife, and the fearful struggle of 1850. As Congress deemed it wise and prudent to refrain from deciding the matters in controversy then . . . by any act declaratory of the true intent of the Constitution . . . so your committee are not now prepared to recommend a departure from the course pursued on that memorable occasion . . . by any act declaratory of the meaning of the Constitution in respect to the legal points in dispute . . . it is apparent that the compromise measures of 1850 affirm and rest upon the following propositions — First: That all questions pertaining to slavery in the territories, and in the new States to be formed therefrom, are to be left to the decision of the people residing therein. . . .

"Second: That all cases involving title to slaves, and "questions of personal freedom" are referred to the adjudication of the local tribunals, with the right of appeal to the Supreme Court of the United States."[22]

[20] Cong. Globe, 30th Cong., 1st Sess. 988, 989, 1002–1005 (1848). Senator Johnson of Maryland introduced the amendment (p. 1002). It will be noted that his amendment is erroneously reported to read "title to lands" instead of "title to slaves." The matter is corrected in sections 24 and 31 of the Bill as passed by the Senate (pp. 1004, 1005).

[21] McLaughlin, op. cit. supra note 6, at 514.

[22] Sen. Rep. No. 15, 33d Cong., 1st Sess. (1854).

The resulting legislation was the fateful Kansas-Nebraska Act of 1854.[23] In course of the Congressional debates on this Act, the familiar arguments were made in favor of the familiar "clarifying amendments. This time we know on the authority of Senator Judah K. Benjamin of Louisiana, the problem was settled in caucus where:

> "Morning after morning we met for the purpose of coming to some understanding upon that very point [slavery in the territories]; and it was finally understood by all, agreed to by all, made the basis of compromise by all the supporters of that bill, that the territories should be organized with a delegation by Congress of all the power of Congress in the Territories, and that the extent of the power of Congress should be determined by the Courts."[24]

In the course of debate on the Kansas-Nebraska Bill, Senator Brown gives what Allen Johnson calls the southern viewpoint:

> "If I thought that, in voting for the bill as it now stands, I was conceding the right of the people in the territory, during their territorial, existence, to exclude slavery, I would withhold my vote. . . . It [the bill] leaves the question where I am quite willing it should be left — to the ultimate decision of the courts. It is purely a judicial question, and if Congress will refrain from intimating an opinion, I am willing that the Supreme Court shall decide it. But, Sir, I have too often seen that Court sustaining the intentions of Congress, to risk a decision in my favor, after Congress has decided against me. The alien and sedition laws, the bank law, the tariff law have all been decided constitutional. And why? Not, in my opinion, because they were so, but because the Supreme Court, as a coordinate Department of Government, was disinclined to clash with the other Departments. If this question is allowed to go before the Supreme Court, free from the influence of a Congressional pre-judgment, I will abide the result though it be against me."[25]

These remarks by Senator Brown may not be crucial in themselves, though Brown was one of the congressional leaders of his day. But they become highly significant through endorsement by the Chairman of the Senate Committee on the Judiciary, Mr. Butler, who joined in and then supplemented Brown's remarks as follows:

[23] 10 Stat. 277 (1854).

[24] Cong. Globe, 36th Cong., 1st Sess. 1966 (1860). Senator Benjamin said the same thing in greater detail prior to the *Dred Scott* decision. Cong. Globe, 34th Cong., 1st Sess. 1093 (1856). For corroboration by Douglas and Hunter, see Cong. Globe, 35th Cong., 2d Sess. 1258 (1859); 33d Cong., 1st Sess., appendix, 224 (1854). See also letter of Congressman A. H. Stephens, May 9, 1860, in Cong. Globe, 36th Cong., 1st Sess., appendix, 315–316 (1860). As to the "clarifying" amendments see, for example, the efforts of Senator Chase, Cong. Globe, 33d Cong., 1st Sess. 421–423 (1854).

[25] Cong. Globe, 33d Cong., 1st Sess., appendix, 232 (1854); Johnson, Stephen A. Douglas 247 (1908).

"I am willing . . . to trust judges upon the bench who are sworn to administer the law and observe the Constitution. I am therefore perfectly willing to trust this bill to fortune under the impulse of justice."[26]

Accordingly what the Douglas Committee on Territories called the "great principles" of the Compromise of 1850 were embodied in the Kansas-Nebraska Act. After declaring the Missouri Compromise "inoperative and void" the measure in Section 14 provided that:

"[It is] the true intent and meaning of this act not to legislate slavery into any territory or State, nor to exclude it therefrom, but to leave the people thereof perfectly free to form and regulate their domestic institutions in their own way, *subject only to the Constitution of the United States.* . . . [italics added]."[27]

The second great principle of the 1850 settlement relating to appeals to the Supreme Court on slavery questions was reproduced verbatim in the Kansas-Nebraska Act's Section 9.

Two years later, in July, 1856, only eight months prior to the *Dred Scott* decision, Senator Lyman Trumbull of Illinois, in the course of a debate on the admission of Kansas as a state, offered what was probably the last "clarifying" amendment. Trumbull wanted the above quoted "true intent and meaning" clause of the Kansas-Nebraska Act glossed with the assertion that the latter

". . . was intended to, and does confer, upon, or leave to the people of the Territory of Kansas full power at any time, through its Territorial Legislature, to exclude slavery from said Territory, or to recognize and regulate it therein."[28]

This, of course, was simply the Northern view, repudiated by the South, that Congress and hence by derivation the Territories, had power under the Constitution to regulate territorial slavery.

Senator Cass of Michigan answered Trumbull in the following terms:

"It is said there is a difference of construction between the North and the South on the Kansas-Nebraska Act. . . . The difference does not result from the words of that bill, but from the nature of things. The North and the South construe the Constitution differently. . . . The different constructions of . . . [the Kansas-Nebraska Act] result from no equivocations of it, but from the fact that here is an important constitutional question undetermined by the supreme judicial authority; and in the meantime individuals in different sections of the Union put their own constructions on it . . . . There is no power which the Senator from Illinois can use—no words which he can put into an Act of Congress, that will remove this constitutional doubt until it is finally settled by the proper tribunal."[29]

[26] *Id.* at 240.
[27] 10 Stat. 227 (1854).
[28] Cong. Globe, 34th Cong., 1st Sess., appendix, 796 (1856).
[29] *Id.* at 797–798.

Senator Douglas whose genius got the Compromise of 1850 and the Kansas-Nebraska Act through Congress, suspecting that his colleague from Illinois was attempting to get commitments that would destroy Douglas at home, answered Trumbull as follows:

"My opinion [on slavery in the territories] . . . has been well known in the Senate for years. . . . I told them [in the Kansas-Nebraska debates] it was a judicial question. . . . My answer then was and now is, that if the Constitution carries slavery there [into the territories] let it go . . . but, if the Constitution does not carry it there, no power but the people can carry it there. . . . I stated I would not discuss this legal question, for by the bill we referred it to the Courts."[30]

Thereupon the Trumbull amendment was voted down.

Was reference of the slavery extension issue to the judiciary understood and acceptable outside of Congress? One month after the Trumbull amendment debate, and some seven months before the *Dred Scott* decision, which he was to condemn so bitterly, Abraham Lincoln said in a public speech at Galena, Illinois:

"Do you [Democrats] say that such restrictions of slavery [in the territories] would be unconstitutional and that some of the Statutes would not submit to its enforcement? I grant you that an unconstitutional act is not a law; but I do not ask, and will not take your construction of the Constitution. The Supreme Court of the United States is the tribunal to decide such questions, and we [Republicans] will submit to its decisions. . . ."[31]

There had been some doubt as to whether President Pierce would sign the Kansas-Nebraska Act for he had been suspected of free-soilism. To resolve any such doubts Secretary of War Jefferson Davis arranged a conference between the President and a number of leading Senators and Congressmen where administration support for the measure was secured.[32] Indeed as it turned out the President personally believed the Missouri Compromise unconstitutional, but rather than repeal by the Kansas-Nebraska Act he favored a "guarantee of rights of persons and property in accordance with the Constitution, and would leave it to the Supreme Court to decide what those rights were."[33] In his last message to Congress on December 22, 1856, President Pierce in effect endorsed the *Dred Scott* decision in advance:

"All that the repeal [of the Missouri Compromise by the Kansas-Nebraska Act] did was to relieve the statute book of an objectionable enactment, unconstitutional in effect and injurious in terms to a large portion of the states."[34]

[30] *Id.* at 797.

[31] Speech at Galena, Illinois, July 26, 1856, II Collected Works of Abraham Lincoln 354–355 (Basler ed. 1953).

[32] Simms, A Decade of Sectional Controversy 59–60 (1942).

[33] *Ibid.*

[34] 5 Richardson, *A Compilation of the Messages and Papers of the Presidents* 403 (1903).

Pierce had nothing but the highest praise for the Kansas-Nebraska Act. In a historical review of the slavery controversy he condemned the Missouri settlement as conducive to sectional strife and attributed Buchanan's victory in the presidential election of the preceeding month to the desire of the people to have a termination of that difficulty.[35]

In his inaugural address two days before the *Dred Scott* decision President-elect Buchanan, referring to the problem of slavery in the territories, said:

> "[I]t is a judicial question, which legitimately belongs to the Supreme Court of the United States before whom it is now pending, and will, it is understood, be speedily and finally settled. . . . The whole Territorial question being thus settled upon the principle of popular sovereignty — a principle as ancient as free government itself — everything of a practical nature has been decided."[36]

Clearly the treatment of slavery in the territories as a judicial question by important political figures on such occasions indicates a rather general public acceptance of that mode of settlement. Similarly in his first public mention of the matter after the *Dred Scott* decision Douglas explained that by the Kansas-Nebraska Act Congressional power over slavery in the territories had been referred to the Supreme Court.[37] The latter having spoken, it was the duty of all good citizens to accept the decision. Indeed, Douglas praised the Court for having passed over mere technicalities and turned its decision upon the true merits of the issue.[38]

We must now go back to trace the history of Dred Scott's litigation.[39]

[35] *Ibid.*

[36] *Id.* at 431. These remarks are famous in connection with evidence now available which indicates that Buchanan had advance notice of what the *Dred Scott* decision was to be. On this aspect of the matter see Swisher, Roger B. Taney, c. 24 (1935). Whether he had advance notice or not, the thoughts expressed in that public utterance make it quite plain that on the eve of the *Dred Scott* decision there was nothing unusual in the proposition that slavery in the territories was a constitutional question for the judiciary to settle.

[37] Speech to the Grand Jury, Springfield, Illinois, June 12, 1857. See Milton, The Eve of Conflict 260 (1934). It will be noted, of course, that it was Douglas who won the Lincoln-Douglas debates, in the sense that it was he who won the prize at stake, a seat in the United States Senate. In that campaign the meaning and implications of the *Dred Scott* case were thoroughly canvassed by its leading critic and its leading apologist.

Of course the *Dred Scott* case did not arrive at the Supreme Court via the procedural (*i.e.,* jurisdiction-liberalizing) route provided in either the Compromise of 1850 or the Kansas-Nebraska Act, but, as Douglas recognized in the Grand Jury Speech, it did dispose of the substantive issue contemplated by that legislation. Lincoln's recognition of the latter point is implicit in his "House-divided" speech (Springfield, Illinois, June 17, 1858) where he sees a conspiracy between "Stephen [Douglas], Franklin [Pierce], Roger [Taney], and James [Buchanan]" — the main elements of their "plot" being the language of the Kansas-Nebraska Act, the *Dred Scott* decision and the *a priori* endorsements thereof by both Presidents.

[38] *Id.* at 260.

[39] See 2 Beveridge, Abraham Lincoln c. 7 (1928); Swisher, *op. cit. supra* note 36, c. 24; and 3 Warren, The Supreme Court in United States History c. 26, 27 (1923).

Having lost a decision in the Supreme Court of Missouri,[40] Scott in late 1853 began a new action in trespass in the federal court at St. Louis against a resident of New York who claimed to be his master. Admitting that he had been a slave, the plaintiff claimed that when he was taken into territory made free by the Missouri Compromise he became free; that he had since acquired Missouri citizenship and was thus properly in a federal court on diversity grounds. Scott won on a plea in abatement which questioned his citizenship, but lost on the merits.[41] The case was argued on appeal in the Supreme Court of the United States in February, 1856.[42] At that time Mr. Greeley's New York Tribune reported that the case would probably be decided against Scott on "the pretext" that his voluntary return from free to slave territory (*i.e.*, the state of Missouri) restored his status as a slave; that the Supreme Court would thus "evade" the real issue (*i.e.*, the constitutionality of the Missouri Compromise), but that "an effort will be made to get a positive decree of some sort. . . ."[43] In April Justice Curtis wrote to a friend that the Court would "not decide the question of the Missouri Compromise line — a majority of the judges being of opinion that it is not necessary to do so. (This is confidential)."[44] On May 12 on the motion of Justice Nelson the case was put down for reargument. Mr. Greeley thereupon assailed the "black gowns" as "artful dodgers. The minority were prepared to meet the issue boldly and distinctly; but the controlling members were not quite ready for such an encounter of authority as could be produced; or perhaps not inclined to open the opportunity for a demolition of the fraudulent pretenses that have been set up in Congress on this question."[45]

Greeley, of course, was fishing in troubled waters and wanted at the very least what he had every reason to believe would be a strongly, pro-Republican opinion from Justice McLean for use in the presidential campaign of 1856. Justice McLean's ambitions for the presidency are, and were at the time, well known. Foiled in his apparent design to make immediate political capital via the *Dred Scott* case, McLean wrote "a long and thoroughly political letter — the letter of a candidate,"[46] publicly indicating his views on the constitutionality of the Missouri Compromise.[47] "It was because of this statement of Justice McLean and of the eagerness and expectation of the Republican press and leaders that the Supreme Court would pass upon the Missouri Compromise in its decision in the *Dred Scott* case, that Lincoln had said in the Fremont

[40] Scott v. Emerson, 15 Mo. 413 (1852).
[41] Dred Scott Collection, Missouri Historical Society, St. Louis, Mo.
[42] 3 Warren, *op. cit. supra* note 39, at 5.
[43] New York Tribune, Feb. 28, 1856.
[44] Curtis, The Life and Writings of Benjamin Robbins Curtis, LL.D. 180 (1879).
[45] New York Tribune, May 15, 1856.
[46] 2 Beveridge, *op. cit. supra* note 39, at 461.
[47] New York Tribune, June 16, 1856.

campaign [the Galena speech, quoted above] that that tribunal was the one to settle such questions, that when it did so, the Republicans would abide by what the Court held to be the law and Lincoln had challenged the Democrats to do the same. If they would not, 'who are the disunionists, you or we?' "[48]

After the presidential campaign was safely out of the way the case was reargued in December, 1856. Two months later, on February 15, Justice Nelson was directed to write the Court's opinion ignoring the constitutional issue entirely and turning the decision on the ground that regardless of Scott's status when he was in free territory he was, according to Missouri law, a slave when he voluntarily returned to Missouri and therefore could not come into a federal court on diversity of citizenship grounds.[49] But within a few days it became clear that Justices McLean and Curtis intended to give extended dissenting opinions emphasizing the constitutionality of the Missouri Compromise.[50] According to Justice Catron, this "forced" a majority of his brethren to take up that issue, and upon the motion of Justice Wayne the Chief Justice undertook to write his fateful opinion for the Court.[51] Something of Justice Wayne's motives and the motives of those who concurred in his motion, is seen in his observation that "[t]he case involves . . . constitutional principles of the highest importance, about which there had become such a difference of opinion that the peace and harmony of the country required the settlement of them by judicial decision."[52] As ex-Justice Campbell and Mr. Justice Nelson put it almost fifteen years later "[t]he apprehension had been expressed by others of the Court [as well as Justice Wayne], that the Court would not fulfill public expectation or discharge its duties by maintaining silence upon these [constitutional] questions. . . ."[53]

In the presidential campaign of 1860 Lincoln and Douglas held the positions they had taken in their famous Illinois debates in 1858 — the one bitterly rejecting the *Dred Scott* decision, the other supporting it. Breckinridge, nominee of the southern wing of the Democratic Party, also endorsing the famous decision, demanded its implementation by a Congressional "slave code" for the territories.[54] This was the South's answer to the Douglas Freeport Doctrine. Clay and Douglas had held the nation and the Democratic Party together by a compromise that removed the most vexing problem of the day from the political to the judicial arena. This entailed an understanding that, win or lose, each claimant would accept the judicial settlement when it should finally

[48] 2 Beveridge, *op. cit. supra* note 39, at 461–462.
[49] 3 Warren, *op. cit. supra* note 39, at 15.
[50] *Ibid.*
[51] *Id.* at 16.
[52] Scott v. Sandford, 19 How. 393, 454–455 (U.S. 1857).
[53] Quoted in Tyler, Memoir of Roger Brooke Taney, LL.D. 384–385 (1872).
[54] 1 Morrison and Commager, *op. cit. supra* note 5, at 636–638.

come. But the North proved unwilling to do so. The Republicans, notwithstanding Lincoln's Galena pledge, repudiated the *Dred Scott* decision outright.[55] The northern Democrats, following the "little giant," attempted escape by a legal quibble — the *Dred Scott* case, they held, ruled only upon the question of Congressional power over slavery. Their platform pledged them to await and accept a Supreme Court decision on the power of the territorial legislatures.[56] Upon the issues so joined Lincoln received 1,866,452 votes, as against a combined total of 2,226,738 for Douglas and Breckinridge. Lincoln's party obtained only a minority in each house of Congress.[57] This could hardly be called a popular repudiation of the principle of judicial settlement or indeed of the *Dred Scott* decision itself.

Shortly after the election, on the eve of Secession, Senator Crittenden, Clay's successor in the Senate as fate would have it, proposed a settlement which would have written an extended Missouri Compromise into the Constitution. He could not even get it through a Senate Committee![58] That approach to the slavery problem had not been politically feasible since the impasse of 1846–1850. Resort to war between the states followed not, as some would have it, because political settlement had been foreclosed by judicial action,[59] but more likely because the issues cut too deeply to be solved either by courts or legislatures. The real misfortune of the *Dred Scott* decision was that, duly distorted, it served as a powerful weapon for the Abolitionists — always a small, fanatical minority. The Court's fault, if it may be so described, lay in accepting the buck which Congress and the statesmen had passed, and in failing to anticipate the partisan, political use which its efforts could be made to serve.

[55] *Ibid.*

[56] Douglas spells out the constitutional theories behind this position in *The Dividing Line Between Federal and Local Authority, Popular Sovereignty in the Territories,* 19 Harper's New Monthly Magazine 519 (1859). His main point is that the territorial legislative power is not derivative but independent of, and broader than, Congressional power in respect to slavery.

[57] 1 Morrison and Commager, *op. cit. supra* note 5, at 637–639.

[58] Hicks, A Short History of American Democracy 363 (1943).

[59] See, for example, Jackson, The Struggle for Judicial Supremacy 327 (1941).

5

ARTHUR BESTOR, born in 1908 and educated at Yale University has taught at Columbia, and the Universities of Wisconsin, Illinois and Washington. In 1957–58 he was Harmsworth Professor of American History at Oxford. His *Backwoods Utopia* received the Beveridge Prize of the American Historical Association in 1950. Professor Bestor's following discussion of the Dred Scott case has been adapted from his provocative essay on the relationship between state sovereignty theories, the territories, and slavery. The author presents a unique treatment of the decision, interpreting it as a fulfillment of southern political drives for *national* protection of its peculiar institution in the territories, and as a stimulant to further southern demands for federal legislative guarantees.

. . . It is a curious fact that though the American Constitution was designed for an expanding nation, the western territories have always been anomalies in the scheme. It is conventional to say that the Constitution created a dual system, composed of the federal government and the states. In reality the Union has always comprised three elements, the federal government, the states, *and* the territories. Only in recent years have the latter declined to a place of relative insignificance in the constitutional structure. All but nineteen of the existing fifty states have passed through a formal territorial stage. Almost three quarters of the continental area of the United States has been, at one time or another, under a territorial government established by federal statute.

The anomalous position of the territories in the constitutional scheme is simply this: Within the parts of the Union fully organized into states, the Constitution recognizes the existence of two governments, state and federal, operating simultaneously but independently and acting directly upon individuals. To each government a sphere of authority is constitutionally assigned. International and interstate relations are the supposed province of federal action. Questions of domestic social policy — involving the exercise of "police powers," so-called — belong clearly to the sphere of action reserved to the states. In the territories, however, no state government, in a constitutional sense, exists. By whose authority, then, are local police powers to be exercised?

Before examining the possible answers, it will be well to take careful note of the practical importance of the question — one that seems, at

5 Arthur Bestor, "State Sovereignty and Slavery: A Reinterpretation of Proslavery Constitutional Doctrine, 1846–1860." *Journal of the Illinois State Historical Society* (Summer, 1961), LIV, 148–74. Reprinted by permission with certain stylistic changes and omissions in text and notes requested and approved by the author.

first glance, to belong to the realm of metaphysical speculation. Under ordinary circumstances, a precise answer was clearly unnecessary. A territory was simply an area in transition from unsettled wilderness to complete statehood. Whatever government existed *de facto* within a territory was bound to wield a police power for the time being, simply because it was charged with maintaining order. A rough and ready practicality, untroubled by elaborate theories about political structure, sufficed for carrying on the everyday affairs of a territory and handling (or postponing) its relatively simple problems. Territorial status was a temporary one. In the end, statehood would operate as an act of oblivion, curing or obliterating any theoretical irregularities that might have belonged to the territorial period.

This was true in most circumstances, but not in all. Slavery created problems of precisely the kind to convert these abstract and apparently trivial questions of constitutional theory into practical and momentous issues of constitutional law. The police power was, among other things, the power to deal with slavery. It was through their police powers that the slaveholding states enacted slave codes, it was through theirs that the free states abolished slavery. Whether or not slavery expanded into the territories thus depended upon how (and by whom) the police power was exercised there.

In the nature of the case, moreover, a decision on slavery during the territorial period would have permanent, not temporary, effects. If the police power were employed at the outset to protect the property rights of slaveholders, then slavery was likely to become so entwined with the institutions of the locality as to be in practice ineradicable. On the other hand, if the police power were used in such a way as to discourage the bringing in of slaves, then the territory would almost certainly produce a free-state majority when the time came to write a permanent constitution and seek admission to the Union.

Both parties to the controversy understood perfectly these implications. Lincoln, in a speech at Peoria on October 16, 1854, presented the antislavery argument against vesting the power of decision in the first settlers:

> Another important objection to this application of the right of self-government, is that it enables the first FEW, to deprive the succeeding MANY, of a free exercise of the right of self-government. The first few may get slavery IN, and the subsequent many cannot easily get it OUT. How common is the remark now in the slave States — "If we were only clear of our slaves, how much better it would be for us." They are actually deprived of the privilege of governing themselves as they would, by the action of a very few, in the beginning.

Proslavery spokesmen were equally opposed to allowing the settlers to decide. James S. Green of Missouri stated the reasons in a speech to the Senate in 1860. Unless slave property is protected in the territories from the beginning, he argued,

> nobody will go there except those who do not own slaves; and when they come to the determination of the question, there will not be an interest sufficient to justify the adoption of the law of holding slaves. The consequence, the inevitable consequence, will be — not another slave State, no expansion of the South, no outlet to the South; but cramped and confined within her present limits, she may prosper for a while, but she will ultimately languish for the want of the power of expansion.

To opponents and defenders of slavery alike, it seemed clear that the first decisions made in the territories would be the determining ones. However significant in theory might be the sovereignty of the state when eventually admitted to the Union, in practice this power — plenary but deferred — might well prove meaningless so far as slavery was concerned. Long before a state attained full standing, its social system could have been irrevocably fixed by decisions already made. Control of the police power during the territorial stage was thus the crux of the entire issue.

It was the Wilmot Proviso of 1846 that brought this issue to the forefront of American politics and thus began the fifteen-year crisis that finally swept the nation into civil war. Under debate was an amendment to a two-million-dollar appropriation bill requested by President James K. Polk, for the purpose, as he said, of paying "for any concessions which may be made by Mexico" in a future peace treaty. The principal object, the President hardly needed to explain, was "the adjustment of a boundary between the two republics" — in plain language, territorial cessions by Mexico to the United States. During debate in the House of Representatives, in the evening of August 8, 1846, David Wilmot of Pennsylvania moved the following amendment:

> *Provided,* That, as an express and fundamental condition to the acquisition of any territory from the Republic of Mexico by the United States, by virtue of any treaty which may be negotiated between them, and to the use by the Executive of the moneys herein appropriated, neither slavery nor involuntary servitude shall ever exist in any part of said territory, except for crime, whereof the party shall first be duly convicted.

The House adopted the proviso almost immediately, by a vote of 83 to 64. The Senate refused to accept it, then or later. But the fat was in the fire.

What made the Wilmot Proviso controversial? The answer requires a careful discrimination among constitutional principles. The proviso was in complete accord with the *law* of the Constitution, as understood up to that time. In banning slavery, the proviso used language almost identical with that of the Northwest Ordinance of July 13, 1787, adopted by the Continental Congress while the Constitutional Convention of 1787 was still sitting. After the adoption of the Constitution, Congress immediately re-enacted the ordinance and thereafter included the same prohibition, in virtually the same language, in a series of five territorial acts, from 1800 to 1838, and in the Missouri Compromise of 1820. The *power* to act on the matter had not, prior to 1846, been seriously challenged.

The principle that the Wilmot Proviso thrust aside was not a *law* of the Constitution, but a *custom* of the Constitution, which dated back to the First Congress. On December 22, 1789, North Carolina ceded its western lands to the Union, to be governed according to the principles of the already re-enacted Northwest Ordinance, "*Provided always* that no regulations made or to be made by Congress shall tend to emancipate Slaves." Congress accepted the condition and set up a Southwest Territory (later the state of Tennessee), explicitly providing that the antislavery section of the earlier ordinance should not apply. Thereafter, from 1798 to 1822, Congress organized various southern territories in like manner, such acts roughly balancing in number those in which it prohibited slavery.[1] Moreover, the Missouri Compromise of 1820 established the parallel of 36° 30′ north latitude as a dividing line through the territories that had been acquired by the Louisiana Purchase and that remained in territorial status after the admission of Missouri to statehood. North of this line slavery was prohibited; south of it there was no restriction. The established *custom* of the Constitution, before 1846, was thus to apportion the territories in an equitable fashion, so as to permit slaveholding in the southerly portions and prohibit it in the northerly.

The conservative position on the Constitution, throughout the entire crisis, was that the *law* and the *custom* of the Constitution (as here defined) were equally binding — in other words, that Congress had an indubitable *power* to prohibit or permit slavery in the territories, but that it had a corresponding *obligation* to consider the interests of the slaveholding states in legislating for the southern territories and the

---

[1] In the list that Justice Curtis included in his dissent to the Dred Scott decision, 19 Howard 393, at 618, five territorial acts of this character from 1798 to 1822 were cited. These neatly balance the five territorial acts from 1800 to 1838 in which slavery was prohibited. Such a balance, however, is somewhat artificial, for many acts permitted slavery simply by remaining silent. More significant is the fact that seven states had emerged from the territorial stage before the end of 1846 with slavery as an established institution, namely: Tennessee (admitted 1796), Louisiana (1812), Mississippi (1817), Alabama (1819), Missouri (1821), Arkansas (1836), and Florida (1845); whereas five had emerged as free states, namely: Ohio (1803), Indiana (1816), Illinois (1818), Michigan (1837), and Iowa (1846); and another was in close prospect: Wisconsin (admitted 1848).

wishes of the free states in legislating for the northern.[2] In immediate reaction to the Wilmot Proviso, this position was asserted in several substitute amendments that would have extended the Missouri Compromise line across all territories subsequently acquired. Each of these proposals was promptly voted down in the House of Representatives. It was this rejection of the traditional approach to the problem that led to an intensive re-examination of constitutional precedents and postulates by all concerned, and hence produced the great constitutional crisis of 1846–1860.

The precedents went back to a period before there was a formal constitution. Indeed, a conflict over the western territories blocked, for almost four years, the ratification of the first written instrument of federal government, the Articles of Confederation, drafted in 1777. Certain states claimed sovereignty over extensive areas in the West; certain others possessed no such claims. The latter insisted that these great unsettled areas become the property of the Union, rather than of particular states, and be developed for the common benefit. The log jam was broken in 1780, when various states (commencing with New York) began to cede their western claims, and Congress adopted a resolution promising that these lands would "be settled and formed into distinct republican states, which shall become members of the federal union, and have the same rights of sovereignty, freedom and independence, as the other states." The smaller states were satisfied. On March 1, 1781, the last

[2] One of the ablest statements of the conservative position is a little-known book by Sidney George Fisher, published anonymously in November, 1859, *The Law of the Territories* (Philadelphia, 1859); see especially pp. 78–83. The conservative position (as here defined) was the one taken by Justice Curtis in his dissent in the Dred Scott case, wherein he rejected three alternative constitutional views that had been presented at the bar of the court. These he succinctly summarized as follows: "One is, that though Congress can make a regulation prohibiting slavery in a Territory, they cannot make a regulation allowing it; another is, that it can neither be established nor prohibited by Congress, but that the people of a Territory, when organized by Congress, can establish or prohibit slavery; while the third is, that the Constitution itself secures to every citizen who holds slaves, under the laws of any State, the indefeasible right to carry them into any Territory, and there hold them as property." 19 Howard 393, at 620. Obviously these were the positions, respectively, of the Republicans, of the "territorial sovereignty" Democrats under Douglas, and of the extreme southern Democrats (whose senatorial spokesman was Jefferson Davis). The fourth position (that is, the conservative one, which Curtis by implication accepted) was presumably the position of the Constitutional Union Party in 1860, though its platform and the speeches of its candidates were frustratingly vague. It was clearly the position of Senator John J. Crittenden of Kentucky, whose famous compromise resolutions, proposed in the Senate on Dec. 18, 1860, represented essentially a return to the constitutional understandings of the period prior to 1846, which he sought to put beyond question by embodying them in formal constitutional amendments. The crucial first article would have restored the Missouri Compromise line for all territory "now held, or hereafter acquired." *Congressional Globe,* 36 Cong., 2 Sess., 114.

state gave its assent to the Articles of Confederation, and the United States began to live under its first written federal constitution.

The obvious — indeed, the necessary — assumption was that Congress would provide governments for the new territories. In doing so, it was morally bound to accord to actual settlers some degree of participation in territorial government and to advance them as rapidly as possible toward the fully self-governing stage that statehood would represent. Throughout the 1780's there were sharp conflicts of opinion about the proper balance to be struck between federal authority and local autonomy in the territories. But there was not the slightest hint that the individual state should play a separate and independent role — apart from the constituted organs of the Union — in governing the territories they had already ceded, thereby surrendering (in the words of the Virginia deed of cession) "all right, title and claim as well of soil as of jurisdiction."

The real territorial question of the early republic was the degree of local self-government to be granted the inhabitants of a territory. On one side was Thomas Jefferson, who drafted the first land ordinance in 1784, and who proposed to give the settlers, from the very beginning, almost complete control over their own affairs. On the other side were the more conservative groups who shaped the Northwest Ordinance of 1787. This enactment specified a virtually colonial type of government, by federally appointed authorities, during the first stage of territorial existence; during the second stage it permitted the inhabitants some direct participation in territorial government; but it withheld full powers of self-government until the time for statehood arrived. The latter pattern prevailed, for the Ordinance of 1787 superseded the Ordinance of 1784 and became the prototype of all later territorial acts.

Divergent as were these two philosophies of territorial government, they reached an identical conclusion so far as slavery was concerned. Jefferson's original draft of 1784 included a prohibition of slavery in *all* the western territories. The Ordinance of 1787 applied a similar prohibition to the particular area with which it dealt, "the territory of the United States North west of the river Ohio." Jefferson's prohibitory clause was eliminated from the Ordinance of 1784 before enactment by Congress,[3] but its subsequent inclusion in the Ordinance of 1787 showed

---

[3] The matter came to a vote on April 19, 1784. The motion was put in such a way that an affirmative majority was needed to retain Jefferson's prohibition of slavery. The motion was to strike out the section, but the question was put as follows: "Shall the words moved to be struck out stand?" Six states voted in the affirmative, against only three in the negative, but the rules of Congress required an affirmative vote of seven states, and the provision was lost. Actually the seven states from Pennsylvania northward were unanimously in favor, fourteen of their delegates in all voting aye. One of these states (New Jersey), however, was represented by only a single delegate, insufficient for a quorum; hence the state could not be counted. Among the southern states, only two (Maryland and South Carolina) were unanimously against the provision. In North Carolina the delegation was evenly

that the dropping of the provision did not imply a lack of power to adopt it.

There was, it is true, a subtly different philosophical basis for the two abolitionary clauses. In the Northwest Ordinance, Congress was simply legislating for the territories. This legislative power might, without question, be exercised in an opposite way, to permit slavery, and it was so exercised in 1790 when Congress created the Southwest Territory. In the Jeffersonian scheme, on the other hand, the prohibition of slavery did not represent an exercise of federal legislative power, for Jefferson assigned virtually all legislative power to the inhabitants of the territories themselves. Instead, the prohibition of slavery in the territories was, in Jefferson's mind, simply a vindication of the principle of natural and unalienable rights.[4] Slavery denied the fundamental right to liberty. To eliminate this violation of natural rights in the older states would require time, but there was no reason why slavery should not be banned from the beginning in new territories that were to grow up "in republican forms."[5] The prohibition of slavery was to be part of what Jefferson labeled a "Chapter of Compact" — in effect a primordial bill of rights, and, as such, "fundamental" and "unalterable." Whether the abolition of slavery be regarded as a legislative measure or as a constitutional protection of fundamental rights, the fact was that by 1787 it had entered clearly into the system of law being evolved for the territories.

---

divided; hence the vote of the state could not affect the decision. Within the Virginia delegation, too, there was division, and, by a bitter irony, Jefferson's affirmative vote was overridden by the negative votes of his two colleagues. Delaware and Georgia were absent. Altogether, only seven individual delegates were opposed to the provision, against sixteen in favor, two of the latter from southern states. *Journals of the Continental Congress,* XXVI: 247. Few issues so momentous have ever been decided by so unsatisfactory a ballot.

[4] Cf. the exclamations in his *Notes on Virginia,* written at this very time: "With what execrations should the statesman be loaded, who [permits] one half the citizens thus to trample on the rights of the other. . . . And can the liberties of a nation be thought secure when we have removed their only firm basis, a conviction in the minds of the people that these liberties are of the gift of God?" The way, he hoped, was "preparing, under the auspices of heaven, for a total emancipation." Jefferson, *Notes on the State of Virginia* (William Peden, ed., Chapel Hill, N.C., 1955), 162–63. He still hoped that Virginia would pass legislation he had earlier favored, which would "emancipate all slaves born after passing the act." *Ibid.,* 137; see also Julian P. Boyd, ed., *The Papers of Thomas Jefferson,* II (Princeton, 1952): 472n.

[5] Phrases promising "a Republican Form of Government" echoed through all the documents of the founding period. See, for example, the resolution of Congress of Oct. 10, 1780, on the cession of western lands (cited in n. 82 above); Jefferson's draft ordinance of 1784 (from which the phrase in the text is quoted); and the Constitution itself, Art. IV, sec. 4. Such guarantees furnished one basis for the view that the federal government should exercise a general superintendence over the institutions that might develop in the territories — including the institution of slavery. Thus Timothy Fuller of Massachusetts declared in the House of Representatives on Feb. 15, 1819, that "the existence of slavery in any State is so far a departure from republican principles." *Annals of Congress,* 15 Cong., 2 Sess., 1180.

In terms of the American concept of constitutional law — which grants priority to the language of the written Constitution over any mere tradition of constitutional action — the basic question was whether the Constitution of 1787 validated the measures that had already been taken respecting the territories. If not — and especially if the Constitution could be construed as forbidding these measures — then the policy (no matter of how long standing) could be reversed on constitutional grounds. This was precisely the result at which the defenders of slavery aimed in the constitutional doctrine they developed after 1846. They built up, from state-sovereignty premises, a theory of the Constitution that denied the legality of every measure prohibiting slavery in the territories that had ever been enacted from the time the Union was perfected in 1787–1788.

They were aided in doing so by the undeniable vagueness and ambiguity of the single clause of the written Constitution that dealt with territorial matters:

> The Congress shall have Power to dispose of and make all needful Rules and Regulations respecting the Territory or other Property belonging to the United States. . . .

Though legislative power can be described as the power to make rules and regulations,[6] nevertheless the language of this clause was obviously weaker than that employed in giving Congress the power "to exercise exclusive Legislation in all Cases whatsoever" over the District of Columbia and over such federal sites as forts and dockyards. Moreover, by referring to "Territory or *other Property*," and by emphasizing the power "to *dispose of*" both, the clause might be interpreted as referring to real-estate transactions rather than to territorial government.

By making the most of these ambiguities, proslavery theorists could argue either that this particular clause did not apply to the situation at all or that it delegated to Congress such limited authority over the territories that no legislative interference with slavery was permissible there. A different kind of power — a non-legislative power, deriving from a different constitutional source — could then be assigned to Congress. And this power, being a creation of pure constitutional theorizing, could be so defined that it would be capable of protecting slavery in the territories without, at the same time, subjecting it to the hazard of hostile legislation.

If full legislative power over the territories had not been vested in Congress by the Constitution, then surely the power must belong to the inhabitants themselves. This had been the Jeffersonian alternative. And it was the alternative that Stephen A. Douglas supported with vigor

---

[6] Certain of the most important powers of Congress were delegated to it in this language, including the power "to regulate Commerce." Constitution, Art. I, sec. 8, clause 3; also clauses 4, 5, 11, 14.

and consistency under the name of territorial or popular sovereignty. To most supporters of slavery it seemed, for a decade after 1846, the best defense against the hated Wilmot Proviso. But as events in Kansas gradually pointed, in the later 1850's, toward an ultimate free-state victory there, proslavery forces turned venomously upon the author of the Kansas-Nebraska Bill and repudiated his doctrine and all his works. The theory of state sovereignty came to full fruition in the brief period that followed. And it showed its imperious quality by the peremptory way in which its supporters rejected every vestige of the idea that the people of a territory were sovereign or self-governing. Typical was a speech in the House of Representatives in 1859 by Otho R. Singleton of Mississippi:

> Sovereignty, as I understand it, and as it is defined by lexicographers, is the highest power — the supreme power in a State; and, if this definition be correct, (and I apprehend nobody will controvert it,) when Mr. DOUGLAS and his followers undertake to put the Territorial Legislature upon the same footing with a State Legislature, in my judgment they are guilty of a most egregious blunder. Now, let me ask what sovereignty is there — call it squatter sovereignty, popular sovereignty, or whatever else you please — belonging to the people of a Territory? Can they organize a territorial government for themselves? . . . Can they elect their own officers without the special permission of the Congress of the United States? Every act that is passed by the Territorial Legislature is subject to the revision of Congress, and liable to be annulled by that body, and there is not a single act a Territorial Legislature can perform showing it to be sovereign.
>
> But the gentlemen claim that the Legislature of a Territory has the same powers as the Legislature of a State. Why, sir, never was a more erroneous proposition asserted. A State Legislature may perform a thousand acts of sovereignty, its power being controlled by no superior. . . . The people of a State select their own officers, establish their own judicial tribunals, alter or abolish their State government at will. And when gentlemen undertake to put a State and Territory upon the same footing in respect to sovereignty, they involve themselves in difficulties which they cannot meet successfully.

The doctrine of state sovereignty was as hostile to local self-determination in the territories as to the exercise of federal legislative power there. But what other alternative could there be? It was in answering this question that the theorists of state sovereignty revealed their extraordinary ingenuity. And the foundation of their argument was the extra-jurisdictional (or extraterritorial) principle that has already shown itself to be the most significant corollary of state sovereignty.

In legal terms, as we have seen, the question at issue was the source of the police power in the territories — the power that might determine, among other things, the existence or nonexistence of slavery. The state-sovereignty argument began by pointing out that the exercise of a police power is the prerogative of a sovereign. The people of a territory had not attained sovereignty, and the federal government had not received, by delegation, those attributes of sovereignty that would enable it to wield a power of local police. The idea that the federal government might exercise such powers in the territories — by default as it were — was rejected as untenable. The federal government is a government of delegated powers, and local police powers are precisely the ones not delegated to it, but "reserved" by the Tenth Amendment. And they are reserved to the full-fledged sovereign states of the Union, and to them alone.

One finds it hard to imagine how the several states could exercise any power of police in territories beyond their boundaries and outside their jurisdictions. And if they attempted to do so, each projecting its sovereignty into the same area, what possible result could there be but conflict, commotion, and chaos? The answer of state-sovereignty theorists was to assign to the federal government a peculiar, extraconstitutional role in the territories. It was to act there not as the government of the *United* States, but as the agent of the united *States*.

This ingenious dualism solved, with the elegance of Euclid, the constitutional problem that confronted the defenders of slavery. In traditional federal matters, the government of the United States was a *government*, with a legislature capable of determining federal policy, an executive capable of enforcing it, and a judiciary sworn to uphold federal statutes as part of the supreme law of the land. In territorial matters, on the other hand, the federal government was not to be deemed a government at all, but a *trustee*. It was a trustee for the sovereign states, responsible to them severally, charged with giving extraterritorial effect to their laws, and denied any deliberative or discretionary power of its own. It had duties to perform and it possessed the power to perform them. But the power to act did not imply the power to decide. The proslavery constitutional theory succeeded in preserving a centralized authority powerful enough to enforce the rights of slaveowners outside the jurisdictions of the slaveholding states. At the same time, it denied to this central authority any power to make policy with respect to slavery in any place or in any manner.

It is time to examine the various — and extraordinary — features of this fully developed doctrine of state sovereignty. The first point to be noted is that the theory did *not* propose a lessening of federal authority in the territories. Federal powers were to be kept in being — even enhanced — in order to protect the exposed flank of slavery. But these powers were so defined as to be capable of employment in only one way. President Franklin Pierce stated the ultimate and desired conclusion in a message to Congress in 1855. "The General Government," he said, "was forbidden to touch this matter [slavery] in the sense of attack or offense" but was obliged to act upon it "in the sense of defense against either invasion or domestic violence." Senator John M. Berrien of Georgia was even more explicit. "Congress," he asserted, "may legislate upon this subject in the Territories, *affirmatively*," that is to say, "to facilitate the exercise of a constitutional right" to own slaves, but it had no power to legislate in such a way as "to create obstructions to the enjoyment" of this right. Speaking for the Supreme Court [in the Dred Scott case], Chief Justice Roger B. Taney reiterated the view: "The Government of the United States had no right to interfere for any other purpose but that of protecting the rights of the owner."

These conclusions — which found expression in all three branches of the federal government — were the product of several subtle but exceedingly important transformations in the realm of constitutional theory.

In the first place, the traditional criterion of constitutionality had been replaced by another. The federal government being a government of delegated powers, the accepted test applied to any federal measure had always been whether or not the power employed was delegated by the Constitution to the federal government. In place of this, a new criterion of constitutionality was insisted upon — a criterion of *purpose*. If a power were used in such a way as to weaken slavery, then it was without constitutional justification, regardless of whether the power, considered as such, lay within the scope of delegated powers. In a speech to the Senate in 1856, Clement C. Clay, Jr., of Alabama, brusquely swept aside as irrelevant, so far as slavery was concerned, the distinction between action that intruded upon the reserved powers of the states and action that fell within the recognized sphere of federal competence. Outright abolitionism, he said, was "less odious and dangerous" than the policy of "those who concede that slavery in the States is beyond the reach of Congress under the Constitution . . . but yet avow their intention and their power to assail it in the Territories, this District [of Columbia], and wherever the national flag floats." Their ultimate goal, he argued, was to "overthrow slavery in the States." The goal itself was unconstitutional, regardless of the means employed. The fact that opponents of slavery approached this goal by a "circuitous" path rendered their conduct not scrupulously constitutional but "insidious and dastardly." "An army with banners," Clement Clay exclaimed, "is preferable to a Trojan horse."

This theory rendered unconstitutional any use of federal power anywhere or at any time in a fashion inimical to slavery. Nevertheless, the theory was still a negative one. Something more was needed: a mandate from the Constitution itself requiring the positive use of federal power to safeguard slavery in the territories. The second great transformation of constitutional theory looked to this particular end. Proslavery theorists undertook to discover in the Constitution itself such a clear guarantee of the rights of slaveowners that Congress and the President would be obliged, whatever their inclinations, to protect the institution of slavery in the territories, without acquiring thereby any concomitant power to debate or decide questions of policy relating to it.

The starting point of this theory was the fact that the Constitution did recognize the existence of slavery. Furthermore, it gave extraterritorial effect to the laws of the slaveholding states in the matter of fugitive slaves. Antislavery leaders, of course, conceded all this, but they considered slavery a tolerated evil, and they regarded the specific provisions of the Constitution as setting the uttermost limits of such toleration. Beyond these limits, they insisted, every constitutional power of the federal government might legitimately be directed against slavery, to limit, weaken, and eventually destroy it. The question whether federal power should be used in this way was a question of policy, not of constitutional law — a question to be decided by the recognized deliberative organs of the federal government.

Proslavery constitutionalists took a diametrically opposite view. The clauses of the Constitution that recognized slavery were to be construed not narrowly but broadly — not as limits on the protection that slavery might enjoy but as tokens of the full protection that the Constitution implicitly promised. By recognizing slavery, moreover, the Constitution necessarily recognized the laws of the slave-holding states and made their principles the controlling ones in every question that affected slavery. No power to legislate about slavery had, after all, been delegated to Congress. But slavery was an institution that must be defined and provided for by law. There was only one place where such law could be found or could be made — in the sovereign states that upheld and protected slavery. Whenever an issue involving slavery arose in the domain of federal responsibility, therefore, the laws of the slaveholding states must take on extra-jurisdictional force, filling the void created by the constitutional incapacity of Congress to legislate on the subject. On all matters affecting slavery, in other words, the slaveholding states, as sovereigns, were to make policy not for themselves alone, but for the country as a whole, except within the boundaries of such sovereign states as had chosen to abolish the institution.[7]

[7] Even there, of course, the laws of the slaveholding states were to operate extraterritorially upon fugitive slaves. Extraterritoriality, one should observe, was to work in one direction only. The freedom that a slave might have gained by being taken into a free state vanished if he was taken back into a slave state. In his concurring opinion in the Dred Scott case, Justice Nelson emphatically rejected the argument "that as Dred Scott was free while residing in the State of Illinois, by the laws of that State, on his return to the State of Missouri he carried with him the personal qualities of freedom, and that the same effect must be given to his status there as in the former State." On the contrary, he said, "No State . . . can enact laws to operate beyond its own dominions. . . . Such laws can have no inherent authority extra-territorially. . . . Now it follows from these principles, that whatever force or effect the laws of one State or nation may have in the territories of another, must depend solely upon the laws and municipal regulations of the latter." Dred Scott v. Sandford, 19 Howard 393, at 462, 460 (March 6, 1857). . . . Furthermore, Nelson went on to treat federal statutes on the same basis, despite the fact that they are, by constitutional definition, part of "the supreme Law of the Land," binding "the Judges in every State . . . , any Thing in the Constitution or Laws of any State

Senator Berrien of Georgia stated the matter succinctly: "Slavery exists in the State where the owner dwells; it exists out of the State where the owner dwells. Once existing, it exists everywhere, until it comes within limits of a sovereignty which inhibits it." The theory of state sovereignty, in other words, made slavery a national institution. Senator James S. Green of Missouri used this very term when he asserted "that the prohibition of slavery in the United States is local, and that the right to hold slave property wherever there is no prohibition is national."

The doctrine of state sovereignty, in the last analysis, was a nationalistic doctrine, not a localistic one. Despite appearances, its real tendency was toward consolidation, not decentralization. By exalting sovereignty, it destroyed the philosophical foundation for a genuinely pluralistic society, in which diversity would be cherished. There was one peculiarity: indivisible sovereignty was ascribed to the several states rather than to the nation. As a consequence, the doctrine exhibited to the world two seemingly contradictory faces. Within their borders, the slaveholding states were invoking a sovereign's immunity from all external control. Beyond their borders, however, they were demanding — as sovereigns — the strictest respect for whatever rights they chose to place beneath the protective mantle of their sovereignty.

Such a view of the Constitution wiped out every policy-making function of the federal government where slavery was concerned. Its powers were converted from legislative to ministerial ones. Congress was to provide ways and means, it was not to deliberate upon ends. The President was not to shape policy but simply to execute the laws. Federal coercive authority, nevertheless, would be kept in being, for the extraterritorial claims of the slaveholding states would collapse without it. But the only branch of the federal government whose powers were to be exalted was the judiciary. The courts were obliged to take their cue directly from the Constitution. They were free to disregard the directives of possible antislavery majorities in the other branches. They could thus be expected to enforce the sweeping mandate that proslavery leaders found in the Constitution — a mandate to safeguard, under all circumstances, the constitutionally recognized institution of slavery.

---

to the Contrary notwithstanding." Art. VI, clause 2. Oblivious to the difference between a federal law operating within the jurisdiction of a member state and a state law operating within the jurisdiction of a fellow state, he rejected the idea that the federally enacted Missouri Compromise (assuming it to be valid) "possessed some superior virtue and effect, extra-territorially, and within the State of Missouri, beyond that of the laws of Illinois, or those of Ohio." Dred Scott case, 463. Nelson did not rule on the constitutionality of the Missouri Compromise; hence he did not involve himself in the flagrant one-sidedness of a majority of his brethren, who accepted his reasoning and then combined it with their own, which concluded that the laws of a slaveholding state followed the slaveowner and protected his property whenever he went out from his own state into the territories that were under federal jurisdiction.

This reliance upon the judiciary — indeed, this almost exclusive reliance — was inevitable, and gave to proslavery constitutional theory its highly legalistic tone. Of the three branches of the federal government, the legislative was least to be trusted. Anti-slavery majorities could already be mustered in the House of Representatives, and sooner or later would be in the Senate. Therefore no discretionary power over slavery could safely be left in the hands of Congress; its every act must be predetermined, so far as aim or purpose was concerned, by the Constitution and by judicial decision. For the moment, the situation in the executive branch was more favorable. Throughout the period of controversy — especially during the administrations of Polk, Pierce, and Buchanan (1845–1849 and 1853–1861) — the proslavery faction were generally successful in committing the President to the policies they demanded. Nevertheless, this control was jeopardized at every election — indeed, the loss of the executive branch to the Republicans in 1860 was obviously a major reason for secession. Executive discretion ultimately was no more to be tolerated than legislative. Only the federal judiciary could be trusted to defend slavery in an active way. The idea that the Supreme Court could not make — and was not, in fact, making — national policy about slavery was a transparent fiction. But it was a useful fiction, from the southern point of view, for it meant that the court was under no obligation to reflect the views of popular majorities. Policy would be made *for* the nation, but not *by* the nation. Power would be neatly divorced from accountability, action from deliberation.

This reliance upon the judiciary paid off in the most important of all the decisions on slavery — that in the case of Dred Scott, decided on March 6, 1857. The ultimate doctrine of state sovereignty, with all its extra-jurisdictional corollaries fully developed and applied, received its most authoritative formulation at the hands of Chief Justice Roger B. Taney, who wrote the opinion of the court in the case. Space does not permit an examination of the many points of this complex and fateful decision. But the heart of Taney's opinion, from the constitutional point of view, was his delineation of the nature of the Union and the conclusions he drew therefrom respecting the power of Congress in the territories and particularly its power over slavery.

The case involved a slave, Dred Scot, who had been taken by his master for an extended sojourn or residence in areas where slavery was forbidden by statute — for two years in the free state of Illinois and for two in that portion of the old Louisiana Purchase which lay north of 36° 30′, and in which slavery had been prohibited by the federally enacted Missouri Compromise of 1820. Having been brought back to the slaveholding state of Missouri, Dred Scott was suing for his freedom in the federal courts. His suit was denied on several grounds. What concerns us here is the pronouncement that Congress lacked constitutional authority to prohibit slavery in the territories, as it had attempted to do in the Missouri Compromise. Each of the nine justices filed a separate opinion. Seven concurred in the final result: that Dred Scott was still a slave. Only six held that the Missouri Compromise was invalid. And only five accepted Taney's reasoning that the measure was actually unconstitutional. The five, nevertheless, constituted a majority of the entire court; hence the constitutional theory about to be discussed became authoritative.[8]

Turning to the written Constitution, Taney could find in it no delegation to the federal government of powers of local government, even over areas that formed no part of any existing state. He denied that such powers were conferred by the clause authorizing Congress to "make all needless Rules and Regulations respecting the Territory or other Property belonging to the United States." Instead of arguing (as most defenders of state sovereignty had done) that the words were inadequate to convey the powers in question, Taney took the curious position that the clause applied only to territory already in the possession of the United States at the time the Constitution was adopted. The effect (and obviously the intent) of this interpretation was to deny the applicability to the territories generally of the antislavery precedent set in the Northwest Ordinance of 1787.

[8] Dred Scott case, 393. In the opinion of the court, Chief Justice Taney (Md.) denied the constitutionality of federal legislation prohibiting slavery in the territories (our present concern) in a lengthy discussion, 431–52. The two dissenting justices, John McLean (Ohio) and Benjamin R. Curtis (Mass.) controverted his views on this point, 538–50 and 604–33, respectively. Of the six justices who agreed with Taney that Dred Scott was still a slave, one, James M. Wayne (Ga.) gave his "unqualified assent" to all Taney's arguments, 454–56. Another, Robert C. Grier (Pa.) concurred specifically with Taney's reasoning on the unconstitutionality of the Missouri Compromise, 469. Two others, Peter V. Daniel (Va.) and John A. Campbell (Ala.) argued this particular point afresh, 487–92 and 500–517, respectively. Accordingly, five of the nine justices subscribed to the doctrines discussed in the text above. One other justice, John Catron (Tenn.), believed the Missouri Compromise invalid rather than unconstitutional, because incompatible with the treaty that ceded Louisiana, and he took emphatic exception to certain of Taney's assertions denying congressional power over the territories, 519–29. The remaining justice, Samuel Nelson (N.Y.), held Dred Scott to be a slave for reasons that did not call the Missouri Compromise in question, 457–69.

Aside from certain technical questions, two other major points were ruled on by the court. (i) Nelson, in an opinion originally prepared to serve as that of the court, rested the case on the principle that it was for the courts of Missouri to decide Dred Scott's status after his return to that state, and hence to determine the effect to be given to his residence on free soil. The precedent for this was the decision in Strader v. Graham, 10 Howard 82 (1850). Seven of the nine members of the court were in agreement on this point. (ii) Taney held that a Negro could not, under any circumstances, be a citizen of the United States and hence that Dred Scott could not sue in the federal courts even if he were free. Only Wayne and Daniel agreed. McLean and Curtis dissented. On this point — profound in its implications — the vote was therefore three to two.

Having rejected as a basis for his argument the one clause in the Constitution that made any reference to territory, Taney furnished himself with the kind of provision he needed by a wholesale discovery of implied powers, reminiscent of the most spacious opinions of John Marshall. The United States had, of course, acquired vast territories without benefit of an explicit grant of power to do so. Since Jefferson himself had swallowed his constitutional scruples in the matter when he consummated the Louisiana Purchase in 1803, no one thereafter was bothered by such scruples. Nevertheless, the possessions so acquired had presumably been sold, as well as governed, by virtue of the clause that spoke of "Rules and Regulations respecting the Territory." Not so, said Taney. The clause in question could not be stretched to include possessions acquired after 1787. Accordingly, Congress had been selling the public land without any written authority from the Constitution. Its power to sell, as well as its power to govern, was inferred from its power to acquire, and this in turn was inferred from the fact that the United States was an independent nation, and, like other nations, an acquisitive one.[9] The Dred Scott decision was a masterpiece of broad construction before Taney changed his course and made it also a masterpiece of strict construction.

The power to govern the territories being an implied power, and not a power derived from the written clause respecting territory, Taney was free to define the power in any way he saw fit. And he saw fit to define it in terms of the dualism we have already examined. Until a territory is ready for statehood, Taney asserted, "it is undoubtedly necessary that some Government should be established, in order to organize society, and to protect the inhabitants in their persons and property." This statement was implicitly restrictive, describing as it did a government with the barest minimum of functions. In establishing this minimal government, moreover, Congress was not acting in its normal capacity as the federal legislature. It was acting simply as agent of the several states, charged with preserving their interests. Taney expressed the idea thus:

> As the people of the United States could act in this matter only through the Government which represented them, . . . it was not only within the scope of its powers, but it was its duty to pass such laws and establish such a Government as would enable those by whose authority they acted to reap the advantages anticipated from its acquisition.

[9] In the Insular Cases following the Spanish-American War, the power to govern, implied from the implied power to acquire, became the basis for a ruling that (in the popular phrase of the time) the Constitution does not follow the flag. "We are also of opinion that the power to acquire territory, but to prescribe upon what terms the United States will receive its inhabitants, and what their status shall be in what Chief Justice Marshall termed the 'American empire.'" In other words, "the Constitution is applicable to territories acquired by purchase or conquest only when and so far as Congress shall so direct." Downes v. Bidwell, 182 U.S. 244, at 279 (May 27, 1901).

This was the concept of trusteeship. The term itself had already appeared in another crucial passage:

> Whatever it [the general government] acquires, it acquires for the benefit of the people of the several States who created it. It is their trustee acting for them, and charged with the duty of promoting the interests of the whole people of the Union.

The territory, he reiterated, "was acquired by the General Government, as the representative and trustee of the people of the United States, and it must therefore be held in that character for their common and equal benefit."

This distinction between legislative power and trusteeship was vital to Taney's argument. If Congress were authorized to legislate (in the full sense) for a territory, then it would stand in the same relation to the people of the territory as a state legislature stands in relation to the people of the state.[10] It could make policy with respect to the domestic and local institutions of the area. It would be empowered, as a state legislature was empowered, to decide upon the existence or nonexistence of slavery in the territory. On the other hand, if Congress were acting simply as trustee for the people of the several states, then it would enjoy no such freedom of decision on matters of policy. It could, of course, perform within the territories the ordinary federal functions that it performed within the states. Beyond this, however, its powers and duties in the territories were those of a temporary caretaker only. The normal legislative power bestowed upon Congress extended only to purely federal matters. No powers of local government — no police powers — were included. Such powers as might be indispensably necessary for the maintenance of order would have to be implied. But these had neither the character nor the scope of the constitutionally delegated powers of Congress. The implied power to provide government for a territory was drastically and peremptorily restricted by the concept of trusteeship.

From this premise, Taney's specific conclusions easily followed. In devising the mere machinery of government, Congress was relatively free to use its judgment. In legislating on substantive matters, however, it was permitted no discretion and no power to decision of its own. "The power of Congress over the person or property of a citizen can never be a mere discretionary power under our Constitution and form of Government." Therefore "citizens of the United States who migrate to a Territory belonging to the people of the United States, cannot be ruled as mere colonists, dependent upon the will of the General Government, and to be governed by any laws it may think proper to impose."

---

[10] [John] Marshall, indeed, had already held that in legislating for the territories, "Congress exercises the combined powers of the general, and of a state government." American Insurance Co. v. Canter, 1 Peters 511, at 546 (1828). Taney distinguished the case. Dred Scott, 444. Marshall's position is unquestionably that of present-day constitutional law. . . .

The federal government, admittedly, was duty-bound to preserve order and protect property. But it was obliged to do so, Taney insisted, in such a way as not to infringe upon any property right enjoyed by an American citizen by virtue of the laws of his own state. Ordinary civil and criminal laws, if common to all the states of the Union, might presumably be enacted by Congress for the territories. But laws that infringed upon a property right recognized by any state would be *ultra vires*. The holding of slaves was obviously such a state-protected property right. No distinction between slave property and other property was authorized by the Constitution, Taney continued, and none could be made by Congress. Accordingly, a federal statute abolishing slavery in a territory was, under any and every circumstance, unconstitutional. The Chief Justice drove the point home by citing — for almost the first time in constitutional adjudication, though not for the first time in the debates over slavery[11] — the Fifth Amendment (and especially its "due process" clause) in defense of vested property rights. "An act of Congress," he asserted, "which deprives a citizen of the United States of his liberty or property, merely because he came himself or brought his property into a particular Territory of the United States, and who had committed no offence against the laws, could hardly be dignified with the name of due process of law."

Upheld in their constitutional views by the Dred Scott decision of 1857, defenders of slavery worked out with logical completeness the program which they insisted the federal government must carry out. The final formulation was in a set of resolutions that Jefferson Davis introduced in the Senate on February 2, 1860, and that he pushed through to adoption on May 24 and 25. The resolutions began by reciting the orthodox postulate of state sovereignty: "that in the adoption of the Federal Constitution, the States adopting the same acted severally as free and independent sovereignties." But the document mounted quickly to a climax in the fourth resolution, which demanded that the powers of the central government be exerted to any extent necessary to

---

[11] It was only a year earlier that the modern concept of "substantive due process" received clear formulation in a New York case, Wynehamer v. People, 13 N.Y. 378 (1856), involving a liquor law. The decision is characterized as "epoch-making" by Rodney L. Mott, *Due Process of Law* (Indianapolis, 1926), 317–18. Taney, who cited no precedents, is often assumed to have had the Wynehamer case in mind, and his application of the Fifth Amendment to vested property rights in slaves is usually regarded as a striking innovation. As early as 1832, however, in the debates that occurred in the Virginia General Assembly over a proposal for gradual emancipation, James H. Gholson argued that any measure taking slaves from their masters would violate property rights protected both by the Virginia Constitution and by the Fifth Amendment of the federal Constitution. He seems, it is true, to have emphasized the clause reading "nor shall private property be taken for public use, without just compensation," rather than the due process clause. See Theodore M. Whitfield, *Slavery Agitation in Virginia, 1829–1832* (Baltimore, 1930), 77.

safeguard slavery throughout all the territories. In Davis's original draft, the section read as follows:

> *Resolved,* That neither Congress nor a territorial legislature, whether by direct legislation or legislation of an indirect and unfriendly nature, possess the power to annul or impair the constitutional right of any citizen of the United States to take his slave property into the common territories, but it is the duty of the federal government there to afford, for that as for other species of property, the needful protection; and if experience should at any time prove that the judiciary does not possess power to insure adequate protection, it will then become the duty of Congress to supply such deficiency.[12]

Davis's resolutions, an election-year manifesto, were adopted in May, 1860. Six months later the election returns were in. The victory of Lincoln and the Republican Party destroyed every hope of achieving the proslavery program for the territories that Jefferson Davis had laid down in the spring. Even without control of Congress, the incoming Republican President would wield powers capable of blocking any measure for protecting slavery in the territories. His veto could strike down a federal slave code, should Congress seek to enact one, and his power to appoint and remove territorial governors (each armed with a veto power) could forestall similar action by territorial legislatures. If Stephen A. Douglas was right when he said that slavery could not exist in a territory without positive legislation in its favor, then slavery in the territories could hardly survive even the calculated *in*action of a Republican administration. Lincoln's election was hardly "an immediate menace to slavery in the states" (as some writers have argued with scanty supporting evidence), but it was indubitably an immediate menace to slavery *in the territories.* And the throttling of slavery in the territories would mean — according to the professed beliefs of opponents and defenders of slavery alike — the ultimate extinction of the institution everywhere. When the election of 1860 ended the possibility of federal protection for slavery in the territories, the principal leaders of the proslavery party chose, or accepted, the long-discussed alternative of secession.

---

[12] After South Carolina seceded, and a month before he himself vacated his seat in the Senate as a result of the secession of his own state of Mississippi, Jefferson Davis offered, on December 24, 1860, the following proposal for amending the Constitution: *"Resolved,* That it shall be declared, by amendment of the Constitution, that property in slaves, recognized as such by the local law of any of the States of the Union, shall stand on the same footing in all constitutional and Federal relations as any other species of property so recognized; and, like all other property, shall not be subject to be divested or impaired by the local law of any other State, either in escape thereto, or of transit or sojourn of the owner therein; and in no case whatever shall such property be subject to be divested or impaired by any legislative act of the United States, or of any of the Territories thereof." *Congressional Globe,* 36 Cong., 2 Sess., 190. All the provisions contained in this comprehensive program for the protection of the slaveholding system were ultimately included in the Constitution of the Confederate States of America, of which Davis became President.

Secession, however, was not in itself a program for the positive protection of slavery. Secession could not be an end in itself. It made sense only as the means to an end. And the end, unconcealed, was to create a new constitutional system, with built-in protection for slavery. To see the character of that system we have only to look at the permanent Constitution of the Confederate States of America, adopted on March 11, 1861. . . .

A GUIDE TO FURTHER READING

Vincent Hopkins, *Dred Scott's Case* (New York, 1951), offers the most complete background account of the case and Supreme Court hearing. It is not, however, as satisfactory in its setting of the political context and analysis of the opinions. Charles Warren, *The Supreme Court in United States History,* III (Boston, 1922), 1–41, presents a broad spectrum of reaction to the decision. There are two very useful historiographical essays: Thomas B. Alexander, "Historical Treatments of the Dred Scott Case," *The Proceedings of the South Carolina Historical Association, 1953,* XXIII, 37–59; and Frederick S. Allis, Jr., "The Dred Scott Labyrinth," in H. Stuart Hughes (ed.), *Teachers of History: Essays in Honor of Laurence Bradford Packard* (Ithaca, 1954), 341–368.

The various constitutional history texts and specialized studies of the Supreme Court contain basic accounts of the Dred Scott case and its immediate effects. Alfred H. Kelly & Winfred A. Harbison, *The American Constitution: Its Origins and Development,* 3rd ed. (New York, 1963); Carl B. Swisher, *American Constitutional Development,* 2nd ed. (Boston, 1954); Andrew C. McLaughlin, *A Constitutional History of the United States,* (New York, 1935); Homer C. Hockett, *The Constitutional History of the United States, 1776–1876,* 2 vols. (New York, 1939); Benjamin F. Wright, *The Growth of American Constitutional Law* (New York, 1942); Robert G. McCloskey, *The American Supreme Court* (Chicago, 1960); Bernard Schwartz, *The Reins of Power* (New York, 1963); and Charles G. Haines & F. H. Sherwood, *The Role of the Supreme Court in American Government and Politics, 1835–1865* (Berkeley and Los Angeles, 1957).

The older surveys of the antebellum period discuss the Dred Scott case at length and, for the most part, are highly critical of the Court. Hermann von Holst, *The Constitutional and Political History of the United States,* VI (Chicago, 1889), 1–46, probably is the most biting. James Ford Rhodes, *History of the United States from the Compromise of 1850 to the End of the Roosevelt Administration,* II (New York, 1892), 249–271, faithfully served the Republican interpretation. Also see James Schouler, *History of the United States of America Under the Constitution,* V (New York, 1891), 373–377; John W. Burgess, *The Middle Period, 1817–1858* (New York, 1901), 449–459; Theodore C. Smith, *Parties and Slavery, 1850–1859* (New York, 1907) 190–208; John Bach McMaster, *A History of the People of the United States from the Revolution to the Civil War,* VIII (New York, 1913), 272–282; and Edward Channing, *A History of the United States* VI (New York, 1925), 186–197. A more modern account, particularly responsive to the "revisionist" arguments, is Allan Nevins, *The Emergence of Lincoln* (New York, 1950), I, 90–118. Also see Vol. II, appendix I on the dissenters' roles.

There are a number of works which deal with the law of slavery prior to the

Dred Scott decision. Indispensable are John C. Hurd, *The Law of Freedom and Bondage in the United States*, 2 vols. (Boston, 1858–1862); and Helen T. Catterall, *Judicial Cases Concerning American Slavery and the Negro*, 5 vols. (Washington, 1937). Mrs. Catterall's essay, "Some Antecedents of the Dred Scott Case," *American Historical Review*, XXX (1924), 56–70, argues that on the basis of the precedents, Taney's "decision [was] unquestionably correct." A good recent discussion of pre-Dred Scott slavery cases is in Donald M. Roper, "Mr. Justice Smith Thompson and the Constitution," (unpublished Ph.D. dissertation, Indiana University, 1963). For the status of the free Negro, see Leon F. Litwack, *North of Slavery: The Negro in the Free States, 1790–1860* (Chicago, 1961). Francis S. Philbrick, *The Laws of Illinois Territory, 1809–1818* (Springfield, Ill., 1950) is a provocative, highly critical analysis of Taney's view of slavery and the territories.

The earliest scholarly account of President James Buchanan's role in the case is in Phillip Auchampaugh, "James Buchanan, The Court, and the Dred Scott Case," *Tennessee Historical Magazine*, IX (1926), 231–240. Philip S. Klein, *President James Buchanan: A Biography* (University Park, 1962), is more detailed and up-to-date. Ex-Justice Campbell offered some revealing insights into the decision-making process in his eulogy of Justice Curtis before the United State Supreme Court. See 20 Wallace's Reports viii-xii (1874). Wallace Mendelson's essay, reprinted here, is the most perceptive analysis of the political maneuverings to secure a judicial decision.

The contemporary commentaries on the decision ranged from a calm, legalistic dissection by a future Supreme Court Justice, to an impassioned assault by a political "elder statesman." Two prominent Boston lawyers, John Lowell and Horace Gray, anonymously published "A Legal Review of the Case of Dred Scott" in the *Law Reporter* in June 1857. Their thorough analysis of the varied aspects of the case established the basis for the contention that overruling the Missouri Compromise was extrajudicial. [Thomas Hart Benton], *Historical and Legal Examination of the Dred Scott Case, etc.* (New York, 1857) continued Benton's long-standing political opposition to slavery expansion. In addition to George Ticknor Curtis's analysis, which is also printed in his *Constitutional History of the United States* (New York, 1896), see Timothy Farrar's review of the published opinion in the *North American Review*, LXXV (October 1857), 392–415. Farrar contended that the only real effect of the decision would be to harm the Court's status in the public mind. Theodore Parker's "sermon," "The Present Aspect of Slavery in America and the Immediate Duty of the North" (Boston, 1858), is an indignant, scorching attack upon the Court. Also see Samuel A. Foot, *An Examination of the Case of Dred Scott, etc.* (New York, 1859); "Cecil" [Sidney George Fisher], *The Law of the Territories* (Philadelphia, 1859); J. T. Brooke, *Short Notes on the Dred Scott Case* (Cincinnati, 1861); Joel Parker, *Personal Liberty Laws, and Slavery in the Territories* (Boston, 1861); and Charles M. Ellis, "Roger Brooke Taney," *Atlantic Magazine*, XV (1865), 151–161. The latter essay, written as the war closed, bitterly assailed Taney and included a "dreadful" play on words: "The end of the dread conflict of battle is the same as the end of the equally dreadful issue of the Court."

The relationship of Dred Scott to the coming of the Civil War receives obvious attention in the literature on the sectional controversy and Abraham

Lincoln. John G. Nicolay and John Hay, *Abraham Lincoln: A History,* II
(New York, 1886), 69–78, established one trend: "The slavery sentiment . . .
flowed in at the open door of the national hall of justice. . . . Against such a
debasement of any living image of the Divine Maker the resentment of the
public conscience of the North was quick and unsparing." Charles Warren's
work, coupled with Albert J. Beveridge's *Abraham Lincoln, 1809–1858,* 2 vols.
(Boston, 1928), may have set the tone for the coming "revisionism" of the
1930's and 1940's. Beveridge seemed somewhat skeptical of the Republican
campaign techniques which exaggerated the meaning of the decision. Such an
interpretation of Dred Scott was essential to the "Repressible Conflict" and
"Needless War" ideas of Avery Craven and James G. Randall. Frank H. Hodder's article (1929) essentially attacking Justice Curtis's motives, similarly
contributed to the historiographical trend. Incidentally, the genesis of Hodder's
thesis can be found in Otto Gresham, *The Dred Scott Case* (Chicago, 1908),
16–20. Also useful, particularly for reviving the *obiter dicta* argument which
Corwin seemingly buried, is Richard R. Stenberg, "Some Political Aspects of
the Dred Scott Case," *Mississippi Valley Historical Review,* XVIII (1933),
571–577. Don E. Fehrenbacher, *Prelude to Greatness: Lincoln in the 1850's*
(Stanford, 1962), 128–142, offers a valuable corrective on the overemphasis
of the Freeport Doctrine. The most penetrating and provocative interpretation
of the relationship between Dred Scott, Lincoln, and the debates with Douglas
is in Harry V. Jaffa, *Crisis of the House Divided: An Interpretation of the Issues
in the Lincoln-Douglas Debates* (New York, 1959). Jaffa's assault on the
Hodder-Randall scholarship is most effective. Paul M. Angle, "Lincoln and
the Supreme Court," *Bulletin of the Abraham Lincoln Association,* No. 47
(1937), is a summary of some of Lincoln's statements regarding the Court.
It fails, however, to deal with Lincoln's whole position, expressed at various
other times in his life. Finally, there is a revealing letter from Taney to ex-
President Franklin Pierce depicting the Chief Justice's state of mind on the
reaction to his opinion. *American Historical Review,* X (1905), 358–359.

   Corwin's analysis of the case should be supplemented with Horace H. Hagan,
"The Dred Scott Decision," *Georgetown Law Journal,* XV (1926), 95–114.
Hagan believed that a determination of the Missouri Compromise could not be
avoided if the Court were to hold Scott still to be a slave. Two years before
Corwin's article appeared, Elbert W. R. Ewing, in his *Legal and Historical
Status of the Dred Scott Decision* (Washington, 1909), offered the first sys-
tematic defense of Taney's position. Ewing's book, in many respects, appears
as a typical turn-of-the-century defense of Southern attitudes which often
found it necessary to rationalize antebellum history. Ewing, with less regard
for scholarly detail, also believed that the Court had to decide the constitutionality of the Missouri Compromise. With no evidence whatsoever, he contended that six justices believed the plea of abatement properly before them.
James Bradley Thayer, the famous Professor of Constitutional Law at the
Harvard Law School, gave a unique treatment to the decision in his 1895
casebook (*Cases on Constitutional Law,* 2 vols.). Instead of highlighting
Taney's opinion, he published Nelson's as the "Opinion of the Court," as it
alone, he said, "limits itself to grounds agreed upon by a majority of the court
and necessary to the disposition of the case." Morris M. Cohn, "The Dred
Scott Case in the Light of Later Events," *American Law Review,* XLVI (1912),

548–577, is the work of a Little Rock, Arkansas lawyer who emphasized, with apparent delight, how Taney's remarks served as the basis for some of the so-called "Insular Cases" in the late nineteenth and early twentieth centuries. Louis B. Boudin, *Government by Judiciary*, 2 vols. (New York, 1932), II, 1–32, focuses on the abuse of judicial power.

The literature abounds with references to Dred Scott as a continuing symbol of judicial indiscretion. See, for example, Carl B. Swisher, "Dred Scott One Hundred Years After," *Journal of Politics*, XIX (1957), 167–183; Robert H. Jackson, *The Struggle for Judicial Supremacy* (New York, 1941); Charles Evans Hughes, *The Supreme Court of the United States: Its Foundation, Methods and Achievements: An Interpretation* (New York, 1928); and, most useful of all, Alexander M. Bickel, *The Least Dangerous Branch: The Supreme Court at the Bar of Politics* (Indianapolis and New York, 1962).

There are abundant materials dealing with the lives of the Taney Court justices or important aspects of their careers. Taney, naturally, has merited the most attention. The earliest biographical study was Samuel Tyler, *Memoir of Roger Brooke Taney* (Baltimore, 1872). While Tyler's work is useless as a critical source, it contains Taney's sketch for an autobiography. Bernard C. Steiner, *Life of Roger Brook Taney, Chief Justice of the United States Supreme Court* (Baltimore, 1922), is in the same vein. Carl Brent Swisher, *Roger B. Taney* (New York, 1935), remains the most complete account of Taney's whole career. Charles W. Smith, Jr., *Roger B. Taney: Jacksonian Jurist* (Chapel Hill, 1936), is a more specialized study and strains a little harder to explain Dred Scott as an anomaly in Taney's career. A recent biography, Walker Lewis, *Without Fear or Favor: A Biography of Chief Justice Roger Brooke Taney* (Boston, 1965), merely adds a few assorted facts to Swisher's work. Perhaps the most perceptive modern analysis of Taney is in Robert J. Harris, "Chief Justice Taney: Prophet of Reform and Reaction," *Vanderbuilt Law Review*, X (1957), 227–257. For some idea of how opinions of Taney have altered through the years, compare the anonymously published, *The Unjust Judge — A Memorial of Roger Brooke Taney, Late Chief Justice of the United States* (New York, 1865) with Charles Evans Hughes's, "Roger Brooke Taney," *American Bar Association Journal*, XVII (1931), 785–790. Walker Lewis, in his recent biography of Taney, offers fairly convincing evidence that Charles Sumner authored the former piece.

The other Supreme Court members, with the exception of Catron, Grier, and Nelson, have been studied in varying degrees. John P. Frank, *Justice Daniel Dissenting: A Biography of Peter V. Daniel, 1784–1860* (Cambridge, 1964), offers useful insights into the mental processes of a Southern "agrarian." Alexander A. Lawrence, *James Moore Wayne: Southern Unionist* (Chapel Hill, 1943), successfully copes with the paradoxes of Wayne's judicial and political life as it pertained to Southern interests. Francis P. Weisenberger, *The Life of John McLean, A Politician on the United States Supreme Court* (Columbus, 1937), stresses McLean's political maneuverings. Henry G. Connor, John Archibald Campbell (Boston, 1920), examines the varied career of one of the Southern justices. Eugene I. McCormac, "Justice Campbell and the Dred Scott Decision," *Mississippi Valley Historical Review*, XIX (1933), 565–571, is worthwhile. Benjamin R. Curtis, whose work on the Court was most prominent, however brief, has had no modern biographer. His son's edition of *A*

Memoir of Benjamin Robbins Curtis (2 vols., Boston, 1879) contains many of Curtis's letters describing the Court at work. Curtis's exchanges with Taney at the time of his resignation in 1857 throw much light on the acrimony generated by Dred Scott. Richard H. Leach, who has an unpublished doctoral dissertation (Princeton, 1951) on Curtis, staunchly defends Curtis's motives in leaving the Court, and particularly counters Frank H. Hodder's charges. "Justice Curtis and the Dred Scott Case," *Essex Institute Historical Collections* XCIV (January, 1958), 37–56. Also see Leach's "Benjamin Robbins Curtis: Judicial Misfit," *New England Quarterly*, XXV (December 1952), 507–523. John R. Schmidhauser, "Judicial Behavior and the Sectional Crisis of 1837–1860," *The Journal of Politics*, XXIII (1961), 615–640, contends that the sectional division in the Taney Court is reflected in a large variety of constitutional law categories. Finally, there are sketches of all the justices in the various volumes of the *Dictionary of American Biography*.

Every historical subject manages to attract a certain amount of sensationalist, if diverting, ideas. The Dred Scott subject is no exception. John Charles Hogan, "The Role of Chief Justice Taney in the Decision of the Dred Scott Case," *Case and Comment*, LVIII (1953), 3–8, argues by a variety of means, including a vocabulary and syntactical analysis, that Justice Wayne actually wrote Taney's opinion. Finally, the most incredible variation on the Dred Scott theme has to be Isabel Paterson's, "The Riddle of Chief Justice Taney in the Dred Scott Decision," *Georgia Review*, III (1950), 192–203. Miss Paterson's essay concerns Taney only in a peripheral way. The Chief Justice, she claims, really desired African colonization for the American Negro, and thus by denying that Negroes were citizens, Taney kept the possibility alive. Actually, Miss Paterson argues, Taney's opinion would have been unnecessary if only taxpayers had been allowed to vote. As noted above, the relationship between this essay and the Dred Scott decision is purely coincidental.